CONTEMPORARY WINE STUDIES

The purchase and consumption of wine, whether in hospitality environments or domestic settings, has huge anthropological significance underpinned by a discourse of wine appreciation. It can be seen as a multi-sensory and symbolically status-rich activity framed by historical, social, cultural and ethical discourses.

This innovative book offers a critical study of wine from social and cultural perspectives. The field of wine studies spans the spectrum of cultural and technical issues concerning the place of wine in society from viticulture, vinification, labelling, regulation, marketing, purchasing, storage and its final consumption. It combines social history and contemporary questions including the notion of *terroir*, the nature of protected wine designations, the pricing of wine and the different motivations for buying and consuming wine. It considers wine as a beverage, as an aesthetic exercise and as a marker of status, as well as its health implications and legal controls.

The title offers a timely contribution into the significance of wine and the role of knowledge, both of which have conceptual and managerial implications in terms of marketing, promotion, consumption and distribution. By offering a holistic and innovative understanding of wine and its consumption, it is a must-read for students and scholars in the fields of wine and social science.

Gareth Morgan holds a Chair at Sheffield Business School, Sheffield Hallam University. He is an experienced wine educator and a specialist in regulatory issues in a number of sectors.

Richard Tresidder is Senior Lecturer in Hospitality Marketing at Sheffield Business School, Sheffield Hallam University. He is a social anthropologist exploring issues of critical marketing in hospitality, tourism and food.

CONTEMPORARY WINE STUDIES

Dancing with Bacchus

Gareth Morgan
and Richard Tresidder

LONDON AND NEW YORK

First published 2016
by Routledge
2 Park Square, Milton Park, Abingdon, Oxon OX14 4RN

and by Routledge
711 Third Avenue, New York, NY 10017

Routledge is an imprint of the Taylor & Francis Group, an informa business

© 2016 Gareth Morgan and Richard Tresidder

The right of Gareth Morgan and Richard Tresidder to be identified as the authors of this work has been asserted by them in accordance with sections 77 and 78 of the Copyright, Designs and Patents Act 1988.

All rights reserved. No part of this book may be reprinted or reproduced or utilised in any form or by any electronic, mechanical, or other means, now known or hereafter invented, including photocopying and recording, or in any information storage or retrieval system, without permission in writing from the publishers.

Trademark notice: Product or corporate names may be trademarks or registered trademarks, and are used only for identification and explanation without intent to infringe.

British Library Cataloguing in Publication Data
A catalogue record for this book is available from the British Library

Library of Congress Cataloging in Publication Data
Catalog record for this book has been requested

ISBN: 978-1-138-78439-0 (hbk)
ISBN: 978-1-138-78445-1 (pbk)
ISBN: 978-1-315-76827-4 (ebk)

Typeset in Bembo
by Keystroke, Station Road, Codsall, Wolverhampton

CONTENTS

List of figures	*vii*
List of tables	*ix*
Foreword	*xi*
Preface	*xiii*
Acknowledgements: our personal wine journeys	*xix*
List of abbreviations	*xxiii*

1	The nature of wine, protected designations and labelling	1
2	Understanding the significance of wine	33
3	Fine wine or plonk?	49
4	Wine consumers	81
5	Terroir	106
6	Wine at home	118
7	Licensing law, duty and the ethics of alcohol	137
8	Marketing of the wine experience	156
9	Wine societies and wine education	174
10	The semiotics of wine	195
11	The importance of wine in contemporary society	214

Index   *220*

FIGURES

1.1	Map of the vineyards of Vougeot in the Côte de Nuits, Burgundy, France	26
3.1	The appellations of the Bordeaux region	66
3.2	The five vineyards of Burgundy	71
3.3	The vineyards of the Côte de Nuits, Burgundy	74
6.1	A typical temperature-controlled cabinet for wine storage in the home	120
6.2	A specially constructed home wine cellar	121
6.3	Various sizes of wine bottles	124
6.4	Decanting a bottle of wine to be served in the home	130
6.5	A 'Vacuvin' wine saver	131
9.1	A wine society tasting	181

TABLES

1.1	Levels of alcohol in the final wine depending on the sugar content of the grapes	4
3.1	Example of timescales for an individual buying en primeur wine produced by a leading Bordeaux château	60
3.2	When very expensive wine is justified	64
9.1	Extract from a list of wines at a tutored tasting	179
10.1	Constituent parts of wine labels	202
10.2	Examples of the semiotic language of wine	209

FOREWORD

Antony Moss Dip WSET MW
DIRECTOR OF STRATEGIC PLANNING, WINE & SPIRIT EDUCATION TRUST (WSET)

Every year many dozens of books are published on the subject of wine, but few of them offer content that expands significantly on what is already available. This is one of those exciting, rare, wine books that open up fascinating directions and dimensions of discussion that will be new to a wider public, though they may be familiar to specialist academics.

Contemporary Wine Studies: Dancing with Bacchus does this in an engaging and accessible way. The book's structure lends itself to dipping into chapters in the order that they interest the reader, and each chapter helpfully provides both a coherent overview of the academic subfield, and pointers to further reading for those who wish to explore further. It is written with care and authority, cautiously separating that which can be stated with a confidence that comes from expert consensus, while elegantly nodding towards those matters where experts disagree.

The subject of wine touches on a huge range of academic disciplines, from natural sciences (chemistry, biochemistry, plant biology ... even human biology and psychology) through humanities (history, geography) and social sciences (economics, sociology) to business management, and areas of philosophy (especially aesthetics and philosophy of language). This can be exciting – or daunting! Either way, a good map or guide is a useful aid to accelerating understanding and enhancing appreciation.

After reading the book cover to cover, the reader will have gained a balanced sense of the 'landscape' of wine studies, with an idea of where the most significant mountain ranges, forests, and rabbit burrows lie, together with knowledge of where to obtain more detailed maps of the features they wish to study further. The success of such a guide depends largely on two things: ensuring the map spans the space, and ensuring it has the appropriate level of detail to be insightful without being overwhelming and confusing. This book by Gareth Morgan and Richard Tresidder succeeds on all counts, and I am delighted with this addition to the wine literature!

PREFACE

Although interest in wine is almost as old as humanity, it is only perhaps since the late twentieth century that 'wine studies' – looking at the place of wine in society as a whole – has emerged as a significant field of research and teaching.

Wine can be studied from the perspective of many different disciplines, including geography, history, geology, plant biology, organic chemistry, food science, marketing and law. There are also huge areas of study in the social sciences and health sciences regarding patterns of wine consumption and the effects of wine on the human body. The production and sale of wine raises many issues of economics, particularly in regions of the world where wine is the most important product in the local economy. Wine is an important theme in many aspects of business and management studies, predominantly in sectors such as hospitality management, retail management, events management, leisure and tourism. For all of these examples wine is often much more than just a product in the supply chain – the provision of wine is often central to the offering.

This book touches on all those perspectives. However, our primary focus is the *culture of wine* in society. Whilst some chapters provide factual or technical background, our key aim is to look at the way we engage with wine using the lens of social anthropology. We explore issues such as the role of wine in social rituals and the symbolism of wine in defining someone's sense of esteem. We look at the semiotics of wine – the messages that are conveyed when a particular wine is served on a particular occasion. We explore the notion of wine hedonism – the role of wine as a source of pleasure (which, for many wine consumers, is about much more than just its alcoholic content). We also look at the place of wine in religion.

We ask why people will sometimes pay huge sums for a very special bottle of wine when other wines from the same grape variety in the same region may be much cheaper. Does it really matter to know that the grapes were grown in a very particular vineyard, and vinified by winemakers drawing on centuries of experience? Is it important to have tight regulations in law that protect the labelling of wine, or is this just a means for those selling wine to command higher prices? We also explore the dangers of wine abuse, and the legal and ethical approaches to preventing or discouraging excessive or inappropriate wine consumption.

Structure

This book is divided into eleven chapters, each of which concludes with some points for discussion and further exploration. Where it is used on taught courses, these may be useful for seminars or as a focus for assignments; readers working in the wine and hospitality trades may find them useful for personal reflection.

The chapters are presented in the order that is likely to be most useful to readers, especially to those new to the field of wine studies, although most chapters can be used independently (cross references are provided where relevant).

Chapter 1 introduces the nature of wine and the broad principles of wine law at a technical level, whilst Chapter 2 explores the significance of wine from a cultural and anthropological perspective. These two chapters act as a foundation for all the subsequent material.

Chapters 3 to 5 explore various issues which differentiate wines and those who consume them. Chapter 3 examines various factors which determine the status or reputation of wines under the heading 'Fine wine or plonk?' Chapter 4 explores the different identities of wine consumers – both from a marketing perspective and in terms of cultural identity, introducing, in particular, the anthropological notion of 'consumption tribes'. However, wine is fundamentally a product of a specific place and the term *terroir* which is so central to issues of wine quality, wine status and its geographical identity is unpacked in Chapter 5.

Chapters 6 to 9 consider four key themes in wine studies regarding the social context of wine, how it is consumed, and how people engage with wine. Behaviour in the home is fundamental to much sociocultural analysis, so patterns of engagement with wine in domestic settings are the theme of Chapter 6. Chapter 7 looks more critically at wine, considering the possible social problems that may be linked to excessive wine consumption, and examines the efforts by society to moderate this. By contrast, Chapter 8 examines the marketing of wine, in particular the marketing of wine as an 'experience' rather than simply as a product. Chapter 9 explores how people learn about wine in general and specifically about the differentiation of wines, ranging from informal wine societies to advanced wine qualifications.

Chapter 10 brings these issues together in an examination of 'the semiotics of wine' – in other words the messages communicated by wine bottles, by wine-related experiences and by wine consumers in contemporary society. Chapter 11 presents a conclusion on the overall role of wine in contemporary society and seeks to articulate the central questions which serve to identify the field of critical wine studies.

The journey – a dance with Bacchus

Our journey in this book is an exploration of the way society dances with the concept of wine – as exemplified by Bacchus, the Greek god of wine – hence the subtitle *Dancing with Bacchus*. Bacchus (or his Roman equivalent, Dionysus) is widely described as 'the god of the grape harvest, of wine and of winemaking' but also as god of 'ritual madness, religious ecstasy, fertility and theatre'. Wine can contribute to all of these aspects of society. Bacchus is widely known for his dancing – his 'wine, music and ecstatic dance frees his followers from self-conscious fear and care' (Wikipedia 2015).

The choices people make about their 'dance with Bacchus' tell us much about how wine is perceived. Some abstain completely from wine, and decline to join the dance at all. Some dance tentatively, keeping Bacchus at a distance, conscious of the risks of being overcome by his ecstatic influences. Some embrace him tightly, in a dance where the joys of wine and of sexuality are closely intertwined. Some insist on the most luxurious wines he can offer before they will agree to dance – others are happy to dance with the simplest drop of fermented grape-must. For some it is a long, slow dance, with many elements: the selection of the bottle, the careful removal of the cork, the delicate process of decanting and subsequent pouring, the assessment of the colour and aromas before the liquid touches the mouth – for others, it is an urgent dance where Bacchus is grabbed from the other side of the dance floor, and his wine is consumed with haste. For some it is a dance that focuses on a much greater God than Bacchus, as when Christians embrace his beverage in the Eucharist or Jews at the Passover meal.

Readership

Drawing on these various contexts where humans interact with wine, we offer a discussion and analysis of the place of wine in society in a way which we believe will be useful to students and to researchers, both on university courses and professional programmes.

This book will not teach you about the details of wines from all the different wine-producing countries of the world – there are many excellent books explaining the wines of the world, and others giving great detail on specific regions: the end-of-chapter references may be useful in signposting other sources. (We discuss one or two wine regions in outline, but this is purely to give examples of how wines are differentiated.) Nor does the book explain the technicalities of viticulture and vinification, except in terms of some points in passing where we indicate possible differences between techniques for the most prestigious wines as compared to those seen as more basic. Likewise we do not cover details of the law on selling and labelling wine in particular countries – where we refer to the law it is generally only by way of example. The book will not tell you how to sell more wine (if that is your aim) – although it will give you some indication of the factors which influence those who buy wine which may be useful to those in marketing roles. Equally we do not offer any simplistic solutions for curbing the excesses of alcohol consumption.

This is a broad-ranging book, considering wine in many societal contexts. In particular, we highlight the many separate human encounters with a bottle of wine which may occur between it leaving the place where it was produced and its eventual consumption: various steps on that road may each involve a separate dance with Bacchus: in the vineyard, in the wine shop, at the screen where an online order is placed, in the restaurant, in the home when wine is received, at the party where the wine is opened and is shared. However, we have tried to avoid assuming that the reader already has extensive experience of wine in all these contexts: many chapters thus include explanations of common practices in the marketing, serving and consumption of wine, or provide background on the legalities of wine classifications and wine sales, in order to provide a context for the subsequent discussion.

Use and limitations

Whilst we believe this is the first book bringing together this spectrum of questions from the field of wine studies in an accessible introductory volume, we appreciate that on many issues we gloss over debates where specialists in areas such as sociology or marketing or wine production could have gone into much more detail: our aim is simply to offer enough explanation to assist a student or researcher embarking on the study of these issues. Moreover, the use of wine and other alcoholic drinks is a well-established domain of study by social anthropologists over more than 50 years: many of the concepts we explore such as why people drink and notions of terroir have received much attention from scholars. On these issues, our aim is simply to introduce some of ethnographic questions raised.

We hope the book will be useful to readers in a wide range of countries, but our specific experiences are rooted in Europe and the UK in particular. In the tradition of ethnographers relying on their own field studies, we focus our examples on what we have observed – but we do not believe readers from elsewhere will find it difficult to translate our examples to their own context. We should also note that, in a few instances, legal and technical details have been slightly simplified to avoid distracting readers with unnecessary background, and we have certainly not been able to cite every writer whose work may have influenced the broad-ranging issues we discuss. Nevertheless, if readers spot any fundamental errors or omissions we would be grateful if these could be brought to our attention so we may remedy them in future editions.

But for professionals (or future professionals) who engage with wine in any form, and for those concerned more generally with the place of wine in society, we hope this book will offer some worthwhile questions and points for critical analysis.

Gareth Morgan and Richard Tresidder
Sheffield Hallam University, UK – Maundy Thursday 2015

Reference

Wikipedia (2015). *Dionysus* [online] at http://en.wikipedia.org/wiki/Dionysus (accessed February 2015).

ACKNOWLEDGEMENTS

Our personal wine journeys

From Gareth Morgan

My first recollection of a special event involving wine was the matriculation dinner for new undergraduates which I attended at Cambridge in 1974. To be served a different wine with each course of a meal, and Port or Madeira at the end, was something I had never experienced, growing up in a household where wine was only drunk on rare occasions. So I must thank the Master and Fellows of Churchill College, Cambridge for initiating me into this field! But it was another 15 years before I began to study wine seriously.

In the meantime, I became fascinated by the approach of social anthropology through studying under Dr Mary Chatterjee in the theology department at the University of Bristol in 1979. But it was not until three decades later, on meeting Richard Tresidder at Sheffield Hallam University (who had already written several articles looking at wine from a cultural perspective), that we first sensed that there might be scope for a broad-ranging wine studies book using these principles. Richard suggested we approached Routledge as a possible publisher, and it is through their encouragement that this book has come to fruition.

However, I could not have attempted to contribute to a book of this kind without some 25 years of support and encouragement in the study of wine, from a huge range of sources. I need to thank the wine retailers and friends who first prompted me to think more about the wines I enjoyed and to start making tasting notes. I especially thank my wife, Sharon, who risked a great deal when she bought me my first wine book: Rainbird (1983) opened my eyes to the diversity and complexity of wine, but also to the mysteries of controlled appellations and classification of estates. Sharon has travelled with me on most of the ensuing journey and has supported me extensively in preparing my chapters for this book.

As a young academic at what is now the University of the West of England, Bristol, in a break from writing up my PhD, I went on my first overseas wine tour, guided by Charles Taylor MW – an experience that drove my passion to learn more about wine, seeing the realities of wine growing and talking directly with wine producers in Bordeaux. Also at Bristol I fell under the spell of the long-established wine merchants Averys of Bristol and had the privilege of attending some fascinating tastings in their cellars and the incredible dinner that marked their 200th anniversary – all presided over by the late John Avery MW.

Over the years I have been hugely influenced by various writers in the wine field, especially Michael Broadbent MW, whose insights both in books and in *Decanter* magazine taught me so much, especially the significance of wine vintages, which has inspired some of my own research. More recently, the critical and highly scholarly work of Jancis Robinson MW has kept me engrossed – in particular, it was her autobiography (Robinson 1997) that first challenged me to consider some of the more critical issues regarding society's attitudes to wine which we explore in this book.

Upon moving to Yorkshire and then taking up my post at Sheffield Hallam University I became involved with the Yorkshire Guild of Sommeliers – a body linking amateur wine lovers with those in the trade. Through their influence I heard presentations from various members of the Association of Wine Educators (AWE) whose profession is teaching about wine, in particular from Richard Goodacre who kindly let me join a number of trips he arranged to key wine regions.

In that context I was persuaded to join a self-study group and sat the exams for the certificate and then the higher certificate of the Wine & Spirit Education Trust (WSET). One or two of the group felt it might be worth attempting the WSET Diploma – I initially felt this was madness for someone not working in the wine trade, but as a university teacher asking students to achieve qualifications I felt it was only right from time to time to subject myself to some study and exams! Much to my surprise I passed the Diploma with strong marks, and for the first time began to reflect seriously on how I could contribute to the wine field. I had no desire to give up my academic career, nor did I wish to take the commercial risks of entering the wine trade, but I could see the contribution made by wine educators. So I started a small freelance venture known as Oinoudidasko Wine Education (alongside my university role) and a few years later I was myself admitted as a member of AWE; I have found the colleagueship with other AWE members immensely supportive. I would particularly thank Laura Clay (ex-chair of AWE) for her comments on Chapter 9 and Antony Moss MW of WSET for comments on various chapters alongside his generous foreword to the book as a whole.

Maps are also central in wine education, and I would like to thank Tony Hoyle (who drew the map in Chapter 1) and the Conseil Interprofessionnel du Vin de Bordeaux and the Bureau Interprofessionel des Vins de Bourgogne for allowing the use of the maps in Chapter 3. Thanks are also due to various friends and colleagues who have shared their wine stories and to the firms and organisations that provided images used in Chapter 6.

Soon after I became active in wine education a fortuitous merger of departments at the University brought colleagues in the fields of tourism, food and hospitality into the business school where I was based, and it wasn't long before some common interests in wine studies emerged. Although my main academic area remained in the field of accounting and regulation (particularly in relation to charitable organisations) the kind encouragement of colleagues in the hospitality area and the support of the faculty leadership meant that I was given the chance to present some wine classes, to organise some wine-related research, and to supervise student dissertations concerned with the wine trade.

Even after the WSET Diploma I had little hands-on experience of wine production, but that changed when I learned of a new commercial vineyard being planted in Yorkshire (at the northern limits of where wine grapes can effectively be grown). Stuart and Elizabeth Smith generously accepted my offer of some limited help at the newly planted Ryedale Vineyards, and appointed me as their honorary 'wine adviser'. This led me into membership of the UK Vineyards Association (UKVA) and to attending a technical course in wine analysis at Plumpton College (part of the University of Brighton) – the UK's leading centre for the study of wine production. Leading figures in UKVA and at Plumpton have been a further source of inspiration on my wine journey.

Over the years I have had the honour to present a huge range of wine events – some introductory, some highly technical sessions for those in the hospitality trade – both through Oinoudidasko and at Sheffield Hallam University. The questions raised by the participants at these sessions have prompted many of the issues explored in this book. But I would also like to acknowledge the influence of my long-deceased maternal grandparents: as strict teetotallers they would be shocked at the extent of my involvement in the field of wine, but their appreciation of the potential dangers of alcohol gave me a keen sense of social responsibility in this field.

I dedicate this book to everyone who has helped and supported me on this exciting journey in the field of wine: this vast range of partners in my own personal dance with Bacchus.

GM

From Richard Tresidder

Unlike Gareth, I came to wine and alcohol at a somewhat earlier age, as I spent most of my childhood living in bars and restaurants. Despite this, I do not purport to be either a wine connoisseur or a wine expert. However, from an early age I was fascinated by wine: I loved their names, the idea of places, but most of all I was fascinated by the way in which people drank, handled wine bottles and how they examined wine labels.

In the 1970s in the UK, wine was still very much seen as a preserve of the wealthy and the well educated; however, by the time I arrived at University in 1988, wine was regularly drunk by my fellow students, friends and peers. At this point, it was clear that a number of these people attempted to use wine and their knowledge of wine as a marker of their identity, status and class. One of these very proudly bought a large Nachtmann red wine balloon glass and an expensive bottle of Bordeaux; he then proceeded to pour the whole bottle into the glass. At this point I realised that we were both reading different signals from the consumption behaviour. It also raised questions as to what type of messages he was trying to send. For me, these little quirks of behaviour tell an awful lot about the person, their identity, their knowledge and who they want to be seen as. He was very proud of the fact that he had found a glass big enough to hold a whole bottle of wine, while I was wondering if he knew what he was doing, as the wine was not shared, it had no opportunity to oxidise and it could be argued that this expensive bottle of wine had been wasted. However, it was clear that he gained insurmountable joy from the consumption process.

So, for the past 30 years, I have been a watcher of wine, people and culture. This watching of cultural activities led to me undertaking both a master's and doctorate in social anthropology and semiotics. Therefore, this book is the result of a lifetime of wine watching.

I would like to thank Jenny Cockhill at Sheffield Hallam University for all of her support and patience, but most of all, for providing me with the time and space to undertake research and writing. And as always, I would like to thank Emmie for proof reading my work and making sense of my mad ramblings and of course putting up with the strange writing hours I keep.

RT

References

Rainbird, George (1983). *An Illustrated Guide to Wine* (London: Octopus).
Robinson, Jancis (1997). *Confessions of a Wine Lover* (London: Viking/Penguin).

ABBREVIATIONS

abv	Alcohol by volume
AOC	*Appellation d'Origine Contrôlée* (France – traditional term equivalent to AOP)
AOP	*Appellation d'Origine Protégée* (French equivalent of PDO)
BAC	Blood alcohol content
°C	Degrees Celsius (also known as 'Centigrade')
CO_2	Carbon dioxide
DO	*Denominación de Origen* (Spanish traditional term for PDO)
DOC	*Denominazione di Origine Controllata* (Italy – traditional term equivalent to DOP)
DOCG	*Denominazione di Origine Controllata e Garantita* (Italy – a higher status than DOC)
DOP	*Denominazione di Origine Protetta* (Italian equivalent of PDO)
EC	European Commission
EU	European Union
g	Grams
GST	Goods and Services Tax
ha	Hectares (a measure of land area equivalent to 100m x 100m – i.e. 1/100th of a square kilometre or about 2.5 acres)
hl	Hectolitres (100 litres)
IGP	*Indication Géographique Protégée* (French equivalent of PGI – the same abbreviation is also used in Italy and Spain)
IMW	Institute of Masters of Wine
kg	Kilograms
l	Litres
m	Metres
mg	Milligrams

ml	Millilitres (1/1000th of a litre)
MW	Master of Wine
NV	Non-vintage
PDO	Protected Designation of Origin
PGI	Protected Geographical Indication
QbA	*Qualitätswein bestimmter Anbaugebiete* (German equivalent of PDO)
QmP	*Prädikatswein* (formerly *Qualitätswein mit Prädikat* – Germany – a higher status than QbA – see Chapter 1)
QW	*Qualitätswein* (Germany – equivalent to QbA)
SO_2	Sulphur dioxide
VAT	Value added tax
WSET	Wine & Spirit Education Trust

1

THE NATURE OF WINE, PROTECTED DESIGNATIONS AND LABELLING

This book is an exploration in the field of contemporary wine studies – in broad terms, the study of the place of wine in modern society.

Such studies can take many directions. Wine studies can lead us into technical questions of where grapes are grown, the methods of viticulture, how they are vinified, and the qualities of the wine that results. They can lead to questions of law regarding the labelling of wines and how they are sold. In many parts of the world, the livelihoods of large numbers of workers depend on the production or sale of wine, and wine studies can embrace important questions of economics.

But wine would be of little interest were it not for those who buy it, drink it, and share it with others. Although we give some consideration to the technical and legal issues, the central focus of this book is the role of wine in society, drawing especially on the field of social anthropology. Social anthropologists take a particular interest in objects that are given a special place of importance in a social context. Perhaps more than any other food or drink product, wine has a very rich symbolism in modern society in many parts of the world. So we explore questions of how wines are grown, produced, labelled, selected and served from the central focus of wine as a social object. Anthropologists also take great interest in the patterns by which people interact with each other and with objects of significance – patterns that are sometimes described as a dance (see the Preface for more on this theme). So this book is an investigation of how society dances with wine and the implications of that dance for a wide range of social, cultural and ethical questions.

To investigate these issues with any precision, we first we need to understand the nature of wine: the definition of the term, the components of wine, and the rules on how it can be labelled and sold. These issues, sometimes described as the 'oenological system', form the focus of this chapter. We will also explore the principal quality factors that give some wines greater depth than others. Then, building on these principles, Chapter 2 will start to consider the social significance

What is wine?

Many people enjoy a glass of wine without thinking what the term means. In fact, sometimes consumers and even retailers refer to a drink as 'wine' when technically it doesn't meet the legal definition of wine.

Under European Union (EU) law, wine is *the product obtained exclusively from the total or partial alcoholic fermentation of fresh grapes, whether or not crushed, or of grape must.*[1] Similar definitions are used in many other parts of the world. In the United Kingdom, such regulations have the force of law under the European Communities Act 1972: this was the Act by which the UK became a member of the former Common Market – now the EU.

It is worth noting a number of elements of this definition.

- Wine can only be made from grapes – the fruit of the vine. Of course, it is also possible to carry out an alcoholic fermentation on juice obtained from other fruits, but the end product must then be called a 'fruit wine', not just 'wine'. In such cases a fruit name must always appear before the word 'wine' – for example, 'apple wine' or 'blackberry wine'. The word 'wine' on its own always means wine made from grapes. Grapes are a very special product for winemaking: when ripe they have the highest ratio of sugar to water and other compounds compared to all popular fruits. So, when the sugar is converted to alcohol during the fermentation, the final product has a significant level of alcohol – typically 10% to 14%. The alcohol is essential to give body and structure to the wine. In many cases these levels of alcohol are achieved entirely from the sugars in the grapes, without chaptalisation (addition of sugar to the fermenting juice, see p. 5). With other fruits, extensive chaptalisation is generally needed to achieve acceptable levels of alcohol.
- Wine must be made from fresh grapes, or at least grape must. The term 'fresh' is not defined, but it is generally accepted that the grapes must be crushed and winemaking must begin reasonably soon after the grapes are picked; certainly most would say no more than 24–48 hours later. Many leading producers try to keep this time as short as a few hours, if they possibly can, in order to maintain fresh flavours in the wine. If grapes are picked and allowed to rest for long periods they will deteriorate rapidly. (There are some exceptions to this rule – for example, in the production of Amarone in the Valpolicella region of northern Italy, where the grapes are picked and allowed to dry in warm loft areas in the roofs before they are used for winemaking. But the drying process is considered part of the winemaking and the grapes are transferred to the drying lofts quickly after picking [see Belfrage 2004].) It follows that winemaking under this definition must

always take place in the region where the grapes are grown, or reasonably nearby (see the next section on the importance of geographical origins). Where grapes are pressed and the juice is then stored and transported long distances before being used to make wine, the product must be described as 'made-wine' – not simply 'wine'. In some countries, there are specific local terms for made wines, in particular, a made-wine produced in the UK can be labelled 'British wine' – but this is very different from 'English wine' or 'Welsh wine' that is made from grapes locally grown in England or Wales. British wine is largely made from grapes grown in warm Mediterranean countries such as Cyprus.

- For grapes to become wine, there must be an alcoholic fermentation. This involves the action of yeasts which convert the sugar to alcohol, releasing heat and carbon dioxide (CO_2). The definition does not require *all* the sugars to be fermented – in many cases the fermentation is stopped (either deliberately or naturally if the yeast reaches its limit), leaving a wine with some residual sweetness. Sometimes in a dessert wine a high proportion of sugars may remain. If, however, all or nearly all the sugars are fermented, the end result is described as a dry wine – one where there is no obvious sweetness on the palate.

The definition above in the EU Regulation is clarified by a number of supplementary requirements as follows (though there are *derogations* from some of these – in other words, specific cases where the general rule may be relaxed for specific products in specific regions).

However, the definition is of little interest unless wine is agreeable to drink. The pleasure people get from drinking wine depends on the balance of alcohol, water and many other components that contribute to the aromas and flavour of a wine. So the next requirement is to consider these components.

Minimum alcoholic strength

The first additional requirement under EU law is that to be classed as wine, the fermented grape product must generally have an actual alcoholic strength of at least 8.5% (or 9% if it includes grapes from what is defined as 'zone C' in the south of Europe). Note that alcohol levels are always measured by volume – so if a wine is labelled as 12% alcohol or 12% abv ('alcohol by volume') it means that approximately 12% of the volume is alcohol – so if you drink a 100ml glass of a 12% wine you will be drinking around 12ml of pure alcohol. (Because alcohol is less dense than water the proportion of alcohol would be lower if one measured the content by weight or mass – the normal approach for food products.) However, beware of treating the alcohol level on a wine label as a precise measure, as the figure on the label is allowed to vary by up to 0.8% from the actual abv – this is to save producers having to reprint labels simply because the abv has changed slightly from one vintage to the next.

The reason for having a lower limit is that characteristics we associate with wine are generally lost if the alcohol is less than 8.5%. So the various 'low-alcohol wines' available in retailers, although potentially beneficial if they reduce alcohol consumption (see Chapter 7), are not technically wines. Some low-alcohol products are produced by blending wine with unfermented grape juice, some are made by stopping the fermentation at an early stage (both of these approaches leave a drink with considerable sweetness), and some rely on advanced methods for removal of alcohol from a finished wine.

Simple calculations and tables enable winegrowers to estimate the final level of alcohol that will be achieved, depending on the sweetness of the grapes. This is critical in deciding when the grapes are ready to pick – in fact, an experienced winegrower can have a good idea purely from chewing individual grape berries in the vineyard. More systematic approaches involve measuring the sugar content by squeezing juice into a hand-held refractomer (the more sugar in the grapes, the more light is bent) or by crushing a quantity of grapes and measuring the density of the juice (the must) with a hydrometer (the hydrometer floats higher in must with more sugar). See Table 1.1 for examples.

In most wine-growing regions the need for at least 8.5% alcohol presents no problem, but in the coolest regions there will often be years when the grapes do not ripen sufficiently to generate 8.5% alcohol once fermented.

This is not necessarily a problem, however, because, under the EU rules, the 8.5% minimum alcohol level does not have to come solely from the sugar in

TABLE 1.1 Levels of alcohol in the final wine depending on the sugar content of the grapes

Density (specific gravity) of the must[1]	Sweetness measured in degrees Oechsle (Oe)[2]	Sugar content in degrees Brix[3]	Potential alcohol (abv) in the wine if the must is fully fermented
1.045	45	11.3	6%
1.060	60	14.8	8%
1.075	75	18.1	10%
1.089	89	21.4	12%
1.103	103	24.5	14%

Source: Compiled using calculations from Musther (2014) and additional information from Riesling Rules (2014).

Notes:

[1] Specific gravity (SG) is the density ratio as compared to pure water. However, the density of almost any substance is affected by temperature – in winemaking, most tables assume must at 20°C.
[2] The Oechsle scale is widely used in German- and English-speaking countries. It is simply the number of thousandths by which the SG exceeds 1, as shown by the examples above.
[3] The Brix scales is used in a number of countries. It is a measure of the sugar percentage in the juice (i.e. the number of grams of sugar in 100 grams of solution). Different sugars have different densities, so the scale measures sugars in sucrose equivalent.
All these calculations have to make assumptions about the proportion of matter in the juice other than sugar and water, so slightly different versions of these tables appear in different publications.

the grapes. In general a measure of *chaptalisation* is permitted – in other words, the addition of sugar to the fermenting grape must as a form of *enrichment*. The sugar added by chaptalisation is converted to alcohol by the yeast alongside the natural sugars in the grapes, so giving a higher level of alcohol in the final wine. The process is named after Jean-Antoine Chaptal who promoted the process in France in the early nineteenth century with a view to improving the quality of wine (Unwin 1994).

But whilst chaptalisation can give wine additional body by increasing the level of alcohol, it also dilutes the natural flavours of the grapes, and it is generally accepted that the best wines are made with little or no chaptalisation. Top winemakers will generally avoid chaptalisation or only chaptalise by a minimal amount. In high-quality wine regions where grapes normally ripen sufficiently to produce wines with acceptable levels of alcohol, chaptalisation is generally prohibited for quality wines, and even elsewhere it is subject to strict limits. Under the EU Regulation, chaptalisation is permitted by up to 3% alcohol in zone A (Northern Europe – this includes the UK and the northern half of Germany), up to 2% in zone B which includes northern France, Austria and the south of Germany, and up to 1.5% in zone C (the main wine regions of France, also Italy, Spain and other Mediterranean countries).

However, even if the maximum 3% chaptalisation is used by a zone A producer, it follows that the grapes must have sufficient ripeness to deliver at least 5.5% alcohol (increased to 8.5% in the final wine by chaptalisation). In years with exceptionally cold weather, the European Commission can increase the 3% maximum level of chaptalisation in zone A to 3.5%. But most producers, even if they choose to chaptalise, would aim to keep well below these limits.

Nevertheless there are a few exceptions to the 8.5% minimum alcoholic rule. Some classic wines such as Asti DOCG – the famous lightly sparkling wine of the Piedmont region of Italy made from the Moscato Bianco grape – typically has only around 5% alcohol. So if the definition above were rigorously applied, Asti would not be classed as wine! Asti is fermented in closed vats known as *autoclaves* (so the carbon dioxide is retained, creating the fizz) but the fermentation is stopped at around 5% by refrigerating the fermenting must to a temperature where the yeast can no longer work (Belfrage 2004). It is one of the great styles of sparkling wine, much appreciated for its delicacy. (The low level of alcohol in the final wine is because a good deal of the sugars are not fermented – grapes picked for Asti would have well over 8.5% alcohol if fully fermented.)

It would clearly be a disaster for producers in the region if Asti were not classed as wine, because of having less than 8.5% alcohol in the final wine. However, the EC Regulation states (by means of a derogation from the general principle) that the 8.5% lower limit of alcohol is reduced to just 4.5% in the case of wines with a *protected designation of origin* (PDO) or a *protected geographical indication* (PGI) (see pp. 25–9 for an explanation of these terms). It follows that where a classic style of wine from a particular region has a lower level of alcohol, it can still be classed as wine (provided all the rules of the PDO or PGI are followed).

A further derogation states that Tokaji Eszencia is also classed as wine, even though the alcohol level may be very low indeed – maybe only 1% or 2%. Tokaji Eszencia is made from the juice of super-ripe grapes from the Tokaj region of Hungary – but the sugar levels are so high that fermentation stops soon after it starts because the yeast cells find it almost impossible to work with such a sweet environment.

Nevertheless, these are exceptions. The normal principle is that wine must have at least 8.5% alcohol (of which at least 5.5% must come directly from the grapes).

Maximum alcoholic strength

The EU regulation also specifies a maximum alcoholic strength of 15%, on the grounds that a product with alcohol above this level does not, to most people, taste like wine. It is worth noting from Table 1.1 that a wine with 14% alcohol, if it is unchaptalised, requires grapes measuring 24.5 Brix – in other words nearly a quarter (almost 25%) of the grape must is sugar! Going much beyond this leads to a wine where the alcohol is so dominant that many of the other flavours we associate with wine are diminished.

Wine products about 15% abv are generally fortified wines (or *liqueur wines* as they are called in the EU Regulation) where distilled alcohol is added at some stage to the wine – see p. 13.

In the past it was widely believed that 15% was effectively the maximum alcohol that could be reached by the normal process of yeast fermentation on wine grapes, and that anything with more than 15% alcohol was likely to be a fortified wine. However, it is now accepted that in some of the warmer regions of Europe and other countries, grapes may ripen sufficiently to give alcohol levels of 16% or even more, and the EC Regulation now allows for the possibility of a wine with up to 20% alcohol, if it is made in appropriate areas where this is normal and provided the wine is completely unchaptalised. This enables winemakers such as those producing DO Montilla-Moriles in the south of Spain to label their products as wine.

Other content in wine

Water and alcohol account for the largest constituents in almost all wines, but a blend of alcohol and water does not make for a very interesting drink! The character of wine – the flavours, aromas and colour come very much from the other components. The most important other components are acids, polyphenols (which include tannins) and minerals (Bird 2000).

Acids

Acids are a crucial component in all fruits, and a significant proportion of acids must be retained in the final wine to give a sense of freshness. Under the EU law,[2] a finished wine must have at least 3.5g/l of acidity. In practice such a wine will generally taste quite 'flabby' – an acidity of at least 7g/l is much more common. There will be many different acids in a wine, but measurements are based on 'tartaric equivalent' – in other words, how many grams per litre of tartaric acid would lead to the measured result (tartaric acid is the most common acid in wine).

Getting the right balance of acidity is a key issue in winemaking. As grapes ripen, in broad terms the sugars rise and the acidity falls. A winemaker in a hot region such as southern Italy or much of Australia will often chose to harvest the grapes before they have reached the maximum sugar levels in order to maintain sufficient freshness. This is especially important for white and rosé wines – we say a wine tastes 'crisp' if it has a lively acidity.

On the other hand, in cooler regions such as the UK and northern Germany, acids may be uncomfortably high, particularly in a year when there has been less sunshine than expected or extensive rains that have hampered ripening. If nothing is done about this, one can produce a wine with such raspingly high acidity it is hard to drink.

It is permissible under EU wine law to adjust the acidity – in hot regions by adding acids and in cool regions by deacidification. If so, most of the acidity adjustment must be done with the must, *before* fermentation, although a small further adjustment is allowed on the final wine if necessary. But every adjustment upsets the natural balance of other characteristics in the wine, so winemakers will always seek to minimise the need for adjustments of this kind.

Moreover, most people do not naturally taste acidity on its own – what we notice on the palate is the balance of sweetness and acidity. In a completely dry wine, too much acidity tastes unpleasant, but if the wine has some sweetness we need a good deal of acidity if the wine is to taste fresh and fruity (otherwise it will just taste like dilute treacle – when this happens we say the taste is 'cloying'). Very sweet dessert wines will have very high levels of acidity to balance.

So, in cool regions where the wines have high acidity it is common to add some unfermented grape juice (often known as *süssreserve* – the German name) to the final wine just before bottling. The sweetness in the süssreserve helps to balance the acidity and give a rounded wine. But, like chaptalisation, the addition of süssreserve is a form of enrichment – adding sweetness that was not natural to the grapes when picked – and is subject to strict limits. The limits mentioned above – for example, the rule allowing potential alcohol to be increased by up to 3% in zone A apply to the chaptalisation and süssreserve additions combined.

But even in cool regions, wines made without any sugar adjustments are often seen as the best. In Germany, such wines are labelled *Prädikatswein* (formerly *Qualitätswein mit Prädikat* or QmP) – this is above the normal level of quality wines that are labelled QbA (*Qualitätswein bestimmter Anbaugebiete* – quality wine from a specific region).

Acids are crucial to the structure of a wine, and especially for white and rosé wines, enabling the wine to be kept for a period of time (including further development in bottle).

Tannins and other polyphenols

Polyphenols are complex organic molecules that provide crucial character to wines. The full range of polyphenols is still being researched, but the most common and important polyphenols, especially in red wines, are *tannins* and *anthocyanins*.

Tannins are the drying bark-like flavours that come mainly from the skins of grapes and also from the pips and stalks. In red wines they are crucial to give the wine structure and stability. Red wines normally have less acidity than whites (we do not usually want a red wine to taste too fresh and fruity) but the tannins (with the alcohol) give them a sense of body on the palate.

It is difficult to describe the flavour of tannin, but it is often the main characteristic we pick up on a red wine with plenty of flavour – especially when we say a wine has plenty of depth to stand up to rich food. Tannins are most obvious as a drying sensation on the lips and the sides of one's mouth after tasting a red wine, especially when we have swirled it around the mouth.

In white wines, a winemaker will try to minimise the amount of tannins by crushing the grapes and separating the juice quickly from the skins and stalks. De-stemming (to remove the stalks) and gentle pressing of the grapes (to avoid crushing the pips) are often used to avoid significant amounts of tannins entering the wine.

However, red wines are made by fermenting the juice on the skins and stalks, so that the maximum amount of colour and flavour (including tannins) is extracted.

The best quality wines, both red and white, may be aged in oak casks, which adds further tannin from the wood; however, the very gentle exchange of oxygen through the walls of a wooden cask enables a wine to develop and, in particular, enables tannins to soften. But it is important to get this right. Putting a delicate white wine in new oak barrels kills the wine with heavy oaky flavours. When white wine is put in oak, the casks are usually several years old so that only the slightest exchange of tannins takes place. On the other hand a robust red wine made from grapes like Cabernet Sauvignon or Syrah may be able to take a good deal of oak.

A young red wine will often have too much tannin for comfortable drinking – the tannins can make it taste very heavy or even bitter and drinking several glasses of the wine (especially with insufficient water alongside) can easily lead to headaches.

Also, young tannins are sometimes described as tasting 'green' or 'stalky' – the sensation is almost as if one is biting into a tree! As a red wine develops in cask or in bottle, the tannins will develop into softer more complex flavours (and the rough tannins may be released as they turn into solids and form a sediment). The ideal of a top-quality well-developed red wine is to have tannins that taste smooth or velvety on the palate. But that is usually only achieved with the best grapes from the best areas, aged for exactly the right time in oak, and then given a good deal more time to develop in bottle. (See Chapter 3 for more on what makes a quality wine.)

EU wine law does permit the addition of tannins artificially, but this is prohibited for most quality wines and it can give a 'stewed tea' taste, so the vast majority of winemakers would avoid doing so. Tannins can be removed to some extent by subjecting the finished wine to a very fine filtration, but that will also remove much of the character of the wine, so the best wines normally only have a very light filtration (if any) before bottling, and tannins thus only soften very slowly through the natural ageing process above. So winemakers will normally take care to manage the level of contact with the skins and stalks (and the amount of contact with oak if applicable) to achieve the tannin level desired.

Many other polyphenols contribute to the style of a wine, especially anthocyanins which give the colour to red wines. The colour in wine comes almost entirely from the grape skins (even with red grapes, the juice is normally white – that is why white wines such as Champagne can be made from red grapes such as Pinot Noir). In a red wine, which is fermented on its skins, factors such as the length and temperature of the fermentation have a big impact on extraction of anthocyanins and other polyphenols. Likewise, the extent to which the juice is pumped over the cap of skins and stalks (which naturally float to the top) has a big impact on the final colour.

In the case of rosé wines, a key skill for the winemaker is to keep the juice in contact with the skins for just enough time to extract enough anthocyanins to give the required pink colour. This depends very much on the grape variety and the density of colour in the skins, but often just a few hours' contact is sufficient.

Minerals

As a vine grows it draws up water from the soil which may include a rich array of minerals. It is often said that these find their way into the grapes and give character to a wine – although the whole notion of 'minerality' in wine remains a major field of research. The mechanisms by which soil characteristics affect the flavour of a wine are still not fully understood.

Nevertheless, it is clear that the best wines normally come from vineyards where the geology, drainage and soil structure lead to a greater complexity in the finished wine. These issues – the unique properties of the physical location – are all part of the notion of *terroir* (explored in Chapter 5). The differences between terroirs are the main reasons why wines made from the same grape varieties using similar winemaking techniques can taste very different depending on where they are grown.

Different grape varieties are better suited to different soils – for example, the best Chardonnay in regions like Burgundy and Champagne comes from chalky slopes. Even amongst the chalky soils in various locations, specialists distinguish the different geological ages, and the presence of fossils, as having a major impact on the style of wine. The pronounced minerality in wines of Chablis is a prime example of this. By contrast the Gamay grape is generally considered to give its best result on granite soils, as in the Beaujolais region.

But in all regions, the grapes will have the greatest concentration of minerals if the vine has to work hard to draw up moisture – so vines planted on a well-drained slope will generally give a much better wine with more complex flavours and minerals than vines planted on flatter land.

However, minerals can also be a challenge to the winemaker. In particular, after fermentation, the alcohol reduces their solubility (Bird 2000) and they may precipitate out, forming crystals in the wine. This is especially an issue with tartrates – whilst they are harmless, consumers may reject a wine with tartrate crystals thinking there is broken glass in the wine. To address this, larger wineries will often put their wines through a cold stabilisation process where the wine is held at a very low temperature (typically $-4°C$) to encourage crystallisation of the tartrates so they can be filtered before bottling. But this is an expensive process, and in any case every additional treatment can affect the final character of the wine.

Other regulatory issues

Although the EC Regulation 479/2008 does not have any specific provisions regarding tannins or minerals in the definition of what is meant by 'wine', the regulations on oenological practices and the rules for specific regions place many additional demands on winemakers, especially to ensure that the finished wine does not contain harmful amounts of substances.

In particular, most winemakers use sulphur dioxide (SO_2) at various stages in winemaking and bottling to maintain hygiene, but there are strict limits on the amount of SO_2 that can be included in the finished wine, as it can trigger allergic reactions, especially in people who are asthmatic. In most cases the total SO_2 cannot exceed 200mg/l (slightly higher limits are allowed for sweet wines), but most producers would aim for much less than this. Even within these limits, the label must show 'contains sulphites' to warn consumers.

However, there are many other requirements for wine labelling, as outlined later in this chapter.

A natural product

We have seen that wine is fundamentally a natural product: grapes are picked, crushed, and through the natural actions of yeasts, sugar is converted to alcohol. In many regions there is sufficient natural yeast on the grapes to bring about fermentation once the grapes are crushed, but even where specific yeasts are added, yeast is a naturally occurring single-celled plant. Almost all winemaking uses variants of *Saccharomyces cerevisiae* that readily multiplies in sugary liquids such as grape must.

This process of collecting grapes, breaking them up, and enabling them to ferment in a suitable container due to the action of yeast is the essence of all winemaking. Of course it helps to have suitable facilities to crush and press grapes, tanks of different sizes for fermentation, and a means to control their temperature that can greatly improve the style of wine that results. A winery also needs facilities to pump wine from one tank to another – especially for 'racking' when the wine is drawn off the lees (the 'lees' refers to the pips, skins and dead yeast which remain at the bottom of the tank). One also needs a means of putting the finished wine into bottles, and possibly some filtration on the way. If the wine is to be aged before bottling – especially if oak barrels are to be used – the winery needs a lot of space to hold all the wine in an environment with cool temperatures, which is why many wine producers use underground cellars. (See Chapter 3 for more on these quality issues.)

It takes many years to become a top winemaker, in order to make the key judgements regarding the ripeness of the grapes, fermentation times and temperatures, choice of yeast, when and how often to rack the wine, and so on. A winemaker may also have to decide on specialist treatments such as barrel-ageing or cold stabilisation or how much SO_2 to use when bottling.

A modern high-tech winery with large numbers of stainless steel tanks, specialist monitoring and temperature control facilities, automatic pumping over, and a sophisticated bottling line can make it look as though the resultant wine is some kind of chemical product. However, all the equipment is simply there to provide a safe hygienic environment for a natural process.

For most wine, the work in the vineyard, pruning and tending vines throughout the year is at least as important as what happens in the winery. Many winemakers say that the quality of the fruit is the most important issue – everything in the winery is secondary to that.

Many winemakers are quite uncomfortable with being described by that term as they do not 'make' the wine in any personal sense. In France, it is rare to meet anyone with the title *vinificateur*, which is the direct translation of winemaker; it is much more common to use a term such as *chef de cave* (the person in charge of the cellar) or *régisseur* (the steward of the estate) or simply *vigneron* (winegrower). Fundamentally, winemaking is simply about supporting a natural process or 'giving nature a helping hand' as many winemakers describe their work.

Red, white, rosé, dry, sweet, sparkling, fortified

So far this chapter has concentrated on the legal definition of wine, and the main constituents. But, of course, wine is much more than a fermented grape product meeting specific technical requirements. There are many factors that distinguish one wine from another. (This chapter focuses on the technical issues, but in Chapter 3 we will refer back to these principles in exploring why some wines are considered superior to others.)

This section first examines the different styles of wine, then considers the choice of grape varieties, then the question of geographical origin, and finally some points on the vintage of a wine. After this overview we consider how the various choices in the vineyard and winery affect the overall quality of a wine.

Colour

The most obvious distinction between wines is that of colour. But this is more than a difference of appearance: red wines and white wines don't just look different – they taste and smell fundamentally different.

This is partly due to the grape varieties: red wines are made from red (or black) grapes, whereas white wines are usually made from white grapes (although, as we noted above, most red grapes have a clear juice and so white wines can be made from red grapes if required).

But the process of winemaking is fundamentally different between white and red wines. White wines are made by crushing the grapes, and then separating the juice to be fermented on its own, typically keeping the fermentation fairly cool to maintain the fresh fruity flavours and elegant floral or mineral aromas. Red wines are fermented on their skins to extract tannins and colour, and the fermentation is allowed to get a good deal warmer in order to help the extraction – whereas winemakers are keen to avoid any significant levels of tannins in white wines.

The winemaker's approach will have a major impact on the final colour – for example in terms of the skin-contact time and whether the wine is aged in oak. White wines can range from water-white, to pale green, to those that have a pronounced straw colour. Red wines can range from very pale reds, which are barely deeper than a rosé, to a wide range of ruby colours or very deep purple colours (occasionally, almost black) where even a small quantity appears opaque in the glass.

Rosé wines are not a blend of red and white, but rather a style in their own right. A rosé wine is made (mainly) from red grapes but using white winemaking approaches – so the grapes are pressed, allowed a short period of skin contact to extract just enough colour, and then the juice is fermented as for a white wine.

Sweetness

As we saw above, wines can be dry (with little or no residual sugar) or they can have varying levels of sweetness ranging from medium dry to extremely sweet. Although small levels of sweetening can be added by the use of *süssreserve* (see p. 7), all high-quality sweet wines rely on significant levels of natural sugars in the grapes. Only some of the sugars are fermented to alcohol – what remains gives a delicate, luscious sweetness to the wine (although good acidity is also essential to give a fresh lively sweet wine – as we noted above, if it tastes too sweet and lacks freshness, a wine is said to be 'cloying' on the palate).

The best quality sweet wines rely on grapes that are picked very late in the season (in the Northern hemisphere this can mean anything from November to January) so that they start to dry on the vines and, ideally, experience morning mists. This can lead to the fungus *Botrytis cinerea* settling on the grape skins. This botrytis (also known as *noble rot* or *pourriture noble*) has the effect of extracting much of the water, leaving the grape berries partly shrivelled with an incredibly high concentration of sugars. But it is also very expensive to produce the very best botrytis-affected wines, as it is necessary to make many passes through the vineyard on different occasions over a period of several weeks, just picking individual berries that show the effects of botrytis (rather than whole bunches). The top wines of Sauternes (in the Bordeaux region of France), from the Tokaj region of Hungary, and wines from any part of Germany where the grapes reach the sweetness for the wine to be classified as *Trockenbeerenauslese* are all made this way.

Fortified wines

For certain styles of wine, as we saw above, additional alcohol may be added, giving a higher abv than can be achieved purely through fermentation of sugars in the grapes. Under EU law, the result is called a *liqueur wine*. The level of alcohol is increased by adding *brandy* – that is, wine that has been distilled. Distillation allows the alcohol to evaporate and it is then condensed. If the resultant liqueur wine is labelled with a European region of origin, only wine brandy obtained from grapes grown in the EU can be used for the fortification (but the brandy does not have to come from the same region as the wine being fortified).

Port is one of the most common fortified wines: very ripe grapes from the Douro Valley in Portugal are picked and crushed and the fermentation starts, but brandy is added and the fermentation stops, leaving some rich sugars in the wine. Most Port is sold at around 20% abv – but that level is only reached by taking fermented sugars from the grapes together with the alcohol added.

Sherry – from the DO Jerez-Xeres-Sherry region of Spain – is likewise a fortified wine, though in that case the brandy is added after the fermentation is complete. This means that the most famous classic style of Sherry – *a fino* – is completely dry (although some styles of Sherry are also sweetened by addition of concentrated grape must).

Sparkling wines

Most wines are still, but some of the world's great wines are fizzy, due to dissolved carbon dioxide (CO_2) in the wine. In most cases, the fizz is a natural result of the fermentation – as we saw above, the process of yeast fermentation of sugars releases heat and large quantities of CO_2. In most winemaking, the fermentation vat is either open or it has a simple valve allowing the CO_2 to escape. But if fermentation takes place in a closed vessel, the CO_2 remains and becomes dissolved in the wine. If such a wine is then bottled the result is a sparkling wine.

The intensity of the dissolved CO_2, and hence and the resulting style in terms of fizziness, is measured by the pressure inside the bottle. Normal atmospheric pressure is approximately 1 bar. A lightly sparkling wine (sometimes called by the French term *pétillant*) may have just 1 bar of pressure beyond normal atmosphere, whereas Champagne and other wines made by the traditional method (see third bullet point down) generally have a pressure of around 6 bar. To withstand this, such wines have to be supplied in much stronger bottles than a still wine.

There are various methods of generating the fizz – three of the most common are as follows, but other variations are possible.

- At the very cheapest end, some basic sparkling wines not carrying any protected designation of origin are made simply by injecting CO_2 into the base wine (as for making soft fizzy drinks).
- Many regions use the *Charmat* or *cuve close* method where the wine is fermented in a large closed vessel so the CO_2 cannot escape. This is widely used in Italy, for production of Prosecco and similar styles of wine. The resulting fizzy wine is chilled, filtered, and bottled under pressure, giving a light, elegant and easy drinking style of sparkling wine, generally with around 11% abv. A similar approach, but with different tanks and with fermentation stopped much earlier, is used for Asti (as mentioned above).
- All the top sparkling wines of the world, including Champagne in France, other French wines using the name '*Crémant*' (e.g. Crémant d'Alsace, Crémant de Bourgogne), Cava in Spain, and the Quality Sparkling Wines of England use the *traditional method* with a secondary fermentation in bottle. (It was formerly known as the 'Champagne method' but that term is no longer permitted due to the protection of the term 'Champagne', which can only be applied to sparkling wines from the Champagne region of France.) A still wine is made from grapes with fairly high acidity. A small amount of sugar and yeast is then added, and the wine is bottled with a temporary closure and left to lie horizontally, preferably in cool cellars, for a considerable time (minimum nine months, but often several years for the best traditional method wines). Towards the end of that time, a process of 'disgorgement' takes place. The bottles will be 'riddled' – either manually or by machine – to bring the dead yeast cells into the neck, the temporary cap is removed so that the yeast plug flies out, and the bottle is topped up with clean wine and possibly a little sweetening (known as the dosage). It is usually then closed with a traditional cork held in place with a wire closure. The final wine is usually around 12–13% abv.

Because of the processes involved, sparkling wines – especially those made by the traditional method – will normally be considerably more expensive than still wines at the same level of quality, and in countries such as the UK they are also subject to a higher level of duty (see Chapter 7).

What to drink when?

The different styles of wine considered in this section are often drunk in different circumstances: indeed the social context where wines are consumed is one of the central themes of this book.

However, there are a number of traditional assumptions. For example, sparkling wines and Sherries are often served as aperitifs, white wines with lighter food dishes, red wines with richer savoury dishes, sweet wines with desserts (or sometimes with cheeses) and Port at the end of a meal. Some people put a big focus on matching particular wines with particular foods, and at a formal meal it may be appropriate to serve different wines with each course.

Moreover, a special occasion may well justify opening a wine such as Champagne that few people would drink with a weekday supper. So there is a clear need for different styles of wine to suit different occasions and foods.

The idea that certain wines must be drunk on certain occasions is rejected by many consumers. Many find they prefer certain styles — for example, some will only ever drink white wines; others stick to red wines; some love rosé wines whilst others hate them, and so on. Much wine is consumed as a social drink rather than with a meal. The choice of which wine to drink on what occasion is much more than a question of wine style — it raises huge questions about price, status, marketing and much more — ideas that we investigate in the following chapters of this book.

But before considering the social significance of wine, there is much more to distinguish wines than the simple issues of colour, sweetness and the choice of still/sparkling. Many other factors help us differentiate and categorise wines, in particular the grape variety, the geographical origin of the wine, and (in some cases) the vintage is also a significant issue.

Grape varieties

The style of wine is determined to a considerable extent by the grape variety. Almost all wines of quality are made using grapes from *Vitis vinifera* — the main species of grapevine that is indigenous to Europe — but there are a huge number of different varieties of grape that can be produced from the vine (see Robinson, Harding and Vouillamoz 2012 for details of 1,368 varieties that have been identified in specific locations). Well-known varieties such as Chardonnay, Pinot Grigio, or Gamay or Cabernet Sauvignon are all varieties within the species *V. vinifera*.

Grape varieties can be distinguished between white and red, those for cool climates and warm climates, varieties yielding different levels of sugar (and hence alcohol), different acidity levels, and between high- and low-yielding varieties (see p. 20 on yields).

Some varieties such as Chardonnay and Merlot are reasonably straightforward to produce: provided they are planted in locations with appropriate levels of sunshine and water they will ripen reliably most years and give a fairly good yield. They are thus highly adaptable and can be grown in many different parts of the world (giving many different styles of wine). Others, such as Pinot Noir or Nebbiolo are much more fickle and are difficult to grow successfully outside their traditional regions, but those who enjoy good wines are willing to pay a little more for wines from interesting and challenging varieties.

However, beyond the technical issues, grape varieties can go in and out of fashion with consumers, which can cause big fluctuations in prices. At one time the well-known international varieties such as Chardonnay, Cabernet Sauvignon and Sauvignon Blanc attracted much higher prices than less well-known local varieties, but by the second decade of the twenty-first century consumers have started to take much more interest in less well-known local or indigenous varieties.

A vine-grower planting a new vineyard has, in theory, a huge potential choice of which varieties to plant. So, in a region where there are a few legal controls, the grower will consider which varieties are likely to grow best in the chosen location (bearing in mind the soil, drainage, climate – the issues that make up the *terroir* of a particular vineyard – see Chapter 5). Sometimes experimentation is needed over many years to see what works best. Moreover, few vine-growers are looking to maximise quantity alone: it is often better to accept a smaller yield from a more challenging variety if the end result is a more interesting and complex tasting wine (which will sell for a higher price).

There will also be some commercial considerations – for example, a grower in a new region of Hungary may be able to get a better price by planting internationally well-known varieties such as Chardonnay or Sauvignon Blanc rather than the local variety Furmint. However, with adept marketing (see Chapter 8) consumers can be persuaded that new varieties offer something different and exciting – so, for example, varieties like Fiano and Nero d'Avola now regularly appear on wine labels from southern Italy. Drinkers of quality Spanish white wines look for varieties such as Albariño or Verdejo, which were unknown except to experts until relatively recent times. Even the Spanish variety Airén, the most widely planted grape variety in the world if measured by area of planting (Robinson, Harding and Vouillamoz 2012:17), has begun to appear on labels, rather than just being included anonymously in generic Spanish white wines.

However, there is usually less choice of variety in established regions subject to protected geographical designations (see pp. 24–9). It may be illegal to plant varieties that do not comply with the rules of the designation – or, even if planting is legal, the resulting wine would not be allowed to be sold under the name of the appellation, which would generally mean a much lower financial return. Such rules go back many years – for example, as long ago as 1395, the 'very bad and disloyal' Gamay grape was banned from the main vineyards of Burgundy (Robinson, Harding and Vouillamoz 2012:384). It found a new home, further south in the Beaujolais region where, growing on granite soils, it gives a much more pleasing result. Nowadays, anyone planting in Burgundy has a simple choice – whether to plant Chardonnay to produce white wine or Pinot

Noir for red (a few other varieties are technically permitted, but very few growers would plant them by choice).

Impact of variety on the taste of wine

There is no doubt that the choice of grape variety has a major impact on the final style of wine. For example, considering some of the major red varieties:

- Cabernet Sauvignon gives an intense flavour, and deep colour (often opaque in the glass), typically with powerful rich black fruit flavours and plenty of tannin.
- Pinot Noir gives a much lighter red with much softer tannins, but great elegance and complex herbal flavours which develop significantly as the wine ages.
- Sangiovese gives a medium-depth red wine, with elegant cherry flavours and plenty of spice.
- Gamay gives a light fruity style of wine, often bright purple in colour, with more acidity and lighter tannins than many black varieties.

When an expert is presented with a wine to taste 'blind' (that is, with no indication of its origin) the first step is usually to identify the variety, and then to consider where it may have come from. The variety is usually the principal determinant of the style and flavour of the wine.

Many consumers express preferences for particular varieties – for example, some people will always choose a red wine made from the Merlot grape, regardless of where it comes from. Some white wine consumers will always go for Sauvignon Blanc. In many entry-level pubs, bars and smaller restaurants, wine lists only show the grape variety and perhaps a brand name for a wine, with no indication of its origin.

But choosing a wine by variety alone is a highly imprecise process, because many varieties give a completely different style depending on where they are grown. A Pinot Noir from Romania or Chile will generally have a much deeper, more leathery character with much more tannin than a traditional light coloured Pinot Noir from the Côte de Beaune or Côte de Nuits in Burgundy. A Chardonnay from the Hunter Valley in Australia that has perhaps been aged for some time in new oak, will taste very different from the minerally style of Chardonnay that emanates from Chablis in the north of Burgundy.

Even experts will make errors in identifying the main grape variety in a wine, because so many other factors affect the final flavour. Also, whilst some regions focus on a single variety, others find the best wines are produced by blending several grape varieties. This is certainly the case in Bordeaux, where the whites are usually blended primarily from Sauvignon Blanc and Sémillon, and the reds are blends of Cabernet Sauvignon, Cabernet Franc and Merlot. The 'Bordeaux blend' – using mainly these three varieties in different proportions – is widely used in many other red wine regions around the world. Blending is also central to the top red wines of Tuscany in Italy.

In many cases, even more important than the grape variety is the geography. Knowing where a wine comes from is the central issue in most of the rules on wine labelling. Some producers, particularly in the New World, suggest this adds unnecessary mystique, and suggest all wines should be labelled by variety. But in traditional European wine regions with well-respected appellations, producers insist there is no need for the label to show a variety, because certain grape varieties are always associated with the particular geographical appellation.

Quality factors in wine

Even consumers with relatively little experience of wine tasting will readily accept that some wines taste smoother, richer or more complex than others. As someone develops more understanding of wine and a more sophisticated palate (see Chapter 9) the differentiation between one wine and another can be enormous.

This section outlines some of what might be considered 'objective' quality factors in wine – in other words, factors unrelated to the perceived status of a wine in terms of its brand or appellation or classification. We consider the implications of producing these high-quality wines in terms of costs of production and hence the impact on the final price – though, of course, some producers whose wines are highly desirable may be able to charge much more than the cost of production (see Chapter 3 for a full discussion of the distinctions in wine quality and status).

The points that follow only offer a brief introduction to these issues: books and articles specifically on the subjects of viticulture and vinification should be consulted for more detail. See, for example, Halliday and Johnson (1992) or Woods (2001) for books discussing issues in wine production from a consumer perspective. For introductory books aimed at wine producers, sources such as Skelton (2007) on viticulture or Bird (2000) on vinification may be useful.

The sensory aspects of a quality wine

Anyone who has some interest in wine will spend time assessing a wine presented to them – looking at the colour and other aspects of appearance (e.g. bubbles in a sparkling wine), then assessing the aromas given off (the 'nose' of the wine), and finally assessing the wine on the palate. The nose and the palate are the clear signals of quality. Even those with no formal training will often realise as they compare one wine with another that some wines are much more intense and give a much more complex nose and palate than others.

Depending on the grape variety and colour, a good wine will normally give very agreeable aromas, with many different 'notes' signifying complexity – sensations of different fruits, spices and minerals. If it has been aged in oak, there will be some additional aromas from the oak. In a top wine the nose will change and develop over time as the wine 'opens up' in the glass due to the contact with the air (oxygenation). By contrast, an entry-level wine, may have a much lighter aroma, often with just one dimension.

There are many factors that a taster will consider on the palate. The characteristics sought are different between red and whites, with more crispiness (acidity) expected on a white and more tannins on a red. However, in both cases, the ideal wine is smooth and velvety, with great harmony between the different elements. One of the most important indicators of quality is the 'length' of the wine – in other words, how long the flavour persists on the palate once the wine has been swallowed (or spat out). A more concentrated wine, made with demanding requirements in the growing and vinification (see next subsection) has much greater length on the palate. A top wine will also have more complexity with many different flavour sensations. It will also change and develop over time if well stored. By contrast, an entry-level wine may taste quite watery compared to a top wine – the flavours are much lighter.

However, the sensorial assessment of wine is a huge field. Whole books have been written on the principles of wine tasting even at the consumer level (see, for example, Goolden 1990; Gluck 1999) and those studying for wine qualifications are taught systematic tasting techniques (Broadbent 1998). See Chapter 9 regarding how such skills are learned. There are also important debates about how far a taster can ever be truly 'objective' when any assessment of the taste of a wine is a subjective process. Simon (2000) provides a helpful analysis of technical issues in wine tasting, and Smith (2007) provides a collection of articles on the philosophical issues in tasting and assessing wines.

The costs of wine production

The costs of producing wine are usually divided between the costs of growing and harvesting the grapes (viticulture) and the costs of making the wine and ageing it if applicable (vinification). However, both stages involve both capital (one-off) costs and ongoing revenue expenditure every year.

In some cases the capital costs can be enormous and may take many years to recover. For example, vineyards in the most expensive winegrowing areas with the right to prestigious appellations on the resulting wine can cost millions of euros per hectare of land – vastly more than normal prices for agricultural land. Similarly, building a top-quality wine production facility with vast underground barrel cellars next to a historic château can be enormously expensive. Sometimes the owner never expects to recover the capital costs through sales of the wine, and simply hopes to build up the value of the property as a long-term investment that can ultimately be sold.

However, revenue costs that have to be met every year have a direct impact on wine prices. Whilst wine producers are used to balancing good years and bad years, no wine producer can continue producing wine in the long term if the wine cannot be sold for a price that exceeds the annual costs of production.

Yields in the vineyard

Yields from vineyards are usually measured in tonnes per hectare (tonnes/ha) – in other words, the total weight of grapes harvested per hectare of land – or in terms of hectolitres of wine produced from each hectare of vineyard (hl/ha), although some countries still use imperial measurements. A hectare is an area of land 100m × 100m (one hundredth of a square kilometre, equivalent to about 2.5 acres). Wines in fermentation tanks are usually measured in hectolitres – 1hl is 100 litres, or enough to produce 133 bottles using standard 750ml bottles if there is no wastage. So 1hl in tank produces 11 cases of wine (12 bottles per case) allowing for losses of around one bottle in the bottling process.

It might be assumed that winegrowers would look for the highest yields in order to produce as much wine as possible, but if the aim is quality, the converse applies. High yields mean grapes with a high water content, which lead to wines that lack flavour and concentration. Properties looking to make top-quality wines take great steps in the vineyard to restrict the yield, for example, by using pruning and training methods that only allow a small number of buds on each vine, or by conducting a 'green harvest' as bunches start to form but before final ripening, where smaller and less promising bunches are removed. The effect of these measures is to produce fewer grapes but as a result the nutrients drawn up by the vine from the soil are spread across a smaller quantity of grapes that remain, giving more concentrated flavours.

Because of this most controlled appellations (PDOs in European law – see p. 26) have rules on the maximum yield allowed and the higher the status of the appellation the lower the yield. For example, in Burgundy, for red wines (made from Pinot Noir) yields up to 55hl/ha are allowed for regional appellations, but for the village appellations a lower figure of 40hl/ha is the norm, and in the grand crus generally only 35hl/ha are allowed. (See pp. 70–5 for the different tiers of Burgundy.) However, these figures are all considerably lower than allowed in many less demanding wine regions from less challenging varieties; for example, in some high-volume wine-producing areas in Germany and in Greece, production of over 110hl/ha is not unusual (though yields would be much lower in the top vineyards).

Lower yields of course mean a higher price for the grapes (and hence for the wine) because fewer grapes are produced from the same land area. Growers concerned for quality will spend much more time in the vineyards than those just seeking to produce average wines, so the labour costs are much higher.

Vineyard location and terroir

Location is critical to the quality of wine. A location where the vines have to put down deep roots, drawing up complex minerals, and where the sun exposure is exactly right for ripening the grape variety concerned, will produce a much more intense and much more complex wine than a site where the focus is simply on getting the maximum possible yields.

Small differences of place can mean significant differences in geology, sun exposure, weather conditions and many other factors, all of which affect the final wine produced. These issues are summed up in the notion of *terroir*. This is much more than just a technical term – it has huge implications in terms of the geographical identity of wine. The concepts associated with terroir are explored in Chapter 5.

Winemaking

The basics of wine production involve picking the grapes (usually the most labour-intensive part of the task), bringing them to a winery, and getting them into some kind of tank for fermentation. Some device is needed to crush the grapes, and a press is highly desirable to allow juice to be extracted from the crushed grapes. At the end of the process the clear wine must be separated from all the solid matter left in the tank (this is called 'racking' the wine) and then it can be bottled.

If the process were as simple as this, costs would be modest and consistent between every wine producer, but within this process there are a huge number of variables to consider. Nearly every step that is taken to increase the quality of the wine will have significant cost implications. Many quality measures will also reduce the final quantity of wine, meaning that the cost of each bottle is proportionally higher.

To give an illustration of the choices, a winemaker seeking to increase quality might choose to take any or all of the following steps.

- Sorting tables are increasingly used at the entrance to the winery. As grapes are received, they are placed on to a conveyer belt that is carefully inspected by trained staff who remove every bunch with any sign of rot or disease so that only the best quality grapes are used for the final wine. In the best properties the sorting is done not by bunches, but rather on every individual grape (after the bunches have been de-stemmed). The top properties are increasingly using optical sorting tables that allow much of this to be automated, but they represent a very substantial cost.
- The choice of press is critical to wine quality. The best presses work with light pressure, to avoid breaking the pips in the wine (which gives a bitter result); they are also designed (particularly for white wines) to minimise the oxygen contact with the grapes. But only pressing the grapes lightly gives less juice to ferment, and the top-quality presses are very expensive, particularly those that operate at speed. It is worth noting that there is no real scope for sharing such equipment between nearby wineries, because all producers in a given locality will generally need to press their grapes on the same day. So much equipment in smaller high-quality wineries is only used for a few days per year.

- Temperature-controlled fermentation is nowadays standard in leading wineries, in order keep the fermenting wine at an optimum temperature to give the best flavours. Fermentation generates heat, so an uncontrolled fermentation would just keep getting hotter and the end result would be a baked wine. Maintaining cool fermentation temperatures is especially important to maintain the freshness of white wines. But heating may also be needed: in a cold autumn it can help to heat the grape must a little to encourage the fermentation to start. However, the fermentation vats with temperature control systems, especially fully automated systems, cost much more than plain tanks. The energy costs in running the temperature control system may also be expensive.
- When a red wine is fermenting, the 'cap' of grape skins and stalks will tend to rise to the top of the tank. So, to extract the maximum depth and colour and flavour from the skins in order to give a rich and complex red wine, it is essential to keep the cap in contact with the fermenting juice. Common approaches include *remontage* (pumping over) – where once or twice a day wine is pumped from the bottom of the vat and sprayed over the cap at the top. But this needs appropriate pipes and pumps linked to each tank, or a labour-intensive approach with a portable pump. Other producers rely on *pigeage* where sticks are used to break up and punch down the cap – but this is physically demanding and can be very labour intensive. (A producer of a basic red wine may therefore avoid any of these options for reasons of cost, accepting that the resultant wine will be lighter in terms of colour and flavour.)
- Racking of wines is important to separate clear wine from the lees. A top producer in a region like Bordeaux may rack wines frequently from one barrel to another, involving considerable labour costs. (A producer who is keen to save costs may rely much more on filtration rather than racking.)
- Once the wines are vinified in tank, the best producers will spend much time on assessing each cuvée and deciding how it will be blended. The top producers will devote a great deal of attention to the final *assemblage* of wines from different parcels of vines that may have all been separately vinified. This means considerable extra costs at harvest time to keep parcels separate. Vats that are felt to be less promising may be demoted and only used for a second wine, sold at a much lower price than the 'grand vin'. In regions like Bordeaux where grape varieties are blended, a great deal of care will be taken with many small-scale assemblages before the final assemblage is agreed. In some cases, decisions are even made barrel by barrel.
- Bottling costs can also be very substantial – this is where the large quantity of wine held in tanks is distributed into the much smaller quantities needed for each bottle. Extremely high standards of hygiene are needed to prevent impurities getting into the wine, and although this can be mitigated to some extent by adding sulphur dioxide, the best producers seek to minimise the use of SO_2 (see p. 10). To bottle large quantities under the producer's

own control, the winery will need a semi-automatic or fully automatic bottling line, normally in its own room. The capital and maintenance costs of bottling lines can be enormous. A small producer may rely on hand-bottling – where each bottle is manually lifted on to a filler and then hand-corked, but this is very labour intensive and it is much harder to maintain the same levels of hygiene. Medium-sized producers in major wine-producing regions can take advantage of mobile bottling lines that are fitted to lorries that travel between wineries. This is more economical than an individual bottling line, but may give less choice as to when the wines are bottled.

Ageing

We have noted that wines develop with age. In some regions such as Spain, it is normal for producers to keep wines for several years until they are considered ready to drink. This means considerable storage cost, and the producer needs space to hold several years' stock. In cash flow terms it may be many years from when the grapes are harvested to when the producer is paid for the finished wine. In some cases (e.g. tawny Ports), the time delay between harvest and final sale may be ten years or more. So ageing wines before release adds considerably to the cost.

The cost can be reduced by expecting purchasers to take on some of the ageing cost – for example, even the top wines of Bordeaux are generally released only just over two years from the vintage, and longer-term storage until the wine is ready to drink is the responsibility of the purchaser – hence the need for home wine cellars or similar facilities (see Chapter 6).

But much of the ageing prior to release may require special facilities – in particular in most wine regions of the world, the best wines are aged in oak barrels. In the case of top white wines, the wine may even be fermented in oak barrels, which is very labour intensive. Oak ageing (or *élevage* in French) is a very important element in the making of quality wines, but it adds considerably to the cost. Oak barrels are expensive to make – indeed, in leading wine regions the coopers often command as much respect as the winemakers as their skills are enormous. Oak trees must be selected from relevant forests, cut down into staves that are aged for at least two years before being made into casks. As the wine lies in contact with the internal surface of the barrel, it picks up flavours from the oak that add to the complexity of the overall wine, and a micro-oxygenation process takes places through the walls of the barrel, so that the wine is able to develop with minute amounts of oxygen.

However, unlike stainless steel fermentation tanks, oak barrels have a finite life, which means the effective cost is substantial. Top estates wishing to give the maximum interaction between the wine and the oak may use mainly brand new barrels each year. This is very expensive – a typical Bordeaux barrel holds 225 litres (300 bottles) so at a typical cost of around £750 for a new oak barrel, the use of new oak adds £2.50 to the cost of every bottle. This is just for the cost of the barrel, without considering all the labour costs of putting the wine into barrels and regular racking, and all the costs of maintaining a large underground cellar where the barrels are stored. If the wine is kept in barrels for more than a year, two separate cellars are needed, each able to hold a full year's production in barrels.

Less prestigious properties may be happy to use barrels that are two or three years old. A common approach in a medium-level cru classé château or a leading cru bourgeois château (see pp. 65–8) might be to use oak barrels of which one-third are new each year. So one-third of the wine goes in one-year-old barrels, and one-third in two-year-old barrels. Some producers wanting a less pronounced oaky character may use barrels four or five years old. But beyond that age, the barrel no longer imparts any significant character to the wine. Other compromises can be made, for example, the use of oak chips placed in the stainless steel fermenting tank, but this is prohibited in many appellations. Even where oak chips are allowed, they do not give the same richness as achieved by oak barrels, because they simply impart oaky flavours without the micro-oxygenation through the barrel wall.

So a producer wishing to age a wine has three main choices: to keep the wine in tank (the cheapest option); to bottle the wine and store the bottles (more expensive as bottles take up more space but cheaper than ageing in oak); or to keep the wine in oak barrels and only bottle shortly before the wine will be released. It is worth noting that even stored in tank or in bottle, a wine will continue to develop: acids will soften slightly, tannins will become more rounded, and the flavour components in the wine will begin to harmonise. But ageing the wine in oak barrels has a much more profound effect.

A producer wishing to age wines for release will usually employ some combination of these approaches. For example, the following approach might be used for a medium-quality red wine. Once the fermentation is finished in November (assuming the grower is in the Northern hemisphere), the wine may be stored for an initial three months in tank until February. Then perhaps half the wine may be transferred to barrels and aged for six months. In August, the barrels are emptied so they can be released for the following year, and the wine goes back into tank for a short period. An assemblage of the different tanks is made (blending oaked and non-oaked components) and the wine is then bottled two months later in October. The producer keeps the bottled wines for another three months before being released in the January – around 16 months after the vintage. However, a producer wishing to minimise costs might bottle the wine a whole year earlier in the January after the harvest and release it immediately.

See Chapter 3 (p. 77–8) for more on wine vintages and ageing, and Chapter 6 regarding the ageing of wine by the purchaser.

The geographical origins of wine

Wine is fundamentally a product of specific *place*. As we have seen, the fruit that is harvested is the most important factor in the final style of the wine – and that is totally dependent on the vines and where they are grown. As two of the world's leading wine writers say:

> There is no other product on earth, agricultural or industrial, where value is as directly and precisely linked to where it grows and is made. Only wine goes to market with the name of a field, a farm, or at least a county ... (Johnson and Robinson 2013:6)

This is embodied in the notion of *terroir* which we explore in more detail in Chapter 5. The term means much more than just the territory or soil on which a wine is grown – the term encompasses issues of soil and geology, slopes and drainage, latitude, altitude, angles of exposure to the sun, rainfall, winds in the various seasons of the year, susceptibility to frost, suitability for particular grape varieties, and history of what has been grown on the site previously. Practical issues like road access and distance from the château or winery may also be highly relevant to the quality of wine that can be made on a particular site. In some regions, the availability of skilled labour and knowledge of winemaking are also regarded as components in the notion of *terroir*.

So, for all these reasons, knowing the geographical origin is crucial in understanding the difference between one wine and another.

Sometimes, it is only necessary to know in general terms where a wine comes from – so it may just be labelled *south-eastern Australia* which can include wines sourced or blended from anywhere in the three states of South Australia, New South Wales and Victoria. But in other cases, because of small differences in soils, or inclination to the sun, there can be substantial differences of intensity and quality between the wines produced from two vineyards on opposite sides of a road or track, and these can have a huge impact on the final price of the wine. There are many examples of this in Burgundy – for example, in the village of Vougeot in the Côte de Nuits (see Figure 1.1) the vineyards immediately above the local D975 road (slightly higher up the slope) fall in the famous *Clos de Vougeot* grand cru vineyard (marked 'A') whose wines would typically retail in the UK at around £100 a bottle at the time of writing, whereas wines from most of the vineyards just below the road ('B') could only be labelled as *Bourgogne*, and would typically retail at no more than £10–£15 per bottle. Yet we are only considering a distance of less than 500 metres between the centres of the two vineyards. See Chapter 3 for more on these distinctions, including more on the price of wine.

Protection of geographical names

Because the geographical origin of a wine is so important, many of the legal controls on labelling and selling wine are concerned with protecting geographical descriptions. Over the centuries, producers of wines from top regions have constantly struggled to prevent wines from lesser areas using their name. Whilst

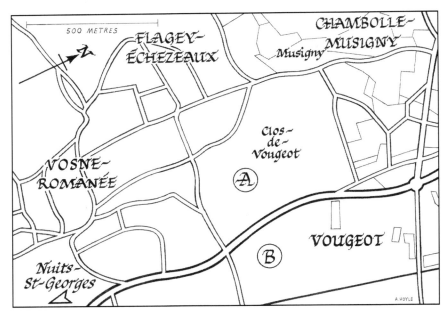

FIGURE 1.1 Map of the vineyards of Vougeot in the Côte de Nuits, Burgundy, France.

litigation sometimes addressed the most severe cases of a wine being passed off as another wine, it is highly problematic if wine producers constantly have to take legal action against rivals. Misleading or fraudulent labelling also presents huge risks for buyers: if I pay out good money for an expensive bottle of wine from the village of Margaux in Bordeaux, I do not want to find I have just got an inexpensive claret from the outskirts of Bordeaux, or even a wine from another region or country.

Some wine regions such as the Douro Valley in Portugal, or the Tokaj region of Hungary were legally demarcated with official maps as long ago as the eighteenth century. But getting effective national legislation for large numbers of geographical names needed more flexible legislation.

To combat the problems of abuse, and to protect geographical names, most of the major wine-producing countries of Europe developed various systems of 'controlled appellations' over the years (the term comes from the French verb *appeler* – to name). Originally these were enshrined in separate national laws – but from 2009 a common EU wine framework was brought into law[3] in all member states of the EU. There are now two levels of protected appellations:

- protected designation of origin (PDO); and
- protected geographical indication (PGI).

These terms apply to a wide range of specialist food and drink products from specific regions – not just wines. In particular, there are many cheeses with PDO status. In every EU country it is an offence to use a PDO or PGI name without meeting all the relevant conditions.

Use of PDO names

PDO is the highest standard of controlled name in EU law, and virtually all the protected names of leading wine-producing regions and villages are recognised as PDOs. This includes names such as:

- in France: Bourgogne, Volnay, Meursault, Champagne, Bordeaux, Margaux, St Émilion, Beaujolais, Chiroubles, Côtes du Rhone, Sancerre;
- in Germany: Mosel, Bernkastel, Urgizer-Würgarten;
- in Italy: Chianti, Chianti Classico, San Gimignano, Barolo, Valpolicella, Gavi, Fruili; and
- in Spain: Rioja, Rueda, Ribero del Duero, Toro, Jerez-Xeres-Sherry.

Many countries have hundreds of controlled appellations recognised as PDOs – for example, in France there are 100 different PDO appellations in the Burgundy region alone.

Countries within the EU are free to translate these terms into their own language, and many have opted to retain traditional terms as legal equivalents. So, most French producers continue to use the term *Appellation d'Origine Contrôlée* (AOC), although those wishing to appear more modern use *Appellation d'Origine Protégée* (AOP), which is the literal translation of PDO. In Italy the usual term for PDO is *Denominazione di Origine Controllata* (DOC) although some producers use the literal PDO translation *Denominazione di Origine Protetta* (DOP). In Spain, the standard term is simply *Denominación de Origen* (DO), and in Germany it is *Qualitätswein* (QW) or sometimes *Qualitätswein bestimmer Anbagebiete* (QbA).

For a wine to be labelled as a PDO (or equivalent in the relevant language) it must be made entirely from grapes grown within the specified geographical area, using specified grape varieties, and produced following a wide range of technical rules essential for the wine to achieve the characteristics associated with the relevant PDO. The rules may include details on the planting density and methods of training for the vines, and the maximum yield permitted (see p. 20), to prevent overproduction and thin, dilute wines. There will generally be rules on the winemaking methods – for example, the types of press that can be used and limits on enrichment or acidity adjustments. In most cases there is an earliest date at which the wine can be released (e.g. 1 July for wines of the previous year's vintage) but for some wines the minimum ageing period before release may be much longer. The rules may specify minimum and maximum alcohol levels, a minimum time that the wine must spend in oak casks, and may even stipulate the size of casks allowed. In the majority of cases a chemical analysis of the wine (to ensure it falls within prescribed limits) and a tasting test (an 'organoleptic assessment') is also needed before the wine can be labelled with the PDO name.

The wine must generally be grown *and vinified* within the PDO geographical area (or possibly vinified in an adjacent PDO). So you cannot pick grapes in Beaune (the central city of Burgundy), ship them hundreds of kilometres to a big production centre, and still label the final wine as 'Beaune'. The protected name is about the local methods of wine production, not just the origin of the grapes. For many PDOs it is also required that the wine is bottled in the region and several regions specify the shape of bottles that can be used.

Some countries have a higher tier for PDOs with additional requirements. For example, in Burgundy the term 'premier cru' may be added to the PDO name if the wine is made exclusively from leading vineyards that have been recognised as premiers crus within the appellation concerned (see Chapter 3 regarding the implication of such terms). In Italy, the top appellations are known as *Denominazione di Origine Controllata e Garantita* (DOCG), in Spain *Denominación de Origen Calificada* (DOCa) and in Germany the best wines with no sugar additions are labelled *Prädikatswein* (or QmP) as explained earlier in this chapter.

Some PDOs are tiny, others cover much wider areas. It is possible to have tightly defined PDO areas whose boundaries lie within a more generic PDO. For example, in Burgundy (see pp. 70–3) within the regional PDO *Bourgogne*, there are a number of sub-regional PDOs such as *Mâcon-Villages*, and village PDOs such as *Vougeot*. If only premier cru vineyards of the village are used, this may be added, giving a modified PDO name such as *Vougeot premier cru*. The very top vineyards in Burgundy are designated 'grand crus' and given individual PDOs purely for one vineyard, as in *Clos de Vougeot*. In a few cases, the production of an entire PDO may be controlled by a single domain or producer – in France where this happens it is called a *monopole* (a monopoly) but there are also instances in other countries.

Use of PGI names

PGI appellations are more flexible: they confirm that the wine is produced from grapes grown in a specific geographical area, but there are fewer rules on the methods of production. Producers generally have a free choice of which grape varieties to use and the methods of vinification.

As with PDO, the term can be translated into local languages, and traditional terms used in place of the formal translation. A few French producers continue to use the term *Vin de Pays* for wines at this level, but most use the literal PGI translation *Indication Géographique Protégée* (IGP). The abbreviation IGP is also used in Italy and Spain.

Many PGIs cover a larger area than PDOs – for example, wines from the whole of the Loire valley can use 'IGP Val de Loire' if they do not meet the rules of any of the Loire PDOs, and a huge range of wines along the French Mediterranean coast can be labelled 'IGP Pays d'Oc'.

Generally PGI wines sell at a lower price than PDO wines, but there are exceptions, particularly where a leading producer develops premium wine that falls outside the relevant PDO rules.

Varietal wines

Some producers are uncomfortable with both the PDO and PGI rules: they may not wish to pay for wines to be assessed under the relevant schemes, or they wish to blend wines from widely separated regions. Such wines can still be labelled with the grape variety and vintage so long as the cellar records enable these details to be checked, but the bottle cannot show any geographical labelling beyond the country. This category replaces the former 'table wine' designation.

For example, a growing number of popular French wines are simply labelled 'Vin de France' (with a possible grape variety and year). Figures show that in the first ten months of 2014, total French wine exports of still wines were classified 43% at the PDO (AOC) level, 32% IGP and 17% Vin de France (the remaining 8% were EU blends) (UBIFRANCE 2015). Similarly, the designation 'Wine of Spain' is widely used for blends sold as house wines in pubs and chain restaurants. A number of smaller English winegrowers use 'Wine of England' (though PDO and PGI systems are well established under EU law, even in smaller wine-producing countries like the UK).

Protected names for non-EU wines

A number of other wine-producing countries around the world have adopted systems of protected geographical names that are framed using similar regimes to the EU PDOs and PGIs. For example, South Africa and Chile both have systems of this kind using the term 'Wine of Origin'.

In many cases these names are helpful to identify wines on export markets, and avoid the problem that until recently European wine names such as 'Chablis' or 'Hermitage' were used to refer to wines that had no link whatsoever to those regions and could not therefore be imported into the EU.

Describing or labelling a wine

It follows from the points covered in this chapter that, as a minimum, the following information is needed to describe a wine in order for someone else to be clear exactly which wine you are referring to. Lists of wines sold by wine merchants or in serious restaurants should always give at least this information:

- the name of the producer (the château, domain, estate, négociant or co-operative);

- the protected appellation of the wine (PDO or PGI) if applicable;
- the vintage;
- any other description needed to distinguish the wine from other wines made by the same producer in the same year from the same appellation. This could include:
  - the name of the grape variety (if the grower produces wines from different varieties);
  - the name of the vineyard (especially if the grower produces separate wines from different vineyards in the appellation);
  - a description to identify particular vines used (e.g. *vielles vignes* – old vines – which will generally give a more concentrated wine than younger vines);
  - a description of the blend or cuvée (if more than one style of wine is produced from the same vineyards) – if necessary this could be a brand name used solely for marketing purposes;
  - any formal classification or status of the château or vineyard – for example, terms like 'premier cru' (Burgundy) or 'cru bourgeois' (Bordeaux).

Here are some examples, all from classic European wine regions:

- *Olivier Leflaive Bourgogne Blanc AOC Les Sétilles 2010*
  - Producer = Olivier Leflaive
  - Appellation = Bourgogne Blanc (from this we know the grape will be Chardonnay).
  - Vintage = 2010
  - Specific vineyard = Les Sétilles (a significant vineyard lying just outside the appellations of Puligny-Montrachet and Meursault in the Côte de Beaune, so it only carries the 'Bourgogne Blanc' appellation).
- *Château Palmer 1996 AOC Margaux – 3ème Grand Cru Classé*
  - Producer = Château Palmer. This is a highly respected château and its status is shown on the wine list by adding the words '3ème Grand Cru Classé' – in other words it is a third growth in the famous 1855 classification schedule of Grand Crus Classés Châteaux of the Médoc – see p. 67. (However, the label on the bottle will generally just say 'Grand Cru Classé'. Producers do not usually advertise their tier in the classification except for first growths, that is, the exclusive wines ranked 'Premier Grand Cru Classé'.)
  - Appellation = Margaux – one of the top village appellations of the Haut-Médoc, in Bordeaux. (As it is a red Bordeaux, we know the main grape varieties will be Cabernet Sauvignon, Merlot and Cabernet Franc. Margaux is usually slightly softer, with a little more Merlot than elsewhere in the Médoc.)
  - Vintage = 1996
- *Fontanafredda Vigna La Rosa Barolo DOCG 2007*
  - Producer = Fontanafreda (one of the leading estates producing Barolo)
  - Appellation = Barolo – from the Piedmont region in north-east Italy. (As it is a Barolo, we know the grape variety will be Nebbiolo.)

- Vintage = 2007
- Specific vineyard = La Rosa (one of the top vineyards in the Barolo region, in the village of Serralunga d'Alba where Fontanafreda is based).

A wide range of other information must also appear on a wine label by law – in particular, the bottle size, the alcohol content (abv) and the producer's name and address. The full rules on labelling of wines is a complex legal area beyond the scope of this book.

However, wine labels often contain much information beyond the legal minimum, and even the choice of colours and fonts for the legal details convey important messages. For further discussion on the significance of wine labels and the social messages they convey, see Chapter 10.

The nature of wine: a summary

In this chapter we have seen what is meant by the term 'wine', we have examined the main constituents of wine, and we have looked at the main factors that distinguish one wine from another, including the crucial role of protected names for wines from specific places and regions.

However, all of these issues have only been considered at an overview level: there are many books going into much more detail on the techniques of viticulture and vinification, and exploring the wines and producers in particular regions. Serious students of wine need to spend much time with books such as Johnson and Robinson (2013), exploring the detailed maps of the various wine regions of the world. More detailed works can then be considered on particular regions – for example, Belfrage (2004) adds much detail on northern Italy, whilst a wine buyer or sommelier dealing with wines of Burgundy will find books like Morris (2010) immensely valuable. Beyond the books, a wine specialist will also need to keep up to date through reading appropriate journals, newsletters, technical articles and regular visits to major wine regions (see Chapter 9 for more on the issues of learning about wine and gaining professional qualifications).

But once someone has grasped the legal definitions of wine, the main differences between one wine and another, and the key issues of geographical origin, they are well placed to consider the wider role of wine in society. This is the focus of the chapters that follow.

For discussion

1 How important is it to have a legal definition of the term 'wine'?
2 This chapter has argued that wine is fundamentally a 'natural' product – where the role of the winemaker is simply to help shape a natural process. Do you agree with this view? Do those who drink wine generally regard it as a natural product?

3 Few people think about the acids, polyphenols and other components when drinking a glass of wine. So in what ways is the science of wine important to the place of wine in society?
4 The production of wine, especially quality wine, is expensive. Should producers focus on quality, even if it means producing smaller quantities?
5 Why do we need laws on wine labelling? Who is helped or protected by such laws?
6 What is the role of quality wine systems – in particular the European PDO and PGI systems? Does the use of protected designations affect perceptions of wine by those who buy it?
7 Does the colour of wine affect its cultural place in society? For example, do red, white and rosé wines have different roles in social settings?
8 Is sparkling wine more special than still wine? Why is it perceived that way?

Notes

1 EC Council Regulation 479/2008, Annex IV, para 1.
2 EC Council Regulation 479/2008.
3 EC Council Regulation 607/2009.

References

Belfrage, N. (2004). *Barolo to Valpolicella: The Wines of Northern Italy* (London: Mitchell Beazley).
Bird, D. (2000). *Understanding Wine Technology* (Newark: DBQA Publishing).
Broadbent, M. (1998). *Michael Broadbent's Guide to Wine Tasting* (London: Mitchell Beazley Pocket Guides).
Gluck, M. (1999). *The Sensational Liquid: A Guide to Wine Tasting* (London: Hodder & Stoughton).
Goolden, J. (1990). *The Taste of Wine* (London: BBC Books).
Halliday, J. and Johnson, H. (1992). *The Art and Science of Wine* (London: Mitchell Beazley).
Johnson, H. and Robinson, J. (2013). *The World Atlas of Wine* 7th edn (London: Mitchell Beazley).
Morris, J. (2010). *Inside Burgundy* (London: Berry Bros & Rudd Press).
Musther, J. (2014). *Vinocalc 3.1* (www.musther.net accessed Sept 2014).
Riesling Rules (2014). *German Oechsle – Brix Conversion Table: Grape Maturity Measurement at Harvest* (Pacific Rim Winemakers www.rieslingrules.com accessed Sept 2014).
Robinson, J., Harding, J. and Vouillamoz, J. (2012). *Wine Grapes* (London: Penguin).
Simon, P. (2000). *Wine-Tasters' Logic* (London: Faber and Faber).
Skelton, S. (2007). *Viticulture: An Introduction to Commercial Grape Growing for Wine Production* (London: Lulu).
Smith, B. (ed.) (2007). *Questions of Taste: The Philosophy of Wine* (Oxford: Signal Books).
UBIFRANCE (2015). French still wine exports. *Drinks Business*, March 2015:41.
Unwin, T. (1994). Chaptal. In: Robinson, J (ed.) *The Oxford Companion to Wine* (Oxford: Oxford University Press).
Woods, S. (2001). *Vine to Bottle: How Wine is Made* (London: Mitchell Beazley).

2
UNDERSTANDING THE SIGNIFICANCE OF WINE

As we saw in Chapter 1, wine is identified through a range of definitions and legal frameworks that can be described as an 'oenological system'. That system recognises the significance of wine, and as such, it is defined and protected in terms of legal definitions of region, use of grapes, label contents, wine names, etc. It may be argued that this demonstrates the economic importance of wine for regions, countries and communities, and that the legal and legislative system that surrounds the wine industry ensures the integrity of the product. However, the contemporary symbolic significance of wine also needs to be assessed and recognised. This adds an additional layer of understanding and meaning to the consumption and appreciation of wine that is generated and comprehended at the social, cultural, religious and individual level.

One of the major aims of this book is to explore why wine has such a significance in contemporary society, why such a simple organic beverage made from fermented grapes is used to celebrate events or successes, used as part of religious ceremonies, used as a means to express our social status, is collected and revered or just simply drunk, enjoyed and appreciated. One of the reasons wines are held in such high regard by society, culture and the individual consumer is that the significance of wine has been embedded in our shared history for the past 10,000 years. This chapter charts the historical evolution of wine, its significance within various religions and how it has gained almost a sacred status in contemporary society, and finally, how wine is used as an expression or marker of regions, places and individuals.

A brief history of wine

Wine in its many forms is central to human history. It is likely that the first wine was produced by accident when a container of fruit from the *Vitis* plant was left in a corner, it fermented naturally, and the result was the beverage we know as wine. As this process was refined, a particular species of *Vitis* emerged, now known as *Vitis vinifera*, which was found to give the best wines. The vast majority of modern grapes, possibly as many as 3,000, are varieties of *V. vinifera*. As there were limited storage options the wine was probably produced quickly and drunk even quicker; however, for many it became a safe alternative to water and other beverages (Tannahill 2002; Lukacs 2013).

By 3000 BC there is evidence that wine was produced and drunk in Mesopotamia; however, it did not become a popular drink until the first millennium BC with the expansion of the Greek Empire. The significance of wine is charted in the philosophical musings of many great classical philosophers such as Plato, Virgil and Horace (Tannahill 2002; Lukacs 2013). The Greek wines fell out of favour when Italy started producing good wine, and by 100 BC, Italian vineyards were able to produce higher quantities from a given area of land as compared to the Greeks. As such, Italian wines came to dominate the market as the quality of the wine available for a given price was considered superior to the wines from Greece. The rise of Italian wines also gathered pace with the expansion of the Roman Empire to the four corners of Europe and beyond (Tannahill 2002; Lukacs 2013).

Although there is a great deal of discussion as to when wine was first produced, there is evidence that the first wine was produced about 8000 BC (Lukacs 2013). According to Riedel *et al.* (2012:402), grapes are one of the oldest fruits and the traditional wine-making processes are an ancient art, which began as early as 1000 BC. Archaeological investigations and discoveries attest that the wine production by fermenting processes took place from early as 6000 BC, whereas other studies from China show that grapes were used together with rice to produce fermented juices as early as 7000 BC (Barnard *et al.* 2011). It is important to recognise that although this wine shared the basic chemical attributes, it was very different from the wine we enjoy today (Lukacs 2013). In charting the modern history of wine, Kennedy, Saucier and Glories (2006) identify that the more formalised development of grape and wine production methods in Western civilisation has generally paralleled other wider technological and agricultural developments such as irrigation and production of pottery and glass. They identify that advances in methods of wine production during the Egyptian and then the Greek and Roman periods (such as vine cultivation, pottery production and winemaking practices) peaked around AD 200 to 400 and laid down the foundations of a system that maximised and formalised production. The advancement in wine production and technology then slowed down for several centuries, and was generally restricted to monastic religious orders in Western Europe (Allen 1961). In the dark ages the drinking of wine was not seen as a luxury, rather it was a necessity. Water was dangerous, so people had to find other ways of quenching their thirst and the only safe available options were wine, ale, beer or cider. However, in the late middles ages, from around AD 1200 onwards, the experience of abbeys and monasteries in producing wine led to huge improvements, and many of the most prestigious European vineyards were identified in that period. According to thirteenth-century manuscripts in areas such as

St Émillion, Chablis and Beaune, wine was drunk regularly as part of breakfast (Tannahill 2002).

The significance of wine has been embedded in all our histories: for thousands of years it provided a safe means to hydrate ourselves. However, the status of wine has also been heightened through its perceived health-giving properties and it has been used in multiple civilisations over thousands of years to treat a variety of diseases (Kennedy, Saucier and Glories 2006). In a recent paper, Gordetsky et al. (2013) examined the evolution and use of wine as a medicine through the ages. The importance of this is not only the actual use of wine for its medicinal qualities, but also the reverence of the way in which wine was recorded by past civilisations. The formalised use of wine as a medicine in ancient Egypt can be evidenced through the medical papyri, carvings on tombs and other texts dating as far back as 2700–2190 BC. In Hippocrates of Cos's (460–370 BC) *Regimen in Acute Diseases*, Hippocrates identifies how to treat ailing patients, describing many healing uses of wine, including its use as a wound dressing, as a nourishing dietary drink, as a cooling agent for fevers and as a diuretic. The use of wine continued to play an important role in the treatment of patients for hundreds of years and was a significant ingredient in ancient Roman remedies. Gordetsky et al. (2013) identify a number of significant physicians during this period, they include Andromachus the Elder, who was chief physician to the Roman emperor Nero (54–68 AD). He attained great notoriety for his concoction, *Galene,* which required 73 ingredients mixed in wine: *Galene* was said to alleviate inflammation of the bladder and kidneys. Pliny the Elder (23–79 AD) in his writings on *Natural History* identified 200 varieties of grapes and 18 varieties of sweet wine listing their differing health-giving properties. Pliny the Elder even went as far as to include a wine-based medicine for the 'conception of beautiful and virtuous children' (Gordetsky et al. 2013:193). Evidence of the medicinal properties of wine exists throughout history, including the notable Spanish physician Arnald of Villanova who in 1310 wrote *Liber de Vinis*, which described 49 medicinal wines used for multiple diseases and remained a best-seller up until the beginning of the seventeenth century.

The benefits of moderate wine consumption is still recognised today. According to Siemann and Creasy (1992) it may reduce cholesterol or even reduce the risk of developing type 2 diabetes and cardiovascular disease (see Chapter 7 for more on wine and health). Our understanding of wine has been formed by many factors; as can be seen from above, wine provided a safe means for people to hydrate and, additionally, it was seen to possess certain health-giving properties. In addition to this, the consumption of wine has been embedded in social and cultural practices throughout the world, the most significant of which is the relationship between religion and wine.

Wine and religion

In attempting to understand the contemporary significance of wine, it is possible to conceptualise wine in a number of contexts that inform, create and perpetuate this significance. One of the reoccurring themes when exploring the history and use of wine is the way in which it has been absorbed and is employed in various sacred (religious) and secular (non-spiritual) contexts to mark events, occasions, rituals and celebrations.

Wine in the sacred world

The use of wine in ceremonies and rituals is probably one of the most common ways in which wine has gathered its contemporary social and cultural connotations. It is almost impossible to separate the drinking of wine from religious ritual or its religious significance, however the role of wine within religious-based rituals or festivals pre-dates Christianity by some 4,000 years. It was often seen as possessing magical or mystical qualities in both its transformation from grapes to wine and the way in which people felt after imbibing. In Greek-speaking areas it was obligatorily, or almost obligatory, to get drunk at certain festivals. The link between wine and religion was forged through the god Bacchus (also known to the Romans as Dionysus). This relationship between wine as a drink and the symbolism of a wine-god (as personified in Bacchus) forms a central theme in this book (see the Preface for further details).

Bacchus or Dionysus is the god of wine, the inventor and teacher of its cultivation, the giver of joy. In analytical terms, Dionysus is the productive and intoxicating power of nature, which transports men away from their usual quiet and sober mode of living, with wine being the symbol of that power (Lukacs 2013). Although he is usually associated with overindulgence and drunkenness, it was also claimed that he cured diseases by revealing the remedies to the sufferers in their dreams and is often evoked against 'raging diseases' by authors such as Sophocles. Dionysus is the Roman version of Bacchus, but the two names are often interchangeable; they undertake the same function and often the same action such as protecting the vines and promoting joy. The festivals and rituals that accompanied the worshipping of both Dionysus and Bacchus were not respectable, but they were legal because they emphasised that normality had a value, there was a conflict in the mundane elements of everyday life, or in other words, they provided a balance between the sacred and the profane. Additionally, the rituals and consumption of wine concentrated upon the euphoria induced by alcohol, the feeling that the worshipper was being transported into the presence of the deity, in fact its followers became so utterly involved it became a complete religion to them (Stanislawski 1975). The religious community's attitude towards the use of wine frequently encapsulates its theological position, and the community's relationship to wine still tells us a great deal about its proximity to other forms of Western religion.

For Christians, wine has a unique role in the Eucharist as the metaphor of Christ's blood. The earliest account of the Eucharist is in St Paul's first letter to the Corinthians, probably written around AD 55 (Bruce 1971:25) – so this is an account written less than 25 years after the original 'Lord's Supper' where the

Biblical accounts describe the institution of the Eucharist on the eve of Christ's death. Paul states:

> For I received from the Lord what I also handed on to you, that the Lord Jesus on the night when he was betrayed took a loaf of bread, and when he had given thanks, he broke it and said, 'this is my body that is for you. Do this in remembrance of me.' In the same way he took the cup also, after supper, saying, 'this cup is the new covenant in my blood. Do this, as often as you drink it, in remembrance of me.' For as often as you eat this bread and drink the cup, you proclaim the Lord's death until he comes (1 Corinthians 11.23–5).

Almost all Christians undertake regular Eucharistic celebrations, normally as the central element in Sunday worship, and some, notably Catholics, will even celebrate the Eucharist on a daily basis. The precise interpretation of the symbolism varies between different Christian traditions, but according to the Catholic doctrine, the bread and the wine used in the sacrament of the Eucharist become the body and blood of Christ, not merely as sacramental signs but in reality (Catholic Church 1994:1376; Wikström 2014). This view is explored further by Bynum (2013:8) who identifies that the bread and wine of the Eucharist are:

> not signs or symbols in the sense of something more or less arbitrarily chosen to refer to something else. Neither index nor icon, they are also not sign. They *are* the divine ... The divine is present 'under the sacrament [*sub . . . sacramento*]' of the bread and wine.

The concept of 'bread and wine' within the Christian context is a particularly pervasive, social and cultural analogy. According to Harvey (2014:213) the significance of this is elevated because:

> Sharing food is among the most intimate acts imaginable ... It is no accident that many Christians have adopted the term 'communion' for a central communal ritual. It is not only the drinking of wine and the eating of bread (whether these are symbolic, representational or something significantly different) but the drinking of tea that indicate that this rite involves more than souls and their deity.

In this context Harvey identifies the role of food and drink as the means or a motive to create a sharing and reflexive moment in time and communing with others and creating a form of communitas between people. Indeed, major Christian theologians affirm this context as the origin of the Eucharist. For example, the German scholar Joachim Jeremias who spent much of his life analysing the accounts of the Eucharist in the New Testament says: 'The "founding meal" is only one link in a long chain of meals which Jesus shared with his followers and which they continued after Easter' (Jeremias 1971:289). For Harvey, the significance of sharing bread or wine with others is deeply embedded within the human psyche as a meaningful or intimate act of communing with others and crosses many faiths and religions. There is also something mystical about the production of bread and wine where through the fermentation and leavening process grapes and flour are transformed into something very different from their base ingredient state. For the people of ancient Greece and Rome there was not a scientific explanation for these processes, but rather, the fermentation of wine and the leavening of bread was seen as a mysterious or mystical process, and significantly was a result of their Bacchus's or Dionysus's intervention between human labour and the spiritual world, in other words, it was seen as a partnership between the profane world and the gods (Hamel 2013). It can be argued that the relationship between the mysticism surrounding the production of bread and wine, and the sharing of bread and wine as part of traditional hospitality marks a communion of sharing or engaging with others. For Wright (2013:27), these ancient Greek and Roman traditions were adopted, adapted and incorporated into early Christian rituals. He goes on to state that the:

> sacrament addresses primarily the sense of taste, this sense itself must be denied in order for complete adherence of the faithful to Catholic theology. To this purpose, the taste of bread and wine, for instance, are situated in the middle of a sensorial network that spiritualizes the body of the faithful just as it directs their attention toward the transubstantiation of the body of Christ. The word of the minister guides such displacement, to which all the sensible elements of the Eucharistic liturgy are subordinated.

However, Bynum (2013:5) also identifies that during the Middle Ages there was also an emphasis on the 'literal presence of the incarnate God in the basic foodstuff of the Mediterranean diet', and this was evidenced through the mystical fermentation, leavening and even bleeding process.

Similarly, within the Jewish tradition, rituals involving the use of wine are designed to cultivate communal affirmation, most notably in the annual celebration of Passover, but also in the weekly Shabbat meal. The sacred texts of Judaism make clear that wine is a sign of God's blessing and that humans should enjoy the 'gladdening of the heart' that wine provides (Genesis 27:28, Leviticus 23:13, Deuteronomy 7:13, Amos 9:14). Within Judaism wine is used to consecrate the altar and foster a sense of community at religiously significant celebrations such as the Sabbath meal where the wine and bread is blessed.

Theologians debate how far the Christian Eucharist is a development of the Jewish Passover or a fundamentally different kind of ritual meal, but the broad ritual purposes are very similar in terms of celebration and the development of community and friendship.

Although the identification of the relationship between bread and wine and the body and blood of Christ is central to the Christian Eucharist, there is much evidence that such linkage pre-dates its Christian adoption. Ritual meals with wine as a central symbol are found in pagan sacramental rites, eulogies and banquets (Stanislawski 1975). It is possible that the link between wine and food and its significance and role in pagan rituals subsequently developed into religious-based rituals. For example, the Jiuxian Temple Fair in China celebrates the patron god of wine-making: the wine made in Dongpu was particularly mellow and fragrant, so the local people believed a Buddha was guarding them, thus they started worshipping the deity. However, the ritual practices of Chinese people are often characterised by their combination of the sacred and the secular in one ritual. The Jiuxian Temple Festival was a communal collective ritual event that took place in a particular time and space, and consequently, there is no clear demarcation between the sacred and the secular, although religious people and non-religious people would have experienced differently what was the sacred and what was the secular in the same time–space (Xue 2014). In Mexico the cactus wine ritual undertaken by the Papago Indians is undertaken by the tribes to encourage rain and the fertility of crops by giving a sacrifice of wine to the gods (Waddell 1976). In an interesting piece of research, Håland (2012:310) explores the relationship between food-based festivals that take place in both modern and ancient Greece. She goes on to state that:

> Religious rituals in which food is a crucial factor are still important. These rituals are not only an excuse to celebrate and have a pleasant time, but are celebrations to secure the future harvest, or as the Greeks say, 'it is for the good' (*gia to kalo*). The significance of the food is a prominent feature in religious rituals in modern Greece.

By investigating the importance of the food in some of the saints' feasts in modern Greece, it is possible to chart their parallels in ancient times in which food and wine were a crucial element of the ritual. Many modern festivals mirror the historical behaviour worshipping of Bacchus in the Greek tradition and Dionysus in the Roman tradition. In assessing the role of wine in contemporary society, it is important to consider how its contemporary significance has been formed, why it is revered or reviled, its perceived health-giving properties, its significance within religious and cultural rituals and its history.

Wine in a secular world

The consumption and purchasing of wine as a commercial activity elevated the significance and symbolism of wine to that of the 'extraordinary' in a way that is in direct opposition to everyday reality. This process is best demonstrated in food and drink marketing. For example, in a recent Marks & Spencer campaign, a bottle of Italian Prosecco is used as a metaphor for the authentic, something that is real, something that has a heritage and provenance, and as such, reinforces the elevation of what is a ready meal to a heightened level of experience, something that is mundane, to the level of authentic or even 'extra-ordinary' (see Tresidder 2011). The presentation of wine within the media as celebratory, sophisticated, authentic, timeless or luxurious allows the significance of wine to be utilised as a social or cultural marker that reinforces the binary relationship between the profane/everyday and the sacred/extraordinary nature of the experience that the consumption of wine supports. We can understand the secular conceptualisation of wine within contemporary society by exploring Durkheim's conception of the 'sacred and profane'.

Émile Durkheim (1858–1917) is widely seen as the father of modern sociology and social anthropology. Rather than accepting the established theological interpretations of the sacred and profane, for Durkheim (1995) the conception of the sacred and profane are socially generated and underline the distinction between social and ordinary experience. As such, we can see the consumption of wine as a marker of the transition from the profanity of everyday life into the sacredness of celebration. Such a transition can take place even in secular traditions such as the use of wine to celebrate birthdays or anniversaries. This transition is also supported by the ritual of consumption that surrounds many aspects of the consumption process, from choosing the wine, opening it, letting it breathe, pouring it, smelling the cork, clinking glasses and statements such as 'good health' or 'cheers'.

In fact there is a recognised ritual and etiquette that heightens and extends the consumption process. We do not just drink wine, rather there is a theatre and a ritual that surrounds wine that does not exist with other alcoholic drinks, and it is this process that heightens expectation and the significance of wine. For Bourdieu (1987) the ritual element is important, but in order for rituals to become culturally embedded or gather significance they have to be repetitive, have rules and contain a social element that are understood by society; in short they are a code of behaviour with a sacred element. It can be argued that the consumer understands the significance of food and wine, as well as the rules and expected or ritualistic behaviour when engaging in them. In addition to this, rituals generally exhibit degrees of 'effervescence, pleasure, games . . . all that recreates the spirit that has been fatigued by the too great slavishness of daily work' (Durkheim 1995:426). What was sacred for Durkheim was society itself; this involved the sacralisation of the social where the object of worship was society itself, as he states 'anything . . . can be sacred' (Durkheim 1995:35) and this includes the collecting and consumption of wine.

As stated previously in this chapter, wine often plays a central role in any form of celebration or ritual. However, according to Genosko (2003:75), 'He (Bourdieu) took great care to outline how the profane needs the sacred, and the regulation, through rites, of the process of consecration in the passage into the sacred from the profane.' Wine is both ritually and materially located in what Caillois (1988:282) defines as the 'sacred sphere of excess'. According to Caillois this sphere of excess provides a glimpse of the sacred within the profane world of everyday lived experience. Thus as consumers we search to justify our existence, or sometimes just simply attempt to escape from the pressures of everyday life, and we achieve this by seeking and finding, 'artificial sources of stimulation ... to make up for the shortcomings of their environment' (ibid:282). The appreciation and consumption of wine can be seen as just one of many artificial sources of stimulation we engage with on a daily basis to escape. However, this sphere of excess is not merely about drinking wine, but it also is concerned with the symbolic historical, religious, social and cultural significance of wine. Thus wine can be seen to fill an important role in society and culture – it is surrounded by a set of rules of rituals that govern its consumption. In understanding the complexity of this, it is important to note that an element of the significance of wine emerges from the embedding of the historical and religious undertones, but also how contemporary culture and society define, contextualise and embed wine in everyday cultural practices.

The embedding of wine

Our conception and understanding of wine is formed through a complex mixture of social, cultural and historical stories or myths that we have encountered through various means, such as our own personal experiences (see O'Connor 2005; O'Gorman 2007). The social and cultural significance of wine is perpetuated by its representations in films (Ferry 2003), arts and literature (Hollander 1999), television and contemporary cultural movements such as advertising and music videos (Ferguson 1998; Magee 2007). These encounters and experiences create a myth and legend that surrounds contemporary understanding and definitions of wine. In fact what this creates is a myth that elevates wine beyond the mundane to the level of the extraordinary. Therefore, to truly understand the significance of wine then we need to understand the context in which that particular wine is located; for example, in certain cultures and societies wine is utilised as a means to express identity and standing, in other cultures wine and its consumption are illegal. What the myth of wine as represented in films and magazines in conjunction with the historical, religious and cultural connotations leads to is what may be defined as 'consensus constructs'. Consensus constructs represent a wide-ranging agreed understanding and definition of the meaning and significance of wine within contemporary society. A good example of this is that Champagne is universally seen as a means to celebrate success. People understand this, and they reinforce this consensus construct through the drinking and buying and giving of Champagne as a means to mark a significant occasion or feat. People just understand it, even though they may have never tasted it or the drinking of Champagne is forbidden within their culture.

One of the major myths that surround wine is the idea of authenticity. There is an idea that wine provides a conduit back to a simpler and more authentic time. This is significant for a number of reasons. We live in a post-industrial society that is dominated by the media, fashions are fleeting and we're continually trying to catch up with the speed of progress of change and technology.

The world we live in is becoming much more inauthentic: foods are genetically modified, intensive farming creates cheap and often tasteless food and we see the use of chemicals and steroids being used to increase production. The idea of wine is something that we draw from the past – perceived to be untouched, more authentic and a clear link back to the past where things were simpler, organic and more authentic, although this may not be the case. Wine provides us with roots in a rootless society. The consumption of wine is not just about taste or bouquet, it is also about how it makes us feel, how a simple sip of wine takes us back to a time, place or experience or a memory. These are what Johns and Pine (2002:127) refer to as the 'authentic environments' in which consumption offers a reflexive space for the individual to escape and to find themselves. For Fantasia (1995) the consumption and presentation of food and wine offers access to the consumer to a world that is artful; it is more than drinking to quench thirst, it is an existential experience that is underpinned by a certain aesthetic that elevates wine to the level of art and the extraordinary. The art of wine consumption is also reinforced through the ritual that surrounds the service appreciation of wine, an aesthetic that is routinely expressed in cultural representations such as this passage from Evelyn Waugh's *Brideshead Revisited* (1945). The main character, Charles Ryder, who is now middle aged, comments on a dinner at a restaurant in Paris:

> I rejoiced in the Burgundy. How can I describe it? The Pathetic Fallacy resounds in all our praise of wine. For centuries every language has been strained to define its beauty, and has produced only wild conceits or the stock epithets of the trade. This Burgundy seemed to me, then, serene and triumphant, a reminder that the world was an older and better place ... that mankind in its long passion had learned another wisdom. By chance I met this same wine again, lunching with my wine merchant in St. James's Street in the first autumn of the war; it had softened and faded in the intervening years, but it still spoke in the pure authentic accent of its prime and ... as at Paillard's ... years before, it whispered faintly, but in the same lapidary phrase, the same words of hope.

Wine can be seen as a means of escape in both the physical and metaphysical sense; this is reflected in Charles Ryder's lament on drinking a 1904 Clos de Bèze (following a 1906 Montrachet).[1] These wines offered an escape to a time and place that was less contrived and shallow. The immersion in the consumption process and the rituals that surround wine and its appreciation facilitates a notion of escape and signifies a time and space that is differentiated from everyday lived experience by its 'extraordinariness', and is differentiated from the routine and often unreflexive consumption of food and drink as merely fuel (Marshall 2005). The way in which the characteristics of a wine is described by a sommelier, by a wine writer and even the description on the back of a bottle may well link back to its terroir, but all create a notion of time and space that elevates the context of the hospitality and food served to that of the extraordinary. For example, Marks & Spencer use a collage of music, settings and dialogue to elevate what is a ready meal to that of fine dining and sophistication (see Tresidder 2011), while the wine is used to reinforce the marketing message about escape and authenticity.

It is within these liminal places or 'pleasure zones' (Fantasia 1995:202) that we find a metaphysical release from our normal social constraints and temporarily enter into a state of communitas which links clearly back to the religious notion of communion. The creation of these 'pleasure zones' offer a delineated space that represents a time, a sophistication in which we may hedonistically explore the experiences of food and wine. This liminality and release enables us to explore wine in terms of senses and the sensual, as an 'intimate frontier' (Dawkins 2009:33). The significance of wine within contemporary culture and society is heightened as the consumption of wine becomes a multi-sensual experience in which we may locate the body, and it enables the individual to explore 'the role of the sensual, the emotional, the expressive, for maintaining layered sets of embodied relationships to food (sic) and place' (Delind 2006:121). Thus, the essence of appreciating wine especially in formal or celebratory spaces is that it is a multisensory gustatory experience, in which the social, cultural, geographical, ecosystem and 'servicescapes' offer a unique sensual experience in which all of the senses are engaged during the consumption process. The link between wine and place, region or terroir can be seen to be part of what Law (2001:266) identifies as a 'sensory geography', this is where the wine expresses not only the climate, soil and rocks in which the grapes were grown, but also the history and culture of the region. We can take this idea of consumption further by building on Curtin's (1992:xiv) notion of a 'food-centered philosophy of human being', interpreted by Martin (2005:75) as meaning that food and wine 'becomes part of the self, it obliges us to re-conceptualize not only the other but also the identity of a self that is so permeable, it can physically incorporate the other'. So in fact what results is an incorporation of place, food, wine and the self in some form of sensual and sensory landscape of consumption.

When we talk of wine offering a multi-sensual experience it is important to explore the complexity of senses and their linking to touch, smell, feel, etc. (see Chapter 3 on the sensory assessment of wine quality, and Chapter 9 for discussion of how such skills are learned). This use of the senses is widely expressed in wine-tasting terms such as references to the 'nose' of a wine, and the use of special glassware or even a 'tastevin'[2] to access the colour and depth of a wine. In technical language it is common to speak of an 'organoleptic assessment' of a wine: using the human senses of taste, smell, etc. to assess a wine. Such assessment can easily be impaired when one of the major senses is compromised through illness or external factors, such as a guest's perfume obscuring the ability clearly to smell the bouquet of a wine. Sutton (2010:217) offers an interesting theory of the senses that once applied to the consumption of wine, which provides us with an insight into how to conceptualise its sensual nature. Sutton in his work introduces the conception of 'synaesthesia', which represents the idea that senses do not operate in isolation, but rather operate in relation to all of the other senses. The significance of this is important when attempting to define and comprehend the oenological experience. Sutton identifies that:

> Synesthesia ... blurs the objectivity and passivity of western sensory models by showing the ways that sensory experience is not simply passively registered but actively created between people. Synesthesia is a reminder of why food (or wine) and the senses should be considered together.

According to Biehl-Missal (2012), we need to consider the impact senses have on our understanding of the world and how they influence our behaviour. She states we gather 'aesthetic experiences through our five senses to create an embodied, tacit knowing that ... can influence behavior' (Biehl-Missal 2012:173). This association between food, wine and sensory experiences is lucidly summed up by Sutton (2010:215), who comments on the significance of the relationship between food and the senses:

> [Food] ... is central to cosmologies, worldviews, and ways of life, and is reflected in the term 'gustemology' as a means of understanding the spectrum of cultural issues that exist around taste and the sensory aspects of food.

The consumption of wine creates a purity of experience and a re-establishment of an awareness of the senses that have been dulled by the act of 'being' in a world. As Levi-Strauss (1983:153, quoted in Sutton 2010:210) affirms in assessing the significance of senses:

> The senses ... are operators, which make it possible to convey the isomorphic character of all binary systems of contracts connected with the senses, and therefore to express, as a totality, a set of equivalences connecting life and death, vegetable foods and cannibalism, putrefaction and imputrescibility, softness and hardness, silence and noise.

Thus, for Levi-Strauss (1983:164), senses are codes that transmit messages and the 'gustatory code' is privileged over other sensory codes. These codes may be seen as codes of consumption that engage all of the senses and the heightening feelings of consumption are reinforced by the rituals and social and cultural significance that inform our understanding of wine.

Wine and identity

There is a clear link between wine, wine consumption and how it expresses identity of a region, people or culture. Additionally, consumers use their knowledge and collecting of wine as a social marker of their own identities.

Wine and personal identity

It is possible to think of senses from two different perspectives: first in terms of synaesthesia and second in terms of the individual's being in the world. There is a strong academic discourse that surrounds the significance of food and wine within society (Cronin, McCarthy and Collins 2012), and is notably reflected by Bourdieu's (1987) use of wine in understanding the individual's habitus, embodiment and aesthetics. Bourdieu explored how the individual's knowledge of food is an expression of their cultural capital, and that food is a part of 'a system of classificatory schemes' (1987:174) that codifies contemporary society. The knowledge of wine, its vintages, provenance and the ritual of consumption are all used as a marker of an individual's 'cultural capital'. We all exchange cultural capital on a daily basis, we use the various 'knowledges' we possess about subjects such as literature, films, brands, etc. as a statement to other people about what type of person we are or want to be, our knowledge and consumption patterns allowing us to distinguish ourselves from other people. We exchange these 'knowledges' with each other and, to a certain degree, the result of this is that we mark our social or cultural position with our peers or the peers we wish to be associated with. How often do we match the wine to the recipient rather than the food at dinner parties? We assess their taste and cultural capital, our wine is chosen to meet their standards or to impress them. As such, we make a 'cultural calculation' about the situation, the identity of the host, the guests and also what message we wish to send to them. In order to successfully achieve this we draw from our reservoir of cultural capital to inform our choice of the wine.

Therefore, if we accept that the consumption of wine and the rituals that surround it create a multi-sensual experience that is a visual, aesthetic and performative practice, then the consumption and appreciation of wine becomes a form of spatial practice in which the consumer can accumulate, express and trade cultural capital (Biehl-Missal 2012). A good example of the consumption of wine and identity is where a new middle class emerges in fast-developing economies such as China or Russia. The means by which individuals mark themselves as members of this new affluent group is to buy European luxury cars or clothes, which are outward markers. Wine is an important cultural marker and clear expression of one's cultural capital: again it links to a more established world of luxury, history and provenance, and wine distinguishes the consumer. Wine has always been used in Chinese society as a marker of class and from the seventh to the tenth centuries was reserved only for emperors (Goody 2007: 60), thus allowing these new social groups to immerse themselves in both European and Chinese forms of cultural distinction. It is interesting to note that countries such as China are amongst the largest consumers of French wine in the world, with the large international auction houses holding regular wine auctions in Hong Kong and Shanghai. Additionally, the globalisation of wine has witnessed the symbolic significance of wine crossing cultures, religions and societies, with many social groups each finding a particular contextualised role for the consumption, collection, evaluation, significance and appreciation of wine.

Terroir and identity

The relationship between wine, its region of origin and the people who produce it is an important aspect of oenology, sometimes summed up in the term of 'terroir'. For the producers and local communities wine is an expression of pride in their region and part of their local identity.

The word terroir is more than just a marker of quality, it is a term that is rich with significance and philosophical meaning. Terroir can be simply defined in environmental terms; however, the origins and significance of the phrase may be located within wider philosophical historical, social and cultural debates that define the soul of a particular locality or region. Douguet and O'Connor (2003:238) state that:

> terroir (an untranslatable word that connotes the local spaces and soils, and also symbolic relations of goods and services production), tends to identify features of their food, cuisine, buildings and wider habitats as 'critical' patrimony in view of their symbolic as well as functional significance . . .

The concept of terroir is so fundamental in the field of wine studies that it forms a whole chapter of the book (Chapter 5). In that chapter, terroir is investigated as a concept, as a means of distinguishing particular wines (especially in terms of the formal classification of wines in the major regions of Europe) and in terms of the central issue of terroir and the geographical identity of wines.

The social significance of wine: a summary

In order to understand effectively the appreciation, marketing or significance of wine to the consumer, it is important that we have the ability to locate it within the surrounding social, cultural and historical discourse that supports the definition of wine as one of the most sensually and symbolically significant products available for purchase. Wine is embedded within all of our histories in one way or another, whether that be our understanding of the role of Bacchus or Dionysus in mythology, as a marker of personal or regional identity or maybe just the joy people attain from drinking wine with friends. When we sip a fine wine, or even when we unscrew a screwcap closure on a bottle we have just bought at a supermarket, it transports us to a more simplistic and organic time, providing a temporary escape from everyday lived experience.

For discussion

1. Attempt to identify the personal significance wine has for you personally. How has this significance been formed?
2. How far can you identify both sacred and secular uses for wine in contemporary society? What is the significance of this, and how far do the two uses merge or overlap?

3 Is it true that wine provides a path to authenticity, in other words, a conduit back to a simpler and more authentic time? How is this expressed in practice?
4 Which sense do you feel is most important in the appreciation of wine?

Notes

1 Both these wines are grand cru Burgundies – see Chapter 3 regarding the significance of this designation.
2 A *tastevin* is a traditional polished metal device, a cross between a spoon and a cup, once used for assessing wines in Burgundian cellars.

References

Allen, H.W. (1961). *A History of Wine* (New York: Horizon Press).
Barnard, H., Dooley, A.N., Areshian, G., Gasparyan, B. and Faull, K.F. (2011). Chemical evidence for wine production around 4000 BCE in the Late Chalcolithic Near Eastern highlands. *Journal of Archaeological Science*, 38(5), 977–84.
Biehl-Missal, B. (2012). Atmospheres of seduction: A critique of aesthetic marketing practices. *Journal of Macromarketing*, 32(2), 168–80.
Bourdieu, P. (1987). *Distinction: A Social Critique of the Judgment of Taste* (Nice, T., transl.) (Cambridge, MA: Harvard University Press).
Bruce, F.F. (1971). *1 and 2 Corinthians* (London: Marshall, Morgan & Scott).
Bynum, C.W. (2013). The sacrality of things: An inquiry into divine materiality in the Christian middle ages. *Irish Theological Quarterly*, 78(1), 3–18.
Caillois, R. (1988) *L'homme et le Sacré. 1950* (Paris: Gallimard).
Catholic Church. (1994). *Catechism of the Catholic Church* (Vatican City: Libreria Editrice Vaticana).
Cronin, J., McCarthy, M. and Collins, A. (2012). Covert distinction: How hipsters practice food-based resistance strategies in the production of identity. *Consumption, Markets and Culture*, 15(1), 1–27.
Curtin, D. (1992). Introduction. In: Curtin, D. and Heldke, L. (eds), *Cooking, Eating and Thinking: Transformative Philosophies of Food*, pp. 28–55 (Bloomington, IN: Indiana University Press).
Dawkins, N. (2009). The hunger for home: Nostalgic affect, embodies memory and the sensual politics of transnational foodways. *UG Journal of Anthropology*, 1, 33–42.
Delind, L. (2006). Of bodies, place and culture: Re-situating local food. *Journal of Agricultural and Environmental Ethics*, 19, 121–46.
Douguet, J.M. and O'Connor, M. (2003). Maintaining the integrity of the French terroir: A study of critical natural capital in its cultural context. *Ecological Economics*, 44, 233–54.
Durkheim, E. (1995). *The Elementary Forms of Religious Life* (Field, K., transl.) (London: Free Press).
Fantasia, R. (1995). Fast food in France. *Theory and Society*, 24, 201–43.
Ferguson, P. (1998). A cultural field in the making: Gastronomy in 19th century France. *American Journal of Sociology*, 104(3), 597–641.
Ferry, J. (2003). *Food in Film: A Culinary Performance of Communication* (London: Routledge).
Genosko, G. (2003). The bureaucratic beyond: Roger Caillois and the negation of the sacred in Hollywood cinema. *Economy and Society*, 32(1), 74–89.
Goody, J. (2007). *Cooking, Cuisine and Class: A Study in Comparative Sociology* (Cambridge: Cambridge University Press).

Gordetsky, J., Westesson, K., Rabinowitz, R. and O'Brien, J. (2013). Wine and honey: The oldest of medicines. *Journal of Nephrology*, 26(Suppl. 22), 192–97.

Håland, E.J. (2012). When the dead ensure the food. Death and the regeneration of life through festivals, food and social gathering during the ritual year in Modern and Ancient Greece. *Cosmos*, 28, 309–46

Hamel, G. (2013). *A New Economy: The Eucharist Worship* (London: T&T Clark).

Harvey, G. (2014). *Food, Sex and Strangers: Understanding Religion as Everyday Life* (London: Routledge).

Hollander, J. (1999). Writing of food. *Social Research*, 66(1), 197–211.

Jeremias, J. (1971). *New Testament Theology* (Bowden, J., transl.) (London: SCM Press).

Johns, N. and Pine, R. (2002). Consumer behaviour in the food service industry: A review. *International Journal of Hospitality Management*, 21, 119–34.

Kennedy, J.A., Saucier, C. and Glories, Y. (2006). Grape and wine phenolics: History and perspective. *American Journal of Enology and Viticulture*, 57(3), 239–48.

Law, L. (2001). Home cooking: Filipino women and geographies of the senses in Hong Kong, *Ecumene*, 8, 264–83.

Levi-Strauss, C. (1983). *The Raw and the Cooked: Mythologiques*, volume 1 (Weightman, J., transl.) (Chicago, IL: Chicago University Press).

Lukacs, P. (2013). *Inventing Wine: A New History of One of the World's Most Ancient Pleasures* (New York: Norton & Co).

Magee, R. (2007). Food puritanism and food pornography: The gourmet semiotics of Martha and Nigella. *American Journal of American Popular Culture*, 6(2), 26–38.

Marshall, D. (2005). Food as ritual, routine or convention. *Consumption, Markets and Culture*, 8(1), 69–85.

Martin, E. (2005). Food, literature, art, and the demise of dualistic thought. *Consumption, Markets and Culture*, 8(1), 27.

O'Connor, D. (2005). Towards a new interpretation of 'hospitality'. *International Journal of Hospitality Management*, 17(3), 267–71.

O'Gorman, K. (2007). Dimensions of hospitality: Exploring ancient origins. In: Lashley, C., Lynch, P. and Morrison A. (eds), *Hospitality: A Social Lens*, pp. 17–32 (Oxford: Elsevier).

Riedel, H., Saw, N.M.M.T., Akumo, D.N., Kütük, O. and Smetanska, I. (2012). Wine as food and medicine. In: Valdez, B. (ed.), *Scientific, Health and Social Aspects of the Food Industry*, pp. 399–418 (Rijeka, Croatia: InTech).

Siemann, E.H. and Creasy, L.L. (1992). Concentration of the phytoalexin resveratrol in wine. *American Journal of Enology and Viticulture*, 43(1), 49–52.

Stanislawski, D. (1975). Dionysus westward: Early religion and the economic geography of wine. *Geographical Review*, 65(4), 427–44.

Sutton, D. (2010). Food and the senses. *Annual Review of Anthropology*, 39, 209–23.

Tannahill, R. (2002). *Food in History* (3e revised) (Oxford: Headline Review).

Tresidder, R. (2011). Reading hospitality: The semiotics of Le Manoir aux Quat'Saisons. *Hospitality and Society*, 1(1), 67–84.

Waddell, J. (1976). The place of the cactus wine ritual in the Papago Indian ecosystem. In: Bharati, A. (ed.), *Rituals, Cult, Shamanism: Realm of the Extra Human*, vol 2, *Ideas and Actions*, pp. 213–28 (The Hague: Mouton).

Waugh, E. (1945). *Brideshead Revisited* (London: Chapman and Hall).

Wikström, O. (2014). Liturgy as experience: The psychology of worship. A theoretical and empirical lacuna. *Scripta Instituti Donneriani Aboensis*, 15, 83–100.

Wright, R. (2013). *Cosmology in Antiquity* (London: Routledge).

Xue, A. (2014). *Religion, Heritage, and Power: Everyday Life in Contemporary China*. Doctoral Thesis, Edith Cowan University, Australia.

3
FINE WINE OR PLONK?

In Chapter 1 we looked at the legal definition of wine and in Chapter 2 we explored its cultural significance. From these discussions we saw that wines are not all equal. Wine, perhaps more than any other alimentary product, has a huge classificatory system where some wines are accorded a very high status (and price) as social objects and others are looked on disparagingly.

This class system has a major impact on the perception of wine, as embodied in the popular English terms 'fine wine' to describe the best wines and 'plonk' to describe basic or inferior wines. In this chapter we explore what leads people to apply these labels to different wines and what that means for the different roles of wine in society. In particular, we explore why the price of a bottle of wine can vary so dramatically.

Discussing the price of wine

It is impossible to consider the wines that might fall in different classes without some mention of price. In order to give some specifics, all mentions of price in this chapter use the UK as an example, considering typical retail prices including duty and VAT in the year 2015. These prices will vary considerably over time and in other countries; however, the absolute prices are of little significance – it is the relative prices between different wines that matter. But there is no point in simply converting these sterling prices to euro or dollar equivalents, because rates and duty and tax vary enormously between countries – see 'Wine prices and taxation' below and the discussion in Chapter 7.

The UK is a useful market to consider because of the huge ranges of wines available from all over the world, the relatively small domestic production and the fact that wine can be sold by a wide range of outlets (there is no state monopoly as in some countries). Also, as a maritime nation, the UK has a long history of importing wines from across the world and shipping costs are generally reasonable. So there are high levels of competition between wines of different countries and regions and between a wide range of different retail and online outlets. Moreover, whilst there are some slight differences in licensing law between England and Scotland (see Chapter 7) the UK does not have substantial differences of taxes or restrictions on the sale of alcohol that apply between different states of the US, for example.

Even in one market such as the UK, the price of wine can vary considerably from year to year due to changing prices charged by producers (partly due to vintage variation), fluctuating exchange rates affecting wine imports and changing rates of taxation – so the figures below are just a snapshot at one point in time. The examples are based on shop or online retail prices for a single 750ml bottle: restaurant prices will naturally be considerably higher. Higher prices of course apply to wines in larger bottles and lower prices to mini-bottles – see Chapter 6 regarding different sized bottles. Also, some wines are only available for purchase by the case or 'in bond', but unless otherwise mentioned the prices discussed here are single bottle retail prices – so, in the case of wines bought 'en primeur' (ordered before release – see pp. 59–60 for details) we are considering final release prices per bottle (including taxes and delivery).

The price of a bottle of wine

Later in this chapter we consider a class system that helps to distinguish the different levels of wine status between fine wine and plonk, but first we look at some of the main factors that affect the prices of wines.

The range of prices

We might ask how the price of wines can vary so widely. At the time of writing, there are bottles of wine advertised for retail purchase in the UK ranging from as little as £2.99 to as much as £6,900 for a single bottle. (There are some products below £2.99 that may look like wines, but we are only considering products that meet the legal definition of 'wine' as explained in Chapter 1 – so this excludes made-wine, low-alcohol products, and drinks which, although sold in wine bottles, are actually perry or wine blends with other ingredients.)

A number of major supermarkets have wines at £2.99 a bottle (red, white and rosé) – they are sold as blends with no identification of specific grape varieties, no vintage, and no geographical indication beyond the country of origin (typically Spain, although some wines at this price are simply sold under a brand name with small print identifying them as 'a blend of wines from different countries of the European Union').

For retailers seeking to attract customers with little cash to spare, the £2.99 price point is considered very important: great efforts are made to squeeze margins in order to offer wine at under £3 a bottle – though, as explained below, there are no profits to be made at this point and the retailer is likely to be taking a loss. Supermarkets are increasingly trying to avoid selling wines below £4 a bottle, and more specialist retailers may have a minimum price point of £6 per bottle or more.

The wine currently listed at £6,900 is a Château Pétrus 1982 *AOC Pomerol*. The wines of Château Pétrus are often the most expensive in Bordeaux, and the 1982 vintage is seen by many as the highest quality Bordeaux vintage in the late twentieth century. (However, this wine is also available at £4,000 by the single bottle from another wine merchant, and if you were in a position to buy a case of 12 bottles at auction, some Pétrus 1982 changed hands in 2014 for around £3,300/bottle – so, even at this level, savings can be made by shopping around! Nevertheless, buying or selling wine at auction can involve substantial commission charges.)

Pétrus 1982 has an almost legendary status – the wine writer Oz Clarke recalls tasting it on a rare visit (only the most distinguished visitors are received at Pétrus):

> It was my first visit. And the wine we would taste was the 1982. I can remember the shock and exhilaration as if it were yesterday. I can remember the flavours and texture as though the wine stood still, shimmering in the glass in front of me. And I can remember being speechless ... What my memory tells me is that the wine was like a celestial syrup of ripest blackcurrants, blackberries, mulberries, plums and cream, overlaid with mint and tobacco, the heady scent of kabash and some kind of mineral power mined from the deep earth. And also the promise, in time, of the perilous, moist excitement of fresh-dug truffles (Clarke 2012:238).

However, whilst £6,900 is a very high single bottle retail price, it is not the highest price paid for any wine on the UK market. Many would consider the world's most exclusive wine to be a red Burgundy: Domaine de la Romanée Conti *AOC Romanée Conti Grand Cru* (la Romanée Conti is both the name of the domain and the name of its top grand cru appellation – the Domaine is often abbreviated to 'DRC'). In 2014, depending on vintage, cases of DRC Romanée Conti changed hands at auction or online trading at over £100,000 per case, or up to £9,800 per bottle (Drinks Business 2014). But DRC is not normally available to purchase by the bottle on a retail basis: individual bottles generally only find their way into wine merchants when a top wine collection is sold – for example, following the death (or occasionally the bankruptcy) of the owner. Even higher prices are sometimes paid for rare older bottles – though they may be purchased more as collectible works of art than as wines that will ever be drunk.

Wine prices and taxation

Any comparison of wine prices should also consider how much of the price is in taxes and duties as opposed to the price of the wine itself. Many countries impose both a fixed tax on each bottle of wine that is sold (often called a duty) and wine is rarely exempt from sales taxes such as VAT (in Europe) or GST (in many other countries). In some countries such as the USA both State and Federal taxes may apply. (See Chapter 7 for more about duties and pricing.)

At the time of writing, in the UK every bottle of still wine is subject to duty of £2.05 per bottle and VAT at 20% on the final price (including VAT on top of the duty). It is illegal to sell wine below the cost of the duty and associated VAT – so the minimum possible retail price, even if retailers had wine that cost them nothing, would be £2.46.

In the case of a bottle sold at a retail price of £2.99, £0.50 of the price is VAT, leaving £2.49 to cover the wine and the duty. With £2.05 of duty to pay, this means the retailer only has £0.44 left to cover both the purchase of the wine and all their own overheads. Even if we assume the retailer is willing to accept a very small margin of just nine pence per bottle, this means the producer cannot be paid more than £0.35 a bottle. To grow and harvest the grapes, make the wine, bottle it (including the cost of the bottle) and ship it to the retailer for £0.35 a bottle is in practice impossible no matter how efficient the processes. Even the price of the empty bottle and cork will typically cost the producer more than £0.35 – without considering all the costs of growing the grapes and running a winery! So wines sold at this price level necessarily mean selling at a loss. Even with a bottle sold for £3.99, only £1.27 is actually being spent on the wine and the retailer's overheads.

However, for a wine sold at £5.99, £1 of the price is VAT, but the duty remains at £2.05 as with all wines at normal levels of alcohol, so the retailer has a respectable £2.94 to cover their own margins and the payments to the producer. If the wine is sourced from continental Europe, this may mean the producer gets a reasonable ex-cellars price of up to around €2.50 for each bottle: sufficient to produce a wine with some quality if it is from a less expensive region. It follows that a consumer willing to pay £5.99 for a bottle of wine can have a vastly better product than the one who only pays £2.99.

At the upper end, with trophy wines, the duty becomes only a trivial element in the price, but the VAT may be considerable. For a bottle sold at £6,900 the retailer will have to hand over £1,150 to the Government as VAT collected, but even if the wine has only recently been removed from bond, the duty would only be £2.05 leaving £5,748 for the cost of the wine and the retail margin!

It also follows from these principles that cross-border shopping, where wine is purchased in low-duty countries for consumption by those living in high-duty countries, only offers significant gains on inexpensive wines. But on more expensive wines, differences in VAT rates may well have more effect and it may be cheaper to buy in the country where the wine is to be drunk.

We might ask why anyone would ever pay many hundreds or even thousands of pounds for a trophy wine – the answer is that in some circumstances only the very best will do. See the scenario in Table 3.2.

Restaurant prices

Most bars and restaurants will add a considerable margin on to the retail price of a wine in order to cover all their costs of serving wine in a catering environment. So the perceptions of value for money on wine are very different in the on-trade.

Many restaurant operators just apply a simple multiplier to the retail price – often in the range of 2.5 to 3.5 – in order to set the restaurant price of a bottle. So a wine that can be bought for £5 retail may be listed at £15 in a restaurant, possibly much more in a high-class venue (although mark-up calculations using such figures are only meaningful if care is taken to compare VAT-inclusive prices in both cases). Where this approach is taken the consumer has to pay much higher differentials in the restaurant setting between entry-level wines and higher quality wines. This may encourage the majority of diners to choose the house wine or a wine at a fairly low price point on the wine list, even though they might select a more expensive wine when buying on a retail basis.

However, some restaurants work on a fixed mark-up, which makes the differentials on higher quality wines no more than in a retail setting. This is almost essential where a wine list includes very expensive bottles. If a wine would sell at £60 retail it may be difficult to list it at over £200 even in the most exclusive restaurants, but a diner might be very willing to pay £100 a bottle, which still gives the restaurant a £40 margin. Trophy wines are sometimes sold in top restaurants at no more than the retail price especially if the wine has been held for some years in the restaurant's cellars – so in these cases the buyer may be getting a 'bargain' even on wines priced at several hundred pounds per bottle.

Price, quality and scarcity

So, we may ask – comparing two examples at the start of this section – how is it that one wine can sell at more than two thousand times the price of another wine? If you are looking to buy some wine, whether you opt for the supermarket Spanish red or the 1982 Pétrus you will expect to get around 750ml of fermented grape must at between 11% and 13% abv, with water as the largest component, and various acids and polyphenols (see Chapter 1). What makes them so different in the price they will attract?

In Chapter 1 we considered a range of factors that are generally regarded as important in quality of wine. The price of wine, and the distinction between fine wine and plonk, is not just a matter of brand and reputation – there is universal agreement that some wines have much greater depth and complexity than others and are worthy of higher prices. This has been the case for centuries, probably since the dawn of winemaking. Indeed, wine professionals will often deliberately taste wines 'blind' so that their judgements are not affected by the appellation or the name of the producer, so enabling them to focus on what are often seen as 'objective' quality factors (though all wine tasting involves a measure of human subjective assessment).

We saw in Chapter 1 some of the reasons why it costs much more to make a fine wine than an entry-level wine. In this chapter we will consider how those quality factors and a range of other issues affect the status of a wine and the associated semiotics – the message given when such a wine is served (see Chapter 10 for more on the semiotics of wine).

However, the price of wines such as DRC and Pétrus, and indeed many other top wines from leading producers around the world that sell at very high prices, are not determined primarily by the cost of production – even though the costs of making top-quality wine will always be high. The price is determined to a large extent by their scarcity, the value created by marketers (see Chapter 8) and the desire of those with wealth to have the very best wines on their table to serve to honoured guests.

This is where the *brand of a wine* is crucial. The term 'brand' does not just refer to large-scale wines sold under well-known brand names – the name of every château or domain is a brand: it identifies wine from a particular producer, using particular vineyards, with a particular reputation. Some producers have a number of brands – for example, in Burgundy, most producers have vineyards in more than one appellation, each of which is separately bottled and vinified and sold at different prices. In Bordeaux it is common for a château to produce a first wine or '*grand vin*' under the name of the château itself and a second wine under a lesser name (sometimes even a third wine, often just sold as a generic wine of the relevant appellation with little or no linkage to the brand of the château). The brand of a wine is a signal of quality, reputation and status.

Once people come to realise that wines from a particular château or domain have slightly more flavour or concentration than those from nearby properties, the owners will find their wines in greater demand and can set a slightly higher price. This will give them more resources to invest for the future: they may be able to invest in changes to the methods of production that give further increases in quality (see next section), which in turn allow the prices to increase further in subsequent years. So leading brands can often become stronger and stronger.

But whilst it is certainly the case that better quality wines cost more to produce, price differentiation in wines is not just due to more successful producers investing more in production costs. Price is also determined by the desirability of a wine, which is influenced by a huge range of factors, not least the producer's approach to promotion of the wine (impressive château buildings, beautifully lit cellars and smart tasting rooms do a great deal to convey and communicate a sense of prestige to visitors). If a wine can be produced that particularly appeals to merchants and independent critics, the affect on price can be very dramatic, especially in the case of a wine awarded '100 points' by the famous US wine writer Robert Parker (McCoy 2008:152). Advertisements in international publications that feature other luxury products may also play a part in building an exclusive wine brand (see Chapter 8 for more on wine-marketing issues).

Some wine regions have formal classification systems enshrined in law – usually influenced by quality assessments built over many years – which enable consumers to differentiate wines that are deemed more special. These necessarily impact on the prices that can be charged for wines. The two most famous classification systems, those of Burgundy and Bordeaux, and a brief mention of a few others, are outlined later in this chapter.

Some producers also seek to manipulate demand by deliberately restricting the quantities of wine released once a wine starts to acquire some kind of reputation, in the hope of being able to charge higher prices in the longer term. In some instances the quantity is limited purely by the size of the property, for example, Château Pétrus only produces around 4,500 cases of wine per year as compared to 68,000 cases for Château Barreyres (a moderately priced cru bourgeois château in the *Haut-Médoc* appellation) (figures from Duijker and Broadbent 1997).

These factors all influence the perceived 'class' or status of a wine, and hence its price. A possible generic class system for categorising wines in price bands in relation to consumer perception is set out below.

A class system for wines

Not all wine falls into the simplistic categories of fine wine or plonk — there are many levels in between. Indeed the term 'fine wine' can include anything from wines just a little better than the norm to the most exclusive wines on earth.

Wine buyers and those responsible for marketing wine will often segment wines into different levels or classes — just as sociologists frequently categorise individuals by social class. As we move up the class scale, the quality of the wines will generally be higher and the occasions on which the wine might be served become increasingly prestigious. This is reflected by increasing price bands, though the price of wine is determined by many factors — as we consider later in this chapter — and it does not always follow that a higher price means a higher quality wine.

Except in certain wine regions which have carefully defined classification systems (see later in this chapter) there is no universally agreed scale of wine classes. But for the purposes of discussion, we consider six levels on a wine class scale:

- I: 'Plonk'
- II: Commercial wines
- III: Mid-range wines
- IV: Wines for drinking on special occasions
- V: Highly exclusive wines
- VI: Trophy wines.

I: 'Plonk'

No one wishing to sell wine would describe it as 'plonk' even if it was priced very cheaply. The term 'plonk' is normally used in a derogatory sense, to refer to wines far inferior to anything one would personally offer.

It is a slang or colloquial term: dictionaries are unclear on its origin, but most English-speaking wine drinkers use it in conversation – usually to refer to wines they would avoid – though occasionally in casual domestic settings, someone might offer a friend 'a glass of plonk' as a euphemism to make the point that the wine on offer was nothing special.

Sometimes people speak of 'plonk' in the sense of high-volume everyday wines that are perfectly drinkable when there is no need for anything special, in other words for lower-end commercial wines (see 'Commercial wines' below). But more often the term is used to suggest a wine which, though not technically harmful, might not be very pleasant to drink. The term 'plonk' could be used for a wine where little could be tasted other than the alcohol and water content. It could also be used for a wine produced so cheaply that it had some slight faults (though only at a level that would be detected by an expert). This might perhaps be due to excessive oxidation giving volatile acidity (wine starting to turn to vinegar), poor storage, excess SO_2 or 'rough' in terms of unpleasant compounds that attack the drinker's throat.

It is not possible to give a price range for plonk because no wine is ever marketed in this way, though even a moderately expensive wine could be described as 'plonk' if it is seen as being below the standard expected.

II: Commercial wines

Whilst no one selling wine would ever use the term 'plonk', there is a huge demand for inexpensive wines. At this level a wine merchant is likely to use a term such as an 'entry-level wine' or in trade negotiations she may say she was looking for a 'commercial wine' – in other words, a wine that will sell in significant commercial volumes as opposed to a specialist wine that will only sell in small quantities to connoisseurs. A restaurateur might say that he was looking to source a 'good value house wine'.

There is no formal definition of the term 'commercial wine' but in the UK market at the time of writing the term would typically be applied to wines selling below £6 a bottle. The wines in this range would span from some very basic wines sold with no more identification than the country of origin (possibly for as little as £2.99 a bottle – see p. 50) through straightforward examples of still wines from most of the major wine regions of Europe and the New World and also some entry-level sparkling wines when offered on price promotions.

Examples would include many high-volume wines from Chile and Australia, many French wines from regions such as Languedoc (often under the broad-ranging appellation *IGP Pays d'Oc*), entry-level wines from the Loire valley, entry-level Bordeaux wines – often négociant blends under the generic appellation *AOP Bordeaux*, wines from much of Italy and Spain (excluding the more prestigious appellations), easy-drinking off-dry German wines, many high-volume wines from Eastern Europe, and some wines from South Africa and the USA.

However, there is no suggestion that any of these regions are *only* producing commercial wines: all of these regions also produce much higher class wines in the categories discussed below.

Most of these entry-level wines will be sourced from co-operatives or large-scale commercial wineries with major economies of scale – smaller producers exporting to the UK market are likely to focus on more premium products.

The vast majority of wine consumers are looking for inexpensive wines – often bought for consumption soon after purchase (see Chapter 6 on 'Wine at home'). More than half of all wines sold on the UK market would come in this class.

III: Mid-range wines

The term 'mid-range wines' is often used to refer to bottles positioned at a level that is clearly superior to commercial wines, but where it would be something of an exaggeration to use the term 'fine wine'. In the UK market this could currently be applied to wines retailing at between approximately £6 and £12 per bottle.

These are the sorts of bottles that will be chosen by consumers taking some care to match a particular wine with the food being served, or looking for something a little better than an everyday wine to serve at a weekend meal or for a romantic occasion or a dinner with guests. The wine will often be bought some time before consumption, either by careful selection from the shelves of a retailer or possibly by mail order. Wines at this level are also likely to be bought by connoisseurs for drinking on everyday occasions (perhaps for weekday meals or casual drinking) or for serving at large parties where the host wishes to offer a reasonable quality wine but where there is no need to serve anything exceptional.

Examples of wines in this class would include higher level wines from New World countries, often with the benefit of careful viticulture with lower yields and oak ageing where applicable, also from more prestigious European appellations such as an Italian *DOCG Chianti Classico* or a Spanish *DOCa Rioja*. French wines in this band would include entry-level wines from Burgundy, from the more prestigious appellations of the Loire such as *AOP Sancerre*, some wines from the Crus de Beaujolais, and Bordeaux wines from petits châteaux, including some of the less expensive cru bourgeois properties (see pp. 65–70 for more on these terms), so rather than just *AOP Bordeaux* this would also include more specific Bordeaux appellations such as Médoc, Graves, and Côtes de Castillon.

The majority of sparkling wines on the UK market would also fall in this band – for example, most Cavas, Proseccos, and even some entry-level Champagne when discounted on promotion (though the normal price of most Champagnes would be well into the next class).

However, this class would generally only include co-operative and négociant wines, wines from relatively large commercial producers and some wines from lesser known individual producers. Wines with more individuality, produced in smaller volumes, would generally fall in higher classes.

Nevertheless, the understanding of what we mean by 'mid-range wine' varies enormously – not least due to different outlets and their policies on price promotions. In the UK, many wines are initially marketed at unrealistically high prices so that they can subsequently be discounted. Just because a wine is listed by a supermarket at £9.99 does not mean it is truly a mid-range wine – this may just be an initial price so it can subsequently be sold on offer at 'less than half price' for £4.99. Likewise, mail-order companies sometimes set relatively high list prices in order to offer vouchers that appear to offer large discounts (e.g. '£40 off any case of wine ordered this month'). Also, prices will vary considerably between outlets – a specialist wine shop might have a wine on its shelves for £15 that is available in a supermarket for £10.50 – but in the specialist wine shop value is added to the wine through the provision of advice on the origins of the wine, and how to serve it (see Chapter 8 'Marketing of the wine experience', for discussion on the creation of value). Moreover, specialist wine merchants, especially those operating by mail order, will frequently offer lower prices per bottle when buying a case (six or 12 bottles) as compared to the single bottle price.

IV: Wines for drinking on special occasions

Once we move beyond the category of mid-range wines, most wine merchants would start to use the term 'fine wine'. But there is a huge difference between wines sold at just a little beyond the mid-range level and the most expensive wines available. So, within the notion of 'fine wine' we initially consider a category that may be called 'wines for drinking on special occasions' – in the UK market this could currently include wines sold at retail prices between approximately £12 and £40 per bottle.

Only someone with a definite interest in wine is likely to spend more than £12 a bottle on a regular basis, though many reasonably affluent consumers may consider occasional purchases of bottles in this range for a special occasion.

A 'special occasion wine' in these terms could be chosen from some of the most prestigious European appellations such as *DOCG Barolo* in Italy, *DOCa Priorat* in Spain, or some of the best Rieslings from leading producers in the Mosel and Rhine valleys in Germany. From the New World, it includes many wines produced in very small quantities by major producers in Australia, New Zealand, South Africa and California. From France, this would include wines from top producers in major regions such as the Loire valley, Alsace and the Rhone valley and a wide choice of wines from the more exclusive appellations of Burgundy and Bordeaux. This would include most of the village wines of Burgundy such as *AOP Volnay*, *AOP Meursault* and *AOP Pouilly-Fuissé* – including many at the premier cru level. In Bordeaux it would include a good range of wines from the most famous appellations such as *AOP Margaux*, *AOP Pessac-Léognan*, *AOP St Émilion Grand Cru* and *AOP Pomerol*. (We are using the designation 'AOP', which is the legal designation in French under modern EU wine law, but most producers of wines at this level prefer the traditional equivalent 'AOC' – see Chapter 1.)

This class would also include leading dessert wines such as Sauternes (from Bordeaux) or Tokaj (from Hungary) or Vin Santo (from Italy). It would also include most of the regular cuvées from the major Champagne houses (though not, in most cases, vintage Champagnes or special premium blends) and the traditional method sparkling wines of England.

At this level, the choice of vintage will also be significant – someone choosing a wine at this price level will almost certainly want it to be ready for drinking when it is served, so, particularly in the case of red wines, it may be stored for some time after purchase before being opened (possibly for many years – see Chapter 6 for choices regarding wine storage at home). In the on-trade, wines at this level will generally only appear on restaurant wine lists in fine-dining establishments (where they might be listed anywhere from £30 to £150 a bottle at restaurant prices). Such establishments either need their own cellars to store wine while they mature, or have to pay a premium to wine merchants to obtain mature vintages.

Wines at this level are widely available in major high-street wine shops and even in supermarkets. Many supermarkets' wine sections have a special area for 'fine wines' or 'premium wines' – often with different styles of display to appear more exclusive, and usually with bottles kept horizontally or at an angle rather than upright on shelves. Whilst the quantities of such wines sold may be small the availability of a small number of relatively expensive wines can be effective in defining the store as a suitable location for up-market customers to choose their wines – and may also help in promoting sales of premium food products.

However, those buying more than the occasional bottle of wine at this level will typically be committed wine connoisseurs, buying through specialist wine merchants through mail order and online offers where it is generally necessary to order a minimum of a case of wine at a time (possibly a mixed case). In some instances at this level (and almost always for the next class), purchases may be made on the *en primeur* system that is widely used for the sale of fine wines from the world's leading wine regions to serious private buyers.

Although some have suggested that the en primeur system is in decline, it is still widely used, particularly for the sales of wines from leading estates in Bordeaux and Burgundy and for vintage Ports, but also for some of the top wines from other regions. Under this system, leading wine merchants attend tastings of wines while they are still 'in their prime' (*en primeur* in French) – that is, after the wine has been vinified and blended but while it is still ageing in barrel and not yet bottled. At that stage, producers announce their prices for release of the wine and merchants add a suitable margin and send offers to their customers, usually supported by tasting notes and comments on the vintage. In the case of Bordeaux these offers are usually issued in around May or June (around nine months after the relevant harvest); Burgundy offers are normally issued somewhat later, often around December/January (around 16 months after the vintage). Customers buying en primeur make payment to the wine merchant at the time of ordering soon after the offer is received – though at this stage they only pay an 'in bond' price – in other words the price for the bottled wine to be brought into a bonded store in their country. A few months later the wine merchant pays most of this over to the producer who then has a major cash-flow advantage in having received most of the payment for wines that are still developing in cask. In due course – sometimes as much as two years later – the wines are bottled, shipped to the purchaser's country, and initially held in a bonded warehouse. The purchaser can either opt to remove them immediately from bond and have them delivered – at which stage the duty and VAT must be paid – or leave them stored 'in bond' (just paying an annual storage charge) and only pay the duty and VAT when they are eventually released. Alternatively, it is possible to pay the duty and VAT and transfer the wine to be stored duty paid – this is a good strategy if the purchaser definitely wishes to drink the wine in due course, but wishes to avoid future increases in rates of duty and VAT. See Table 3.1 for an illustration.

TABLE 3.1 Example of timescales for an individual buying en primeur wine produced by a leading Bordeaux château

- September 2015 – Harvest at the château
- October 2015–March 2016: vinification and initial blending of the wine
- March/April 2016 – Trade tastings in Bordeaux attended by wine merchants
- May/June 2016 – Wine merchants issue en primeur offers for Bordeaux 2015
- July 2016 – 'Andrew' a lover of good red Bordeaux, living in the UK places an order with his wine merchant. He orders one case of 'Château Example' at £300/case (£25/bottle) en primeur and makes payment to his merchant
- June 2017 – Château Example bottles their 2015 vintage
- November 2017 – Château Example ships their 2015 wines to those merchants in the UK who have placed en primeur orders. (Different châteaux will deliver to the UK in different months.) The wines will be held by the UK merchant in a secure bonded warehouse with near-constant temperature as some customers may want the wines to be stored for many years
- March 2018 – Once the merchant has received all shipments of 2015 Bordeaux they contact their customers, including Andrew, asking for their instructions on shipment or storage of the wine
- April 2018 – Andrew advises the wine merchant that he would like to take immediate delivery of the wine: he pays the duty of £24.60 and the VAT of £64.92 (on both the original purchase price and the duty)* and a £10 UK delivery charge – so he pays the wine merchant a further £99.52. The total price of his wine is thus £399.52 for the case, or £33.29 per bottle
- May 2018 – The wine is delivered to Andrew's home and he stores it in his personal cellar. Shortly afterwards, the merchant releases their own stocks of Château Example 2015 for retail purchase at £39/bottle
- December 2023 – Andrew opens the case and uncorks the first bottle to see how the wine is drinking – this is 8 years after the vintage and 5 years after he received it. (By now, very few wine merchants still have Château Example 2015 available for retail purchase, but where it is offered the price is now around £55/bottle.)

* In this example, the duty and VAT are calculated at rates applicable in the UK in 2015.

The en primeur system requires considerable trust between the customer and the wine merchant, as customers are paying for the wines a considerable time before they will ever be received: there have been scandals where wine merchants have closed or gone into liquidation leaving customers seriously out of pocket. Most customers buying en primeur will therefore use a wine merchant with a strong track record and that will only deal with highly dependable producers in the region concerned (some of the leading merchants in the UK who specialise in en primeur sales have been trading for more than two centuries).

However, for serious wines for special occasions, buying en primeur is often the only way to be sure of securing a particular vintage from a particular château, and usually (though not always) those buying en primeur secure a price advantage as in the illustration in Table 3.1.

V: Highly exclusive wines

Although the range of purchasers shrinks considerably once we go beyond about £40/bottle, there is a considerable market for 'highly exclusive wines' which, in terms of the UK market could be defined as wines with a retail price in the range £40 to £100 per bottle.

Wines in this category would include most of the 'classed growth châteaux' of Bordeaux (though not the first growths or even the most highly sought second and third growths), premiers crus from the most prestigious producers in Burgundy and some of the higher volume grands crus (see pp. 65–75 for explanation of terms). This group would also include most vintage and special cuvée Champagnes (though not the very top cuvées) many of the most exclusive wines from producers in the top regions of Italy and Spain, vintage Ports from the top producers, as well as some of the most prestigious names from the New World. Also, many producers of trophy wines (see p. 62) also produce a 'second wine' designed to sell at this level.

The prices of wines at this level (and above) can vary considerably from vintage to vintage, and there is also an extensive market for older vintages, where the price will be often be considerably higher than the original retail price when the wine was first released, especially for the top-rated vintages. (Though there are exceptions – some vintages are felt to be over-priced on release and subsequent prices may fall.)

Wines in this class will be a normal purchase from time to time for committed wine connoisseurs with considerable wealth, with the initial purchase very likely to be made en primeur – though typically with no expectation of drinking the wine for some years, except perhaps in the case of Champagne. (However, sometimes whole cases of such wines are resold without being opened – there is an extensive secondary market in wines at this level.) Purchasers at this level will either have an extensive personal cellar or will be storing whole cases with their wine merchants.

These highly exclusive wines will only be opened on the most special occasions, typically with guests who are likely to appreciate the significance of the wines on offer. If they are served with a meal it is likely that the food will be chosen to match the wine, rather than vice versa. Notwithstanding the costs, a wine connoisseur may arrange to serve a number of such wines together perhaps with a common theme – for example, several vintages of the same wine (a vertical tasting) or wines from several nearby estates from the same year (a horizontal tasting).

Wines at this level are also in demand for the most exclusive restaurants, where a host wishes to be seen to be choosing the most prestigious wines to complement exclusive food with honoured guests. Some high-status bars choose to offer wines of this kind by the glass, or maybe even just by the tasting sample (e.g. where small samples of several wines are offered as a 'wine flight') so enabling customers to have the experience of drinking very exclusive wines without needing to buy a whole bottle.

VI: Trophy wines

Once we move beyond a retail price of around £100 a bottle, it is more appropriate to speak of 'trophy wines'. These are the ultimate in fine wines – they are bought with the intention of acting as a trophy – a symbol that will make a very significant social statement when they are eventually opened and served. For the symbol to be understood, those who will share the wine need to be very knowledgeable wine consumers, or where this is not the case, the host may have to adopt other measures to create the sense of prestige – for example, using a professional sommelier to serve the wine and explain its significance.

This class would include the first growth wines of Bordeaux, the most prestigious grands crus from leading domains in Burgundy and a few top cuvées – often deliberately produced in very small quantities – from a small number of leading producers elsewhere in the world who have spent many years building and developing a luxury brand.

Many wines at this level are simply bought and sold primarily as investments, with no intention that they will ever be drunk – at least not by the initial purchaser (though the purchase of wine purely for investment falls outside the scope of this book). But ultimately most wines even at the trophy level will eventually reach someone who intends to drink them – although many wine lovers will tell of having one or two wines in their cellar that are so special that they never feel the time is right to open them, and eventually the bottles deteriorate (see Chapter 6 on storing wine at home and assessing when a wine is ready to drink).

Most trophy wines are initially sold only through en primeur sales (see p. 60), and for the most prestigious there is typically an 'allocation' system where wine merchants are offered only a few cases of a wine to allocate between their customers. Usually there is a policy of favouring customers – whether individuals or restaurants – who have bought regularly from a particular property, rather than those who just want to buy the best vintages. Sometimes the top wines are allocated on the basis that the purchaser must also buy wines from lesser appellations from the same producer.

Even when such wines are resold, and perhaps made available for purchase by the bottle rather than by the case, they will not normally appear on normal shelves even at top wine merchants. This is partly to avoid pilferage or damage by people handling the bottles, but also because such wines need to be stored in impeccable conditions to maintain their value. For this reason, and because there may only be a few bottles available, they usually only appear on wine merchants' lists of 'fine and rare' wines that must be specially requested – rather than on a normal retail price list. Some of these wines (particularly those in full cases) may still be held in bond, so merchants' lists will generally show each wine as 'IB' (in bond) or 'DP' (duty paid): if wines are bought at the IB price and the customer wishes to receive them, a considerable payment of duty and VAT may be involved, as with taking delivery of en primeur wines. For older wines, additional notes will seek to show the condition of the wines, particularly the level in bottle. A small amount of evaporation through the cork, leading to a visible reduction in the level of the wine in bottle, is to be expected in a wine that is more than 15–20 years old but if the level has dropped significantly the wine is likely to be oxidised and possibly undrinkable.

Trophy wines will often be aged for many years before they are served on the most exceptional occasions. Wine connoisseurs often choose to mark a great occasion by opening a bottle from a specific year that could be decades earlier – for example, the year of birth or marriage or of admission to a specific profession – though only the very best wines can be kept for decades. However, purchasers with wealth but limited wine experience occasionally have been known to buy trophy wines to impress others and end up serving them far too young when the flavours are aggressive and unbalanced.

Top restaurants may choose to include some trophy wines on their wine lists. They may only keep one or two bottles of each wine in stock as orders will be rare, but simply including very exclusive wines on a wine list has a powerful semiotic role in marking the status of the restaurant. Nevertheless, there will be occasions where such wines are ordered, especially by those celebrating major financial successes – see Table 3.2 for an example (based on a true story).

Classifications of wine enshrined in law

The classes of wine suggested above attempted to span all wines available on a specific market (using the UK retail market as an example). As such, the criteria we considered were generalised. But a number of the world's leading wine regions – in particular the two most exclusive regions, Burgundy and Bordeaux (both in France) – have over the years developed very sophisticated local classification schemes to enable buyers to distinguish what are widely regarded as the very best wines. These give rise to terms such as *premier cru*, *grand cru*

TABLE 3.2 When very expensive wine is justified

'Eric' was dining in a top London restaurant with his client 'Fergus' to celebrate the completion of the sale of Fergus's business worth tens of millions of pounds.

Eric's firm had provided professional advice that was crucial to the deal: a great deal of staff time had been involved and Fergus had been advised that the total fee for these services would be around £300,000. As they sat down, Fergus suggested that whilst he was very pleased with the work undertaken, he felt – based on what they had agreed – that a fee nearer to £200,000 would be more appropriate.

Eric suggested they looked at the menu before talking business. He spotted that the wine list included a number of vintages of Château Pétrus from the 1990s that would be in top condition for drinking. He knew that Fergus had some interest in wine, and asked if he had ever had Pétrus. When Fergus said he hadn't, Eric ordered a bottle of Château Pétrus 1998 to go with their meal. It was listed at £850 a bottle (around £1,000 including the restaurant's service charge).

The Pétrus was carefully decanted by the restaurant's sommelier and served in beautiful glasses. Both men realised they were drinking a truly special wine with their meal, and their conversation warmed considerably.

At the end of the meal, they departed without any further mention from Fergus regarding Eric's fee. So, Eric's firm submitted the bill for £300,000 and it was paid in full.

Eric said afterwards: '£1,000 of wine for a business lunch for two may have seemed high – but it was a superb investment. By saving us from a possible £100,000 reduction on our fees, we got a 100:1 return!'

---

or *grand cru classé*, which are so significant in identifying wines that are particularly special. These 'badges of status' are extremely important to wine connoisseurs seeking to offer the best wines to their guests – whether serving wine at home or choosing wines in a restaurant. Because of the importance of these categories in distinguishing fine wines, anyone studying the status of wine in society will find it helpful to understand the main rules. Some other systems are mentioned briefly after discussing these two.

In both Burgundy and Bordeaux, these systems are enshrined in legislation and wine producers cannot claim that their wines have a higher status than that officially allocated to the château or vineyard concerned. Occasionally those seen to be breaching the rules have faced serious prosecutions for fraud.

The subtleties of these classifications are discussed in great detail in specialist wine books covering those regions: the explanations below simply explain the main features to show how the classifications work and their implications for the perceived status of a wine. Authors writing on the details of classifications in Bordeaux include Peppercorn (2003), Duijker and Broadbent (1997), Clarke (2012) and the classic French-edited volume of Bordeaux châteaux known as '*Cocks & Féret*' (Boidron 2014) running to over 2,000 pages, which has been produced since 1850 and appears in new editions every few years. Leading authors on Burgundy include Sutcliffe (1999), Hanson (2003), Pitiot and Servant (2004), and Morris (2010). There are also books and websites going into greater detail on individual appellations and even on individual châteaux or domains.

All parts of France use the term *cru* to refer to a particular vineyard or group of vineyards which produces wine that in some way is distinctive (the term is also used in a few wine regions outside France). Translated literally into English, the word 'cru' means 'growth' – a specific growth of vines – so sometimes wine specialists speak of 'a third growth estate' in Bordeaux as a translation of a château that is rated *troisième grand cru classé*. But the translation means little and increasingly the terminology is left untranslated when writing in English.

It is important to note that a particular term may be used in different ways in different regions. For example, in Burgundy the term 'grand cru' refers to wines at the top of the hierarchy – single vineyard appellations from the most prestigious sites, but in the St Émilion appellation of Bordeaux the term 'grand cru' simply identifies wines that are somewhat superior to a generic St Émilion, as there are three higher tiers in the St Émilion classification.

Classification of châteaux in Bordeaux

Almost every wine-producing property in Bordeaux is called a château. The Bordeaux region has long favoured lists of châteaux ordered by their status and significance. At their simplest such lists can just be compiled by ranking châteaux in decreasing order of the price at which their wines are sold (with the most expensive at the top) – and there is no doubt that prices play some part in a number of the classification systems. But many other factors such as terroir, complexity of the wines, size of the property and history can affect the classification.

However, different classification systems are used in different parts of the Bordeaux region, so it is vital to refer to a map (Figure 3.1). We focus on the two main systems: in the Médoc and in St Émilion.

Classification of the Médoc

The Médoc is to many people the most famous wine region of the world, on the left bank of the Gironde estuary, including the four prestigious appellations (AOPs) of *St Estèphe*, *Pauillac*, *St Julien* and *Margaux* – see Figure 3.1. It is sometimes described as the 'left bank', being on the left side of the Gironde estuary when viewed in the direction of flow of the river. It is home to many spectacular châteaux surrounded by top vineyards with Cabernet Sauvignon, Merlot and Cabernet Franc on largely gravelly soils that force the vines to dig deep, producing wines with great depth, complexity and ageing potential. All but the simplest wines are aged in oak barrels, often for nearly two years, and the top properties will use mainly new barrels every year to maximise the interaction of the wine and oak.

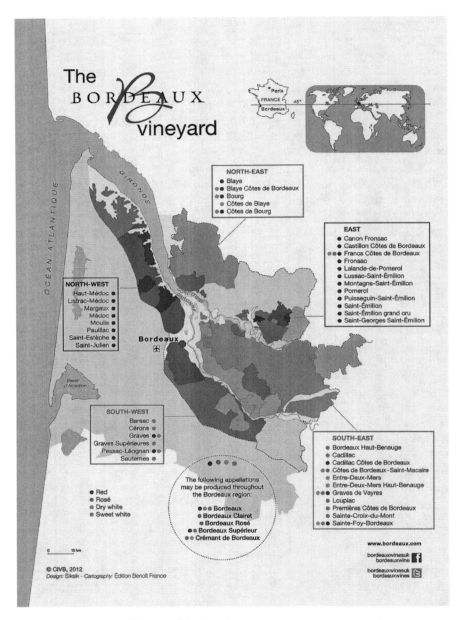

FIGURE 3.1 The appellations of the Bordeaux region.

Source: Conseil Interprofessionel du Vin de Bordeaux.

However, not all châteaux are huge: there are also many smaller family-owned properties that are producing excellent wines within these prestigious appellations. In Bordeaux, vineyards are normally just identified by the name of the château:

they generally lie in close proximity to the château building, and many châteaux are surrounded by their own vineyards.

The rules applicable in the Médoc allow us to distinguish four main levels of producers:

- The co-operatives – producing wines on behalf of growers who do not have their own wineries – although their wines must still meet all the rules of the appellation under which they are sold. The co-operatives account for 15% of the production from the Médoc. Some of their wines just carry brand names – for example, '*La Rose de Pauillac*' from the highly regarded Pauillac co-operative of that name – but co-operative-produced wines can carry a château name on the label where the grapes from a particular property can be suitably identified.
- The so-called 'petits châteaux' – these produce their own wines, though they are not formally classified. Many produce good wines that can be sold with the Médoc appellations and whilst their wines are generally simpler and lighter than the classed growths, their prices are much more affordable. Eleven per cent of the Médoc's wines come from the petits châteaux.
- The 'cru bourgeois châteaux' – these are properties that, though not entitled to the designation 'grand cru classé' are regularly producing wines of a very high standard, normally with good concentration and use of oak. The term *cru bourgeois* has been subject to debate over the years, but a new legal framework took effect from the 2008 vintage and the list is now revised every year. Under the classification for the 2012 vintage (announced in November 2013) some 267 châteaux of the Médoc are entitled to use the description *cru bourgeois* on their labels. Recent figures show 50% of Médoc production coming from cru bourgeois châteaux.
- The 'classed growths' or 'grands crus classés châteaux' according to the 1855 classification. This classification, originally devised for a Paris exhibition, identified 61 leading estates, and placed them in five tiers. Following a revision in 1973 affecting one property, the number of châteaux in each tier is now: 5 × 1er grand cru classé (or 'first growths'); 14 × 2ème grand cru classé; 14 × 3ème grand cru classé; 10 × 4ème grand cru classé; and 18 × 5ème grand cru classé.

This classification has had a major effect in prices over the years. Any wine from a grand cru classé château would be regarded as 'fine wine' and most would fall at least into the class of 'highly exclusive wines' using the six classes outlined above. But prices vary dramatically even within the classed growths: a wine labelled *Premier Grand Cru Classé* can command prices that are at least three times the price of a typical *Deuxième Grand Cru Classé* (although over the years some châteaux in the lesser tiers have invested in standards of production well above their tier and prices have changed accordingly).

The five first growths (*premier grand crus classés*) – Châteaux Lafite-Rothschild, Latour, Margaux, Mouton-Rothschild and Haut-Brion (the latter is actually in the Graves region) are all trophy wines, affordable only to those prepared to spend hundreds of pounds per bottle even in lesser vintages.

A high-ranking château is able to sell its wines at higher prices, which means more revenue to invest for the future – higher standards in the vineyard, more sophisticated selection of grapes at pressing, more expensive techniques in winemaking and ageing – leading ultimately to richer and more concentrated wines. So it is hard for lesser properties to catch up and overtake those at the top. Likewise it is hard for a cru bourgeois château to catch up with the classed growths (although there are a few outstanding crus bourgeois châteaux that sell at similar prices to the lesser classed growths).

So, despite the fact that the 1855 classification has not been revised in over 150 years (apart from the one change in 1973) it remains a widely used benchmark in distinguishing outstanding wines. As such it has a major effect on the price of wines and the status of a wine in terms of the classes considered earlier in this chapter.

If a particular château is rated grand cru classé, that designation applies to all wines bottled under the main château name provided they are sourced from relevant vineyards within the appellation – there is no formal distinction between individual vineyards under the château's ownership, though as we noted above, many châteaux produce a 'second wine' from plots which they do not feel are good enough for the grand vin.

The St Émilion classification

On the opposite side of the Bordeaux region, on the 'right bank', north of Bordeaux city, across the rivers Garonne and Dordogne, a different classification system operates in the appellation (PDO) of *St Émilion* – surrounding the historic town of that name. Here the soils are very different with chalky slopes and some sandy soils so the main grape is Merlot usually with lesser amounts of Cabernet Franc and often only a little Cabernet Sauvignon. The châteaux are generally smaller than in the Médoc, and more are family owned though there are still many prestigious château buildings. The history of wine production in St Émilion goes back much earlier than in the Médoc – the traditional ruling council, the *Jurade de St Émilion*, is widely regarded as France's oldest wine order (see p. 187 for more on the Jurade).

Like the Médoc, St Émilion has a system of classification of châteaux, but unlike the Médoc (with its 1855 classification that has only ever had one change) the classification of châteaux in St Émilion is revised every ten years. It is helpful to distinguish six levels of St Émilion producers – the last four of these represent special classifications which a château may be awarded (above the basic appellation St Émilion).

- Growers who take their grapes to the co-operative (the Union des Producteurs de St Émilion – this is a co-operative with a considerable reputation, producing a number of different cuvées under different labels under both the *AOP St Émilion* and *AOP St Émilion Grand Cru*, see below).
- Châteaux whose wines are simply sold with the AOP St Émilion (though most use the traditional term 'AOC' rather than 'AOP' – see Chapter 1). This group includes several hundred smaller properties, mainly owner-managed, but some owned by larger groups.
- Properties of any size whose wines have greater depth and complexity can apply each year under the regulations of the appellation to use the *AOP St Émilion Grand Cru*. A château whose wines meet the rules each year to be awarded the grand cru appellation will have well-located vineyards with good vinification including at least some oak ageing. Such a producer is sometimes described as a 'grand cru château' but strictly speaking the grand cru classification is only awarded to the wines of a specific year, rather than the château itself. (It has some parallels with cru bourgeois status in the Médoc – though that term is not used in St Émilion.)
- The first level in the ten-yearly classification of individual châteaux is the designation *St Émilion Grand Cru Classé*. Generally the wines from these properties have a lot more depth, complexity and oak ageing than those simply at the grand cru level. The latest classification was in 2012 and there are currently 63 châteaux at this level. Most of these would be priced at a level to fall in class IV in the categories outlined above – wines for drinking on special occasions. (Note that there is no further AOP at this level – even the wines of a château rated St Émilion Grand Cru Classé – or above – are sold under the *AOP St Émilion Grand Cru*. However, the term 'Grand Cru Classé' will almost always appear on the label below the name of the château.)
- Above this are châteaux rated *St Émilion Premier Grand Cru Classé (B)*. These are 'first growths' to use a direct translation of the term, though there are currently 20 châteaux at this level, so it is not equivalent to first growth status in the Médoc. Also, no one would put the 'B' on a label but it distinguishes the second tier within the premier grands crus classés châteaux. These are properties committed to the top standards of production with the best sites, low yields in the vineyard, great selectivity when grapes arrive for processing, and extensive oak ageing with a significant proportion of new oak barrels. Most would fall into the category of 'highly exclusive wines'.
- The four very top properties are designated *St Émilion Premier Grand Cru Classé (A)* – this includes Châteaux Angélus, Ausone, Cheval Blanc, and Pavie (though Angélus and Pavie were only promoted to this list in 2012). They are usually considered equivalent to the first growth of the Médoc and would only be served on the most special occasions – generally they would be seen as 'trophy wines'.

Other areas of Bordeaux

Less well-known classification systems are also used in some other areas of Bordeaux, notably in the Graves and in Sauternes.

However, some parts of the region, notably the Pomerol appellation (on the right bank, next to St Émilion) eschew any kind of formal classification and wines are simply sold on their merits. This has not prevented one or two châteaux of Pomerol achieving 'trophy wine' status, notably Châteaux Pétrus (mentioned above) and Le Pin that usually sell at even higher prices than the first growths of the Médoc and St Émilion. So a formal classification system is manifestly not essential to achieving the highest prices.

Classification of vineyards in Burgundy

The region of Burgundy (*Bourgogne* in French) stretches around 230km north to south on the eastern side of France. The vast majority of Burgundies are either white wines produced from the Chardonnay grape or reds from Pinot Noir. Whilst Chardonnay is grown all over the world, many would see Burgundy as its natural home, producing outstanding white wines with crispness, great length, and often a gentle use of oak. For Pinot Noir, Burgundy is even more seen as the ultimate home, having just enough warmth to ripen but without creating a rich jammy wine that can result when Pinot Noir is grown in warmer climates.

The region is generally divided into five main vineyard areas – from north to south these are: Chablis and the Auxerrois, the Côte de Nuits (north and south of the famous town of Nuits-St-George), the Côte de Beaune (around the famous walled city of Beaune), then further south the Côte Chalonnaise, and the Mâconnais (around the town of Mâcon) – see Figure 3.2. The Côte de Nuits and the Côte de Beaune are together known as the Côte d'Or (the 'hills of gold') – as the steep east-facing slopes of the Côte d'Or give rise to some of the most exquisite (and sometimes the most expensive) wines in the world.

Unlike Bordeaux, there are few large châteaux in Burgundy – the vast majority of producers are simply known as domains. In addition, many high-quality wines are produced under the names of leading négociants who may buy in grapes or newly fermented wine from a range of producers in an appellation. But great emphasis is placed on the location where the grapes are grown – the individual vineyard (*climat* in French). In most appellations, every climat has a name, even though some are very small – often well under a hectare. Moreover, two adjacent climats may have significant differences in their terroir. The climats are often seen as fundamental to the makeup of the vineyards of Burgundy.

Wines from a top domain taking enormous care in the vineyard and vinification will, of course, cost more than other wines from the same appellation. The focus of the classification system is not on the producer, but on the specific location of the vineyard sites, in many cases down to the individual climat.

Fine wine or plonk? **71**

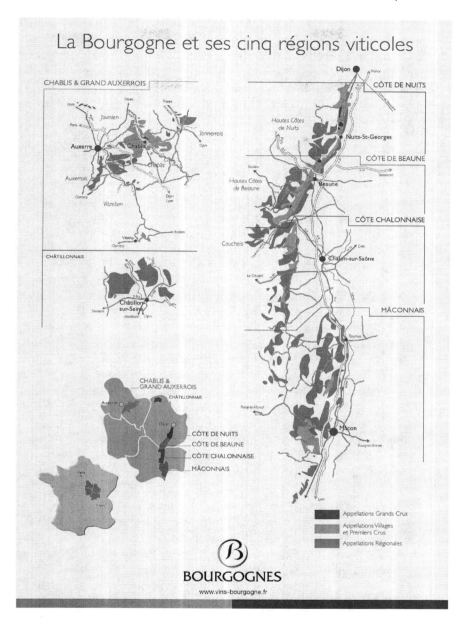

FIGURE 3.2 The five vineyards of Burgundy.

Source: Bureau Interprofessionnel des Vins de Bourgogne.

The region has no less than 100 appellations d'origine contrôlées (PDOs to use the technical EU term, or AOP in French, though most producers keep to the tradition term AOC). These are divided into four levels.

72 Fine wine or plonk?

- At the first tier are the regional appellations, such as *AOP Bourgogne* (which covers the whole region) or sub-regional appellations such as *AOP Mâcon-Villages* (which covers a large part on the Mâconnais). However, there are few really inexpensive wines in Burgundy: most of those bottled under regional appellations would be priced as 'mid-range wines' within the classes suggested above. These account for 52% of all the wine produced in Burgundy.
- The second tier comprises the communal or village appellations – for example, *AOP Pommard*, *AOP Nuits-St-George*, *AOP Chablis*, *AOP Mercurey*, *AOP Gevrey-Chambertin*, *AOP Puligny-Montrachet*. For a wine to be bottled under one of these appellations the grapes must come entirely from vineyards within the boundary of the appellation concerned. Many of the villages have a unique character that can be spotted by experienced tasters even when tasting wines blind. In most cases these would fall into the price band of 'wine for drinking on a special occasion' – to offer one's guest a Puligny-Montrachet, or a Pommard or a Gevrey-Chambertin, whether at home or in a restaurant, is well above the level of most people's everyday drinking. Some of these appellations are solely for reds or solely for whites, in other cases such as Mercurey both reds and whites are allowed. Over the years, many villages have tagged the name of their most famous vineyard, usually a grand cru (see below) – on to the village name. So, for example, le Montrachet is widely regarded as the top climat in Puligny but that does not mean that all wines labelled '*AOC Puligny-Montrachet*' will all come from the climat le Montrachet – they could come from anywhere in the village of Puligny. Thirty-seven per cent of wines from Burgundy are sold under village appellations.
- Within many villages (but by no means all) the top climats are given the status 'premier cru'. Wines from the premiers crus in a village normally have more depth and complexity – they are outstanding examples from the appellation. If a wine is made entirely from premier cru sites within one appellation, this can be shown on the label as part of the appellation (e.g. *AOC Gevrey-Chambertin Premier Cru*). The term is sometimes abbreviated '1er cru'. If the wine is entirely from one specific premier cru site, the name of the climat can also be shown (e.g. *Gevrey-Chambertin 1er Cru Bel Air*). Those who know a village well can explain the different characteristics of the wines from the different premier cru climats. Gevrey is one of the leading appellations of the Côte de Nuits (see Figure 3.3) with wines, especially from the premiers crus climats, which have great depth and ageing potential. Across Burgundy as a whole, 10% of wines are classified as premiers crus.
- The very top climats are known as the grands crus, and have a unique status where each climat is normally an appellation in its own right. So, a wine from the grand cru vineyards of le Chambertin (in the village of Gevrey-Chambertin) will just show on the label '*AOC Chambertin*' and the words '*Grand Cru*'. A wine from le Monrachet will just show '*AOC*

Montrachet – Grand Cru'. The grands crus account for only 1.4% of the production of Burgundy, but in villages that have grand cru climats, they are, of course, the most exclusive wines.

Figure 3.3 gives a detailed map of the Côte de Nuits, where the different levels of shading distinguish the regional, village, premier crus and grand crus sites. It will be seen that the grands crus lie along a thin strip of hillside facing south-east, with superb exposure to the sun. (The same approach is used in Figure 3.2, but the grand crus are so small in relation to Burgundy as a whole that they are hard to spot.)

It is worth stressing that the status of a grand cru – although at the peak of the classification of vineyards – is no absolute guarantee of quality. Some of the larger grands crus such as the Clos de Vougeot (mentioned in Chapter 1) are owned by many different producers, including some families within only a couple of rows, and standards of production can vary. But the words 'grand cru' on the label always allow producers to charge much more than for their village wines, and normally a good deal more than their premier crus.

Nevertheless, when the appellations were established, many villages did not seek the status of 'grand cru' for any vineyard, and in those cases the premier crus are the top wines. Indeed, some top-quality appellations such as Pouilly-Fuissé in the Mâconnais area, do not even have any premiers crus (though at the time of writing there is an active campaign by leading producers to win premier cru status for the top climats of Pouilly-Fuissé).

So, the overall status (and hence the price) of Burgundian wines are determined by a combination of the appellation, the producer and of course the year (as quality varies considerably by vintage).

For a serious wine lover, to be offered a grand cru wine from Burgundy is the ultimate pleasure – especially a good vintage from an acclaimed producer. There is a particular status in some of the small grands crus known as '*monopoles*' (monopolies) where one domain owns the entire climat – so any wine under the relevant appellation is always from that one producer. The example mentioned previously of la Romanée-Conti – the famous grand cru vineyard in the village of Vosne-Romanée, owned entirely by the DRC domain, is an example of this situation, where prices are exceptionally high (driven by the limited quantities and the demands of investors). But even from a lesser producer, most grand cru Burgundies would be priced as trophy wines.

Use of the classification terminology

Understanding these rules, and which producers or vineyards fall in which categories, is a marker of wine expertise: such terms create a sophisticated and exclusive language. But there are many traps where similar words can be used in very different ways which can separate those with a little knowledge from the serious wine connoisseur.

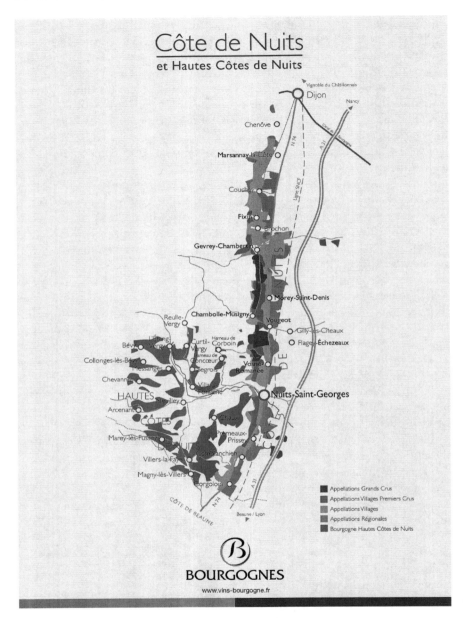

FIGURE 3.3 The vineyards of the Côte de Nuits, Burgundy.

Source: Bureau Interprofessionnel des Vins de Bourgogne.

Wine connoisseurs will expect when they open a trophy wine such as a Château Margaux that their guests appreciate that they are being served a wine from one of the five premier grand cru classés châteaux of the Médoc – as opposed to the offer of 'a bottle of Margaux' that could come from any château of the Margaux appellation or even from a négociant's blend. So, although any wine of the *AOP Margaux* would still be wine for a special occasion, it would be much less special than Château Margaux itself. Likewise to be offered a glass of le Montrachet (arguably the top grand cru white Burgundy appellation – clearly a trophy wine) is much more significant than being offered 'a Puligny-Montrachet'. The latter is still an expensive appellation – in price terms clearly a special occasion wine – but it could come from anywhere in the village of Puligny-Montrachet.

Some connoisseurs learn by heart the names of all the grands crus and even the leading premiers crus of Burgundy. Some memorise every château in the 1855 classification of the Médoc. However, not everyone is inclined to such memory tests, and even serious buyers of expensive Bordeaux and Burgundies will regularly refer to reference books, websites or apps on their mobile phones – or they may be dependent on a close relationship with a particular wine merchant to guide them. But an appreciation of at least the broad principles of these classifications is fundamental for anyone who wishes to be perceived as a wine connoisseur (at least in relation to French wines).

Other areas with classifications of vineyards

The classifications in Bordeaux and Burgundy are probably the most well-known amongst wine buyers and connoisseurs, and it is usually the wines of these two regions that sell for the highest prices.

However, it should be noted that many other wine regions have classification systems for their vineyards where terminology is controlled by law. For example, in the Douro Valley in Portugal, vineyards are classified 'A' to 'F' and whilst these letters do not appear on labels, they affect the Ports that a grower can produce (Robertson 1992:37–9).

In Champagne, vineyards are rated on a 100-point scale known as the *échelle des crus* (ladder of growths), which traditionally determined the prices at which grapes were sold by growers to the producers. Those vineyards rated 90 to 99% are known as premier crus, and those with a 100% rating are grand crus. A Champagne made entirely from vineyards that are rated at least premier cru can use that term on the label (and similarly for grand cru), although many of the top Champagne houses prefer to rely on their brand names as a signal of quality. However, it is worth noting that Champagne is a single protected designation of origin (PDO – see Chapter 1): unlike Burgundy and Bordeaux there are no formal appellations for specific areas.

The term 'grand cru' is also used in the Alsace region of France where around 50 of the top vineyards are entitled to this designation, and many of the best wines are sold with the name of a specific grand crus vineyard on the label under the *AOP Alsace Grand Cru*. This status has only been available since 1975, so is a much more recent classification than Burgundy (and there is no premier cru status below this). However, the grand cru sites have been extended over the years and some Alsatian producers feel the term is not sufficiently rigorous to be worth using on their labels.

In Italy a number of wine appellations have a protected designation of origin, and an inner region, representing the best vineyards at the heart of the regions, where the name *Classico* is added. For example, the *DOCG Chianti* covers a large part of Tuscany, but the *DOCG Chianti Classico* region is limited to the best slopes around the central villages of the region: a black cock symbol (*Gallo Nero* in Italian) is used to signify these wines.

Such geographical classification systems are less common in the wine-producing countries of the New World, where the emphasis is usually more on the reputation of individual properties and there is less willingness than in Europe to enshrine such systems in legislation. However, classification schemes have been proposed in many other regions: in some cases these are controlled by law and in others they are administered by trade bodies.

Other legally controlled classifications of superior wines

Whether or not vineyards are individually classified, many wine regions have protected terms to denote superior wines.

For example, in Germany, much emphasis is placed on the amount of natural sugar in the grapes (i.e. the must weight in degrees Oeschsle – see p. 4). For *Pradikät* (unchaptalised) wines the terms *Kabinett, Spätlese, Auslese, Beerenauslese,* and *Trockenbeerenauslese* may be used for successively higher levels of natural sweetness (German Wine Institute 2013:102). The higher sugar levels can be used either to leave a rich natural sweetness in the final wine, or may be fully fermented (so a dry Auslese will have a high level of alcohol).

In the DOCa Rioja region of Spain, the terms *Crianza, Reserva* and *Gran Reserva* denote minimum periods of ageing (in oak and in bottle), with only the best grapes allowed to be used in a *Reserva* or *Gran Reserva* (Jeffs 1999). However, other regions of Spain use similar terms but in some cases with shorter minimum periods so, as in so many cases with wine classification systems, understanding the rules needs considerable expertise. Much of Italy also uses the term '*Reserva*' to denote higher quality wines with more depth and more oak ageing. However, in much of Portugal, the term '*Reserva*' can be applied to any wine deemed to have additional depth and complexity when formally assessed for the protected designation of origin: it is not linked to a specific period of ageing.

However, many other regions place no formal controls on the terms 'Reserve' or 'Reserva' (including most of France). In these cases producers can choose to label any wine they choose with a term such as 'Proprietor's Reserve' or 'Reserve du Château' or simply 'Reserve'. There are also many terms such as 'grand vin' that have no legal meaning, and even a producer of entry-level commercial wines can put this on the label if it is felt to be helpful for marketing.

The role of vintage in the status of wine

Although the geographical origin and the name of the producer are central in determining the style and quality of a wine, there is another variant that is also extremely important – the year of harvest, or vintage.

Wine is a product of naturally grown grapes, and in many regions of the world, the style of wine can vary dramatically from year to year, because of variations between vintages. This is largely due to the weather – a long hot summer may produce much riper grapes, with more intense flavours than a cool year with a lot of rain. However, both extremes can be dangerous: in a very hot year such as 2003 there were real problems in parts of Bordeaux of vine stress (due to lack of water) and wines being produced with something of a 'baked' flavour, tasting more like jam than fresh fruit flavours. Also if the weather gets too warm very early in the spring, the vine can flower and then suffer frost damage when the weather turns colder, leading to serious loss of production (this was a major issue in Bordeaux in 1991). Winds can also make a big difference and hailstorms can cause massive damage to vines.

In most regions, an ideal year has plenty of sunshine, interspersed with periods of light rain, but avoiding long periods of excessive heat, and with little or no rain in the last two weeks before harvest. However, it is rare to get a 'perfect' year, and the variation from one year to another is a major factor that leads to variations from one wine to another.

Of course, for simple wines to be drunk young there may be no choice of vintage: a buyer may be given the choice of ordering wine from the last year or from two years ago, but there may be no further choice. Also, many wines are sold with no vintage on the label (usually shown as 'NV' in lists), thus permitting the producer to blend wines from more than one year. In some cases this is the norm even for wine from prestigious regions, for example, with Champagne and with Sherry.

But for wines from major properties in leading regions, the vintage is an absolutely crucial element of the label, and it may have a major affect on price. For example, with the top châteaux of Bordeaux, wines from the outstanding vintages of 2009 and 2010 are typically priced at around double the price of a wine from the same château of the more ordinary 2008 vintage. (However, the vintage variation in price is considerably smaller from less prominent châteaux: with major properties the price is affected by the perceived investment value of the wine.)

Vintages and ageing

It is also generally considered that top wines, especially red wines, improve with age, if well stored (in a cool, dark cellar). This may be very important for a connoisseur storing wines at home (see Chapter 6). The fruit flavours develop maturity and harmonise with the oak (if used) and large course tannins combine and precipitate out as a sediment, leaving softer tannins and more silky flavours in the wine. So, for a red wine from a good property, a vintage 8 to 15 years old will usually be much more enjoyable to drink than a vintage that is only two to three years old.

Top wine merchants and leading restaurants may therefore offer a choice of many different vintages from the same château or domain: those who prefer their wines with plenty of fruit and robust tannins may wish to choose a younger vintage than those who enjoy the additional complexity of a wine with some age. (However, it is worth remembering that wines from the Southern hemisphere are generally harvested from January to March, whereas harvest is usually between August and October in the Northern hemisphere. So a wine with a given vintage from Australia or South Africa will be six months older than a wine of the same vintage from Europe.)

Nevertheless, there is a limit to the principle of improvement with age: eventually a wine will start to 'thin out' leaving flavours of fruit acids but little structure, or conversely the fruit may fade but still leave firm tannins giving a style described as 'tough as old boots'! Robinson (1989) in a series of 'vertical tastings' comparing many vintages from top producers, found that a red Bordeaux from a top château in a good year was still generally improving at 15 to 20 years from the vintage, and for a top vintage Port, the wine may not have peaked until 40 years after the vintage – though this is only with perfect storage conditions. However, such studies attempt to assess the optimum age of wines by comparing *different* vintages at one point in time, and more research is needed comparing the *same* wines over extended time periods (Morgan 2007).

For lesser vintages, and for more modest wines with less concentration, the optimum age may be much less than the examples above. But for anything other than a very simple wine, knowing the vintage is essential to understanding the likely style of flavours in the wine. The vintage is thus absolutely fundamental in any listing of fine wines (except in the case of wines that are explicitly sold as a blend of several years – for example, most Sherries or non-vintage Champagne). A trophy wine must generally come from a top vintage, as well as being from a top appellation and a prestigious producer.

The status of wine: a summary

In this chapter we have explored a wide range of factors that distinguish wines in terms of status and quality. We have looked at issues in the production of the wine that affect the final quality, we have considered the role of formal classification systems for ranking wines in regions such as Burgundy and Bordeaux, and we have seen how these factors affect the perceived status of a wine. We have considered a number of issues that affect the pricing of wines, and a generic wine class system has been proposed, based largely on pricing, which considers wines on the market in six categories from 'plonk' at one end to 'trophy wines' at the other.

The principles of wine differentiation considered in this chapter lie at the heart of much discussion in other chapters regarding the status of wine and its anthropological role in the lives of those who drink it or serve it to others.

For discussion

1 In Chapter 1 we saw how 'good' wine costs considerably more to produce than cheap wines. How far are these considerations reflected in retail prices?
2 Is it worth paying more for a wine from a prestigious classification? What does the purchaser get by investing in a wine that is (for example) a premier cru from a leading village in Burgundy's Côte d'Or or a grand cru classé château from Bordeaux's Médoc area?
3 Would other wine regions benefit from developing formal classification systems like those used in the top regions of France? Would it lead to improvement in quality? Or would such systems just enable producers to sell at higher prices?
4 Some people suggest that the classification rules of regions like Burgundy and Bordeaux only serve to create complex rules which no one except an expert would ever understand. Do you agree? How important is the mystique of understanding the rules?
5 This chapter has suggested six classes of wine based primarily on retail prices. How far does price determine the status of a wine?
6 What is meant by the brand of a wine and how does the brand relate its status and desirability?
7 Those who buy or serve the cheapest wines are sometimes treated with derision. Is this justified?
8 Do expensive wines represent value for money? For example, does a £40 bottle of wine give twice the pleasure of a £20 bottle? What about a £200 bottle – could that give ten times the pleasure? If not, why do people buy expensive wines?

References

Boidron, B. (ed.) (2014). *Cocks Éd Féret: Bordeaux et ses Vins* (19th edition) (Bordeaux: Éditions Féret) [English translation available of 17th edition – London: Wiley 2004].
Clarke, O. (2012). *Bordeaux* (revised edn) (New York: Sterling Epicure).
Drinks Business (2014). Fine wine monitor: Shifting up a gear. *Drinks Business*, November, 96–7.
Duijker, H. and Broadbent, M. (1997). *The Bordeaux Atlas and Encyclopedia of Châteaux* (London: Ebury Press).
German Wine Institute (2013). *German Wine Manual* (2nd edn) (Mainz: German Wine Institute).
Hanson A. (2003). *Burgundy* (London: Mitchell Beazley).
Jeffs, J. (1999). *The Wines of Spain* (London: Faber and Faber).
McCoy, E. (2008). *The Emperor of Wine: The Remarkable Story of the Rise and Reign of Robert Parker* (revised edn) (London: Grub Street).

Morgan, G. G. (2007). *Consumer Perceptions on Wine Vintages: Towards a Methodology for Longitudinal Assessment* (Food & Gastronomy Research Conference, Sheffield Hallam University, November 2007).

Morris, J. (2010). *Inside Burgundy* (London: Berry Bros & Rudd Press).

Peppercorn, D. (2003). *Bordeaux* (London: Mitchell Beazley).

Pitiot, S. and Servant, J.-C. (2004). *The Wines of Burgundy* (English translation by Jones, R.) (Beaune: Collections Pierre Poupon).

Robertson, G. (1992). *Port* (4th edn) (London: Faber and Faber).

Robinson, J (1989). *Vintage Timecharts* (London: Mitchell Beazley).

Sutcliffe, S. (1999). *The Wines of Burgundy* (London: Mitchell Beazley Pocket Guides).

4
WINE CONSUMERS

If we are to understand how people make sense of, interact with, consume and purchase wine, we need to explore the different factors or resources they bring to this interaction. It is not possible to make any sweeping statements about wine consumers as each individual brings a myriad of different types of resources that inform their relationship with wine and even their status within the wine community. This chapter explores the various types of resources consumers bring to the purchasing and appreciation of wine and their interaction with wine. Resources are not just measured and understood in terms of the amount of money a person has, but also includes their relationship to their knowledge, cultural capital, access to products, etc.

This chapter consists of two distinct but interrelated sections. The first section ('Consumer resources, risk and segmentation') explores how consumers perceive and mediate risk during the consumption process, and how they engage their consumer resources in their consumption and appreciation of wine; in addition, the subsequent identification of their resources is also used by the wine industry and marketers as a means to demographically define, categorise and identify groups of consumers who possess shared levels of consumer resources. The second section ('Wine, lifestyle and identity') focuses on wine and lifestyle. For Lockshin and Corsi (2012) this can be seen as a subset of segmentation. This section differs very much from the first section as consumers are identified as possessing the ability to create and express their own identities and position in society, through their knowledge and consumption patterns, whereas in the first section consumers have identities and social positions imposed upon them by others.

Consumer resources, risk and segmentation

One of the ways in which wine consumers are categorised, segmented and broken into identified consumption groups is through the identification of the resources they possess as a consumer. Understanding the various levels of resources a consumer possesses enables the specific targeting of groups who share the same levels of resources, thus creating a segmentation group that can be marketed similar goods and services.

Consumer resources

The way in which a wine is perceived or the way it gains value in the commercial sense is not just the result of how good the vintage is or even simply how it tastes. The economic, social and cultural value of wine is not just generated by the producers or marketing companies, but is also dependent upon the various resources possessed by the individual consumer. Integral to both these perspectives are what Vargo and Lusch (2008) call operand and operant resources. Operand resources are those that a consumer acts upon to create value, and would include a marketplace object such as a bottle of wine, or their financial or material resources (Arnould, Price and Malshe 2006) with which to purchase it. Simply, operand resources may be seen as part of the exchange of goods for money, which results in the creation of economic value. Alternatively, operant resources are those that a consumer deploys to act upon operand resources to create value (Vargo and Lusch 2008). For example, the purchasing of a particular rare or scarce vintage may be used as an expression of knowledge and status within a particular community; a good example of this is within Somogyi *et al.*'s (2011) research where wine is used as a means to express status within Chinese society. In other words, the consumer creates a value in terms of group status through a material expression of knowledge rather than just their wealth. In most cases a combination of operand and operant resources are integrated alongside those offered through the marketplace and media to create meanings and value, thus there is a co-creation of value. The way in which value is generated or found by the consumer, or how risk is mediated or reduced is very much dependent upon the various resources they possess.

Financial resources

The most basic of all resources is the resource of money. Wine is a luxury: we can still live if we do not have it, so it is not a necessity. But it is a necessity for consumers to possess surplus financial resources in order to purchase and engage in the appreciation of wine. The amount of this surplus in conjunction with other factors will either open up or decrease possible choices of wines and types of consumption patterns available to consumers. As seen in the work of both Mitchell and Greatorex (1989) and Spawton (1991), there is clear perception that the more you pay for a bottle of wine the better quality it is, and that consequently the risk factors associated with the wine are reduced. The price of a wine remains the one major factor that influences consumers' behaviour (Lockshin and Corsi 2012).

However, the significance of price varies according to the type of consumer. In an assessment of purchase intentions of wine consumers considering the influence of price, price discount and region, Hollebeek et al. (2007) found that region was more important for high-involvement consumers and price more important for low-involvement consumers. This view was also supported by research undertaken by Lockshin et al. (2006) who used simulated choices to measure the importance of price, region, brand and awards. Low-involvement consumers more commonly used price and awards to make their decision, whereas high-involvement consumers combined the various attributes associated with the wine as part of a more complex decision-making process. In short, the financial resources of a consumer provides them with more choice, the ability to shop in specialist wine stores, to visit vineyards, to buy information through books or the engagement of a specialist, and to mediate risk by purchasing expensive wines.

Nevertheless, the financial resources of the customer only play a small part in their interaction with the purchasing and consumption or appreciation of wine. You may be wealthy but be a low-involvement consumer, or you may have limited funds to spend on wines but are a high-involvement customer who searches for great wines that are reasonably priced or are disguised behind a supermarket own-brand label. The resources you engage in the consumption and appreciation of wine consist of a complex set of factors that vary according to each individual's resources and how they wish to engage them.

The resource of time

Consumers possess different levels of time equity or surplus of time: this equity is situationally dependent upon factors such as their occupation, the distance of their commute, the home environment, the pets they own and their family commitments. Although at first sight the resource of time may not be seen as a significant influencing factor in the purchasing of wine, time plays a significant role in defining levels of access and the type of choice consumers have.

If you have limited time resources then your interaction with the various types and vintages available may be limited to the stock held by your local shop or supermarket. If you possess a large surplus of time then it is possible to source, explore and research alternative vintages, to travel to vineyards, specialist wine retailers or dealers, attend events, auctions and tastings, etc. Additionally, the subsidiary industries that surround the wine trade have developed a wide range of knowledge-based resources. These include books, specialist magazines, newspaper and magazine specialist wine sections, wine-specific websites, qualifications, wine tours and even wine tourism (see Chapter 9 regarding the various means for learning about wine). It can be argued that in order to appreciate wine truly, the consumer has to engage in at least some of these knowledge-based resources, however all of them are only accessible if the consumer has a surplus of time.

Space as resource

In conjunction with the other resources identified above, the resource of space also impacts upon the consumer's behaviour, as space will define how much wine can be stored efficiently and, most importantly, the conditions in which it is kept. Good storage of wine is essential if you are to get the best out of wine: in particular, wines with cork closures should be stored horizontally, at a stable cool temperature as this can affect how quickly a wine matures. The recommended temperature for storage is around 10°C–13°C, out of direct light and in an atmosphere that has some moisture in order to stop the corks drying out and exposing the wine to oxygen. Additionally, wine should be subject to as little movement as possible. For a consumer who wishes to lay wine down or to protect and mature a collection, extensive storage facilities may be needed (see Chapter 6). Thus, the potential of consumption and how and what value can be created or experienced will often relate to the scale and scope of accommodation space. The resource of space is thus important as it determines whether a consumer can collect wine, buy by the case or have the ability to lay it down, rather than just buying wine for immediate consumption.

Supporting material resources

It is possible to create an endless list of supporting material resources that assist the collecting, tasting and appreciation of wine, many of which can enhance the wine experience. The material resources possessed or the consumer has access to will influence the type of wine experience they can have. For example, access to wine books and guides, decanters, wine funnels, corkscrews, or sommelier knives provide a certain degree of access, while ownership of other material resources such as aroma sets for developing one's olfactory abilities provide a higher level of access and engagement. Those organising wine-tasting events will also need professional ISO tasting glasses,[1] spittoons and bottle covers for blind tasting (see Chapter 9 on wine education activities).

Some consumers may already possess such items, but if this is not the case then the first step towards immersing oneself in the oenological world would be able to access such material resources. At the most basic level, anyone wishing to share fine wine in a social context needs a matching set of wine glasses of a suitable size and shape with sufficient space above the liquid to contain the aroma: there is no point in investing in a special bottle wine without suitable glassware. The possession of such material resources also acts as a social marker to one's peers, suggesting that the consumer enjoys high levels of both knowledge and financial resources, while simultaneously creating further value and meaning to the wine experience.

Social resources

The appreciation and consumption of wine is largely a social activity often taking place with other individuals or within identified and selected groups (as seen in Chapter 9). The type of wine experience, and even which wine is chosen, is often the direct result of the social context of a particular time or event. Without the possession of social resources in the form of friends, colleagues or partners, the social element of the wine experience is limited.

Social resources can be broken down into three very broad categories:

- People and networks from which consumers seek referral, knowledge or information about a product or service, such as friends, colleagues, acquaintances, social media, blogs, etc.
- Those resources that are either integral to the episode of consumption itself, or those involved in the delivery of the wine experience. This includes wine dealers, wine clubs and societies, educators, sommeliers and staff in wine bars or shops.
- The third category of social resources is of particular importance as it denotes a personal or collective realisation of value and meanings, through the association with celebrities, newspapers or magazines, lifestyle groups, critics or authors as an individual expression of personal membership of a particular social or cultural group. Thus, following the wine recommends in a particular newspaper or magazine such as the *Financial Times*, *The New York Times* or *GQ* may be an individual expression of sharing the values of those publications, a means of belonging expressed through consumption patterns.

What is clear is that wine consumption and appreciation provide membership of particular identified lifestyle groups (see Brunner and Siegrist 2011; Olsen, Thach and Nowak 2007; Ritchie 2007). But in order to access these groups and add value to the wine experience, it is imperative that the consumer possesses the social resources to do this.

The resource of knowledge

It could be argued that engagement with wine as marketed in contemporary society demands a particular kind of knowledge and set of skills to understand how to read a wine label, and to understand even at the basic level what type of wine is being purchased. In short, without developing skills and knowledge one cannot be a competent and successful consumer. As stated previously, there is a great deal of angst in making the right choice when buying wine, so consumers frequently undertake research to reduce the risk of purchasing the wrong wine, to understand the language that surrounds wine (see Chapter 10), and to follow the correct etiquette or ritual of wine consumption that confirms membership of a particular group. Having the ability to read a wine list in a restaurant or just choosing the correct choice of wine for event, meal or occasion (Atkin and Thach 2012:54; Rubio, Oubiña and Villaseñor 2014) demands a certain level of wine knowledge.

The common theme that links all of these issues is the reliance on different types of knowledge to know how to behave in the correct manner or to engage in the full appreciation of wine. Even though a consumer may possess the financial resources, the material resources, the social resources and the spatial and temporal resources to enjoy wine, unless they also possess the requisite levels of knowledge to utilise these resources, then the resources all lose any significance they may have had.

Knowledge is gathered in various ways, through experience, through study, through reading the plethora of lifestyle wine books and magazines, watching television and films, listening to radio programmes, engaging with societies or even engaging in wine tourism. As we go through life we collect these different types of knowledge, they add to our individual 'cultural capital'. Just like financial capital, we save it, amass it and, in the case of cultural capital, we exchange it with others as an expression of our knowledge and status within a particular group. The knowledge collected and exchanged is a form of cultural capital and very much defines who we are. Wine is and has always been an important means of expressing one's cultural capital, status and intellect. A person may have a surplus of financial, time, social and spatial resources, however if they cannot utilise all of these resources in a knowledgeable and informed manner then interaction within the field of wine appreciation and formalised wine networks is limited.

Risk

The individual mobilizes their own level of consumer resources when purchasing wine. Gluckman (1990:45) asserts that the 'act of purchasing wines is clouded with insecurity' and that customers are unlikely to ask for help, thus they need to find other strategies to mediate levels of risk. Wine is also often used as a social marker of identity and the conspicuous consumption of wine is a means for consumers to express their status, wealth and knowledge. As such, in order to reduce the risk of purchasing an inappropriate wine for a particular event, consumers collect and build resources that will reduce the risk. Many authors identify that the purchasing of wine can sometimes be a stressful exercise; it is underpinned by a concern that the purchaser 'will select the wrong bottle which could result in negative social perceptions' (Atkin and Thach 2012:54). As such, according to Rubio, Oubiña and Villaseñor (2014), there is a functional risk related to the performance (quality) or perceived utility (use context) for the wine. There is also a financial risk – the potential loss of money that can occur in any transaction – and a social risk – the bad image that consuming the product may give an individual in the eyes of others. These risks apply whether wine is being bought in a retail environment, with the intention of being served to others or presented as a gift, or when ordering wine in a restaurant.

Risk perception is thus one of the most important drivers of wine purchasing behaviour. It is difficult to assess if a wine is a good wine or a bad wine, as there are a number of characteristics that are often difficult to quantify (as discussed in Chapter 3). As wine possesses a high proportion of characteristics that can only be assessed during consumption, apart from the relatively few cases where wines are offered to taste before purchase, the ability of the consumer to gauge quality prior to purchase is very low. Consumers have to rely upon intrinsic and extrinsic clues to aid them in the evaluation of the quality, characteristics, and often even the social or culinary context of the wine. As a consequence, they are forced to rely upon the semiotic extrinsic attributes contained within the marketing of the wine, which will typically be through assessing the brand name, style or even the shape or colour of the bottle as a denotation of the quality and suitableness of the wine (see Chapter 10 for discussion on the semiotics of wine).

The notion of risk is not a fixed concept, rather it differs according to the individual consumer's cultural traits or the type of event or the occasion for which the wine is being purchased. For example, Somogyi *et al.* (2011) identify that Chinese cultural traits mean that Chinese consumers are unwilling to take high levels of risk, so they participate in various strategies of risk avoidance within their purchasing behaviour. As a result, the Chinese wine market is heavily drawn towards established brands and the more traditional Old World wines or are reliant on recommendations provided by friends, colleagues or family and the reputation of traditional wine-producing countries. This is also the case for Japanese wine consumers, where the country of origin is of particular importance (Bruwer and Buller 2012). In less risk-averse cultures such as the UK, the Netherlands, Germany and Australia, wine consumers are more willing to take a risk on products they have never seen or consumed before.

The purchasing of wine involves both risks and social benefits. It is interesting to note that much of the literature surrounding risk concentrates on the social risks involved in the purchasing of wine and rarely considers the taste of the wine as a risk. Risk is often measured in terms of selecting the 'wrong wine' in relation to the social benefits of choosing a wine that others admire, rather than the wine's characteristics. The levels of perceived or associated risk in the purchasing of wine is also governed by the context of the event or occasion. Bruwer, Fong and Saliba (2013:374) identify seven different contexts in which the risk element will differ:

- intimate occasions
- occasions with friends
- family occasions
- business occasions
- gift-giving occasions
- celebratory occasions
- at-home consumption.

It is not possible to say whether any of these carry higher or lower risk, as the concept of risk (what is meant by risk, what constitutes risk and its impact) is an individually formulated exercise. For example, you would think that the risk would be low if you were buying a wine for friends; however, if you and your friends participated in competitive aspirational dinner parties, where you were continually trying to keep up with the food and wine served by your friends or even surpass their hospitality, then the social risks could be quite high. Alternatively, if you were sat in front of the television eating a pizza, drinking cheap red wine with close friends, then you would assume the risk may be less; however, this may not be the case because you still would not want to make a choice that would make you look like a cheapskate or generate a feeling that the hospitality you provide is poor. Rather, risk can only be measured through the connections between individual perceived risk and individual risk dimensions. It is possible to say that there are always elements of risk in buying wine, as until the wine is opened there is always the chance that it has spoiled, etc. Therefore consumers generally employ risk-reduction strategies.

Strategies for reducing risk

As a result of the perceived risk factors that surround the purchasing of wine, consumers employ a number of strategies to reduce risk. Most studies use either Mitchell and Greatorex (1989) or Spawton's (1991) analysis of risk-reducing strategies as the foundations of their research. Mitchell and Greatorex (1989) identified that there were six forms of risk-reduction strategies utilised by wine buyers, in decreasing order of importance, through the wine purchase process:

1 *Consumers seek information*: the search for information ranges from word of mouth, to magazines, to wine books.
2 *Brand loyalty*: remaining loyal to a known brand.
3 *Store image*: using the image of the retailer to judge product worth.
4 *Well-known brands*: using top-of-mind brands in unfamiliar product segments.
5 *Price*: paying more than a reasonable price.
6 *Reassurance*: getting reassurance through trials such as tastings and samples.

A number of these factors are considered in some detail in Chapter 3, especially the role of price as a perceived indicator of wine status. We also saw how the designation of wine in a protected appellation or with a formal classification such as 'premier cru' can assist in distinguishing fine wines. However, according to Mitchell and Greatorex, the label as a means of gaining information about the wine is an underused resource by consumers, and the six categories above are more important in defining buying behaviour. For Spawton (1991), with the exception of a few connoisseurs at the high end of the market, most wine purchasers are highly risk sensitive and their subsequent purchases are governed by risk-reduction strategies. Consequently 'consumers govern their wine purchase behaviour by following expectation and risk-reduction strategies that they employ in order to reduce post purchase cognitive dissonance' (Spawton 1991:16). Possible approaches to reduce risk in buying decisions include:

- selection of a known brand
- use of recommendation
- advice of retail assistants
- wine appreciation education
- pricing
- packaging and labelling.

Although there are some similarities between Mitchell and Greatorex's and Spawton's risk-reduction strategies, Spawton adopts a more contextualised approach within wine studies with a clearer identification of the role of wine books, magazines and critics in reducing risk factors as well as recognizing the significance of wine education and the wine label. However, for all of these authors, risk-reduction strategies assume that consumers possess certain resources.

Segmentation and the wine consumer

Traditionally, marketeers segment wine purchasers by the traditional approach of breaking consumer groups into age, educational background, geographical location, income, etc. However as discussed in Chapters 2 and 8, wine has different social, cultural and individual meanings, significance and uses. As such, there may be ten people all with the same income, same educational attainment, living in the same city, but their relationship with wine may be very different.

As a response of the failure of the traditional demographic approach to adequately understand the segmentation of the wine market, Spawton (1991:17) suggests four categories that can be formulated from the consumer's expectations and risk-reduction strategies, which can form the basis for segmenting the market of those who purchase wine. These segments are as follows:

- *Connoisseurs*: This is the wine-knowledgeable segment, the primary purchasers of fine wines. These people consume wine on a regular (often daily) basis. They have a broad spectrum of tastes and like to experiment, although adoption of new tastes may be slow. They are brand loyal – either in relation to particular producers or particular regions and appellations. They have strong preferences and make their decisions in advance of purchase. They prefer to purchase from specialist wine merchants and auctions, or directly from the wineries. These consumers see wine education as a hobby, read wine journals avidly, and are less price-sensitive than the other segments.
- *Aspirational drinkers*: Members of this segment are concerned with the social aspects of wine drinking. They purchase fashionable wine styles and are attracted to the more fashionable brands and labels. Brands act as symbols of status and reassurance. These buyers are highly risk averse and will spend considerable time in the search process. They will often seek the advice of a retail assistant to give them confidence and will, therefore, choose outlets dependent not just on convenience but also on their confidence in the

reputation of the retail store. Aspirational drinkers are strongly influenced by wine writers, journalists, and opinion leaders. They are likely to attend wine appreciation courses.

- *Beverage wine consumers*: These are avid wine consumers with little desire to appreciate wine. They are loyal to a wine style and are not prepared to experiment. They buy wines in an impersonal supermarket environment. They are brand loyal to a range of 'safe brands', where choice is dependent on a consistent taste, price and price-related promotions. When dining out they may order the same wine each time, rather than seeking variety.
- *New wine drinkers*: These are the young who are attracted to wine based on the behaviour of their parents or peer group. Preferences are not yet established but sparkling wine and 'coolers' (wine blends with soft drinks) may feature strongly in the choice of product consumed. Wine is purchased at social occasions and often on the premises at pubs, discos, parties and restaurants. They are strongly influenced by the occasion where wine may be consumed. They are unsophisticated and have limited parameters for choice, but often use price as a determinant for purchase (adapted from Spawton 1991:17).

In addition to these categories, there are also significant numbers of consumers who never buy or consume wine, and others who may consume wine when it is offered by someone else but never buy it themselves. In many households, the majority of wine purchasing decisions are made by one person, typically the person with the greatest wine knowledge resources. In many societies, wine buying has traditionally been a male-led activity, but this is changing rapidly and some studies have found that females buy more expensive wine than their male counterparts (Bruwer *et al*. 2005).

These segments of wine consumers can be described as *consumption tribes*, that is where groups of consumers are brought together through shared consumption practices, value systems and knowledge (see Cova and Cova 2001; Cova, Kozinets and Shankar 2007). Kozinets' (1999, 2010) research focused on the way in which individuals interacted with online consumption communities and the motives that direct their interactions and behaviour within these groups.

It is possible to contextualise this work within a wide range of modern wine consumption communities, by considering the consumer resources possessed and the social positions adopted by the members of the groups. Such analysis enables us to unpack three main categories of individuals in terms of their engagement with wine (Tresidder and Hirst 2012):

- *Minglers*: A mingler is more active in the social aspects and life of the community, becoming a participant. Although drawn into the search for product knowledge and information in similar ways to the consumer, the motive branches out to be inclusive of congenial interaction, interpersonal experience and value. The mingler will thus use the community as a resource to build virtual friendships, social capital and relationships. Importantly, in this case, the social experience will be considered to be equally if not more valuable than the information role and resource that the community provides. In most cases, the social experience will transcend the very reason as to why the mingler was drawn to the community in the first place, and although the group or society initially provided a platform for them to learn and explore wine, a major by-product of this was the membership to a social group and, resultantly, the social contextualisation of wine. Accordingly, the membership to groups and the socialisation of the wine experience eventually becomes more important than the wine, or the personal desire to develop oenological knowledge (Cova 1997). Under these conditions the social resource itself ultimately ends up providing the majority, if not all, of the value and meaning for the consumer.

- *Devotees*: The next category is the devotee, whose interest and interaction with the community is fully consumption orientated and product related. Devotees will be engaged mostly with the endorsement and critique of wine and services and occupied in protracted discussions related to consumption experiences with others (often not devotees). In view of this, devotees will typically hold a great deal of influence over other less knowledgeable wine consumers: they achieve this by providing the majority share of product-related information and reviews within the community through organising wine events and writing articles and blogs. This will be compounded by their commanding self-positioning as 'specialist' consumers, which will be communicated and reinforced through their knowledge that is expressed through their dialogue, interactions and use of the 'semiotic language of wine' (see Chapter 10). Access to them also becomes an important specialist 'knowledge resource'. The gathering of wine knowledge from devotees is also a means to gather cultural capital that may be shared and exchanged at a later date with other consumers.

- *Insiders*: These are extremely active in both realms of experience in the community. They engage in product- and consumption-related dialogue in a manner on par with a devotee and, like the mingler, insiders are similarly active in the social aspects of the community. In this respect the insiders have multiple motives attached to their engagement with the community. Value and meaning is derived in equal measure from the relational, recreational and informational modes of experience and interaction. As a result, the insider is an important and critical social resource for all of the other participants and interlocutors engaged in online consumption-orientated activity and engagement, making them, along with devotees, an important target for marketing activity. What is more, they have manifold roles that encompass friendship, play, community maintenance and information disseminators. In that sense that they will be perceived to have expertise, be less prone to bias and, consequently, be considered as more trustworthy (adapted from Tresidder and Hirst 2012:73–4).

In addition to these categories we can also think about 'outsiders'. These are consumers that do not engage in collecting knowledge surrounding wine and its appreciation, nor belong to any of the above wine communities. This group is probably the largest group in terms of wine consumption, as their resources in terms of wine knowledge is fairly low (although they may possess high levels of resources in any of the above categories) so their social and knowledge resources exclude them from the above groups. Their consumption and purchasing patterns are influenced by other characteristic such as the style of the label, accessibility, promotional offers, colour and country preferences, alcohol content or as a direct reaction to advertising. In short, in this context, the outsiders' interaction with wine is similar to their relationship with other alcoholic beverages.

Value creation and meaning production

As discussed in Chapter 2, the consumption of wine is largely a social process and it is used as part of celebrations, social gatherings, events and even religious rituals. As such, sharing a wine experience with our social resources (i.e. friends, colleagues, acquaintances, as well as members of physical and consumption communities) provides a context and social significance for the wine; it adds value by adding an experience to the consumption process. Thus value, significance and meaning is generated through the consumption of wine, but also through the people you share it with, and as such is critically dependent upon the actions and interactions of those inclusive to that consumption. The social community or unit is integral to the experience and is therefore an important consumer resource. It can be argued that the consumption and appreciation of wine is a socially mediated experience and bad company, service or disagreements can very easily ruin a good wine.

Service delivery personnel as social resource

It is important to think about the service provider as a social and knowledge resource for the consumer. Winsted (2000) submits that there is a direct correlation between the service experience and value creation; for example, it is not unknown for devotees to invite an expert to come to their home and introduce a wine, to decant it for them and to serve it, to create a sense of theatre around the experience. Access to this type of expertise is a means of value creation and to elevate the experience to that of the extraordinary.

Winsted goes on to identify three different forms of behaviour that are exhibited by service providers that generate value to the consumption process: concern, civility and congeniality. Consumers can draw on such behaviours and role performances in the following ways:

- A consumer may seek information, advice, clarification or reassurance about the suitability of a wine from a wine dealer or sommelier, including advice

on its compatibility with food or whether the wine could be laid down. At this moment, the consumer is engaging with a transfer of knowledge as a resource, so that they come away with both a suitable wine and a piece of knowledge that becomes an element of their cultural capital that can be exchanged with their guests at the point of consumption.
- It can be argued that the greater the exchange of physical or financial resource, the greater the expectations of the levels of service expected by the consumer in order to feel valued and to have a sense that the level of service is appropriate. For example, an individual retaining a wine merchant to help build a cellar or purchasing a bottle of wine at a Michelin-starred restaurant with the aid of a sommelier expects a very high level of personal service commensurate with the financial resources being invested. By contrast, poor service devalues the experience and the significance of the consumption process.
- A consumer may engage in social intercourse to pass time or strike up a convivial conversation. In this respect being able to engage in idle conversation with a member of the bar or waiting staff could be significant to enhancing the experience and memories of the consumption process, thus generating additional value.

Tresidder and Hirst (2012), drawing on the work of Arnould, Price and Tierney (1998), extend this framework and add a fourth category, i.e. *communicative staging*. Communicative staging is of particular importance as it includes all forms of communication and media that constitutes a servicescape or environment: this includes elements such as the décor, the type of wood used, signs and paintings or advertisements, as well as the commercial 'performance' of the staff. In terms of these latter aspects, communicative staging can range from a highly scripted and commercially punctuated performance through to flexible and authentic dialogue, but fundamentally it is a semiotic exercise that stages the wine experience for the consumer so as to enhance their experience (see Chapter 10). Service delivery providers act as gatekeepers and signpost the experience or values of the company or organisation they work for. For example, in fine restaurants a good sommelier brings the experience of wine alive for participants through discussions about the origins of the wine, how it was produced and its terroir, which help the consumer to wallow in the experience and adds another dimension to the consumption process. An account that links the production and consumption of a wine (e.g. its terroir or its history expressed through narrative framing and storytelling) is particularly important. It provides an enhanced authenticity to the wine, as stated previously.

The wine itself only plays one part in the appreciation of wine experience; 'servicescapes' also play a part in the individual reliving of traditions and cultural memories (Chronis *et al*. 2012). Additionally 'servicescapes' play an active role in generating new experiences, traditions and intimate moments so that wine experience becomes an artefact of joint cultural production (see Kozinets *et al*.

2004; Peñaloza 2000) between the consumer, fellow consumers and the 'servicescape'. In this co-production, the notion of terroir is the fulcrum around which experience moves and is generated. It can be conceptualised as a cognitive category (Aurier *et al.* 2005) that mediates experience and that is negotiated by the customer in their appreciation of wine.

Consumers as resources for other consumers

Next we consider the role of consumers as resources for consumers. In a similar manner to service personnel, consumers act as resources for other consumers, and this is a particularly important element in the consumption of wine. In a discussion with 25 sommeliers, Hoffman (2013) found that 18 of them associated the best wine they had ever drunk to a particular circumstance or social context where the personal significance of the wine elevated it to a high level even though it may have been a bottle of non-vintage Champagne rather than a rare fine wine. The people with whom a wine is shared are integral to their staging and production. Ultimately customers play a decisive role in creating the experience for others.

For instance, Bitner *et al.* (1997:195) outline a variety of roles that consumers play in this process, these being:

- *The customer as a productive resource*: For example, where customers create an atmosphere in an empty restaurant.
- *The customer as intrinsic to quality, satisfaction and value*: This is seen when a customer needs to perform a specific role himself or herself for the services to take effect and be evaluated positively. Ordering from a menu, negotiating the supermarket to fill the shopping basket or using a self-service till is reflective of this.
- *The customer as a competitor to a service organisation*: For example, where a customer publicly complains about the service or meal, thus causing a scene and devaluing the product and experience for others.

Thus, as we can see from above, other consumers or even friends, social contacts, family or loved ones are important in adding value to the wine experience. However, through the adoption of forms of negative confrontational behaviour by other parties it is possible to devalue or even destroy the experience. This is also the case both in terms of 'servicescapes' and in the communicative staging of experiences. Ineffective development in wine service and communications can mean that the context of a wine event or occasion becomes lost, as does the significance of the wine for the consumer.

Traditionally, wine consumers are often understood only in terms of their demographics, but it is important to understand the diverse factors that influence their behaviour, define their interaction with wine and the ways in which they can be broadly classified.

It is only once we truly understand the wine consumer that it is possible to market effectively, bearing in mind that consumers are typically seeking not just a wine product, but often a 'wine experience' that requires education or meaningful interaction with them. Significantly in the case of wine, purchasers need resources to mediate perceptions of risk. So even at a basic level, it is important to have the ability to understand and assess the consumer's resources, whether that be their social, financial and supporting resources or their resource of wine knowledge. Personal levels of knowledge inform the type of images, words, colours and description of the wine used in both marketing and in terms of the contents and structure of wine labels, how it is distributed and how sales people or service staff interpret the wine for the consumer.

In recognising the various types of consumers, whether we adopt Spawton's (1991) classification of wine consumers as connoisseurs, aspirational drinkers, beverage wine consumers or new wine drinkers, or the idea of devotees, insiders and minglers, these approaches allow for the social and cultural profiling of wine consumers. Such profiles are driven and constructed through understanding their knowledge, resources and how they define their relationship with wine and, most importantly, the role it plays within their lives. Such approaches enable a more in-depth and holistic understanding of the market, compared to traditional demographically orientated segmentation approaches that are utilised to predict and understand the behaviour of wine consumers. However, there is another way of understanding the behaviour of wine consumers and that is through understanding how consumers use wine as a part of a particular lifestyle, to express identity and to cement membership to groups.

Wine, lifestyle and identity

We have noted throughout this book that wine is elevated to a higher cultural level than almost all other food and beverages. However, wine is so full of subtle variations and symbolic meanings that according to Crane (2007) it can be thought of as an 'aesthetic object'. Just like the appreciation of art, the appreciation of wine can be understood and interpreted at various levels. These levels are governed by the experience of the consumer, their knowledge of the language, history, geography and culture of wine, and the development of their palette and other sensory skills. The knowledge of wine, like the knowledge of art, is often perceived as belonging to people who have high incomes, are well educated and even sophisticated. Thus expressions of your knowledge of wine is a means to express to people what type of person you are, or more importantly the person you want to be seen as. This is not a new phenomenon as throughout history certain consumption patterns have always supported perceptions of social class (Holt 1998).

Therefore the definition of wine as an aesthetic object places it within a world where expression of taste and the accumulation and exchange of cultural capital are important elements of lifestyle, which reflects a 'symbolic hierarchy' that is defined and maintained by society (Allen and Anderson 1994:70). This hierarchy enables groups of consumers to distance or make themselves distinct from other individuals or groups by defining trends, consumption patterns or expressions of taste. The expression of wine knowledge as an expression of taste becomes an integral aspect of our own identity, as well as a symbolic and social resource that has power to define status within particular groups of consumers (Belk 2010). As Allen and Anderson (1994:70) state: 'taste becomes a "social weapon" that defines and marks off the high from the low, the sacred from the profane, and the "legitimate" from the "illegitimate"'.

This exploration of taste and lifestyle is not just a theoretical missive, it has real-world implication for the marketing of wine, the production of knowledge-giving books and magazines, and of course the structure and nature of wine education programmes and societies, as it enables the tailoring and development of products and experiences within specific fields of consumption based on cultural knowledge and capital.

Cultural capital and knowledge

One of the most important social and cultural elements that the individual gains from the consumption or appreciation of wine is the generation of what can be termed 'cultural capital'. This is simply the additional social and cultural benefits we may gain from appreciating wine with others. We are continually exchanging our cultural capital with others. This is achieved by sharing knowledge about wine, literature, art, music, travel, culture, etc. We exchange our knowledge or cultural capital with friends, family and peers, and the amount of cultural capital we are judged to possess by these groups identifies where we are placed hierarchically within the social group. Our expression of cultural capital may cement our position or it may place us in a position whereby people look up to and wish to emulate us. We can think of cultural capital as analogous to money: we earn it, save it and spend it. The process of cultural capital is the same, and just as there are different types of currencies, there are also different types of cultural capital. Cultural capital can be simply defined as the amount of knowledge you have collected, and the sharing of this knowledge with others whether that be in the form of speaking a second language, wearing a type of clothing or having the ability to order a bottle of wine and then be able to discuss its origin and merits. Holt (1998:3) claims that: 'Cultural capital exists in three primary forms: embodied as practical knowledges, skills, and dispositions; objectified in cultural objects; and institutionalized in official degrees and diplomas that certify the existence of the embodied form'.

Significantly for Holt (1998), the sharing of this cultural capital attracts the esteem of others, and it also plays an important role in shaping consumption patterns of others in an attempt to emulate the same levels of knowledge. Within wine studies it is possible to see cultural capital in terms of:

- *Cultural knowledge, skills, experience and abilities*: This category consists of various forms of wine knowledge and skills such as the ability to analyse and describe the olfactory aroma or bouquet of a wine. The ability to do this is underpinned by a form of wine knowledge that has been amassed through experience, research and education. This category also includes wine stories or experiences, where an individual will talk about the best wine they have ever drunk, the occasion, setting and the significance of this.
- *Linguistic competence and vocabulary*: Within wine studies this operates at a number of levels. The first is simply having the ability to negotiate a wine menu and to pronounce the name of the wine correctly. The second level is concerned with the possession and understanding of the specialist language that surrounds the study and appreciation of wine. This specialist language enables you to discuss and analyse wine using the appropriate words and phrases (see Chapters 1, 3 and 10 for further information).

We all possess particular levels of knowledge about different subjects and experiences, in this case wine. This wine knowledge, in conjunction with the actual consumption or collecting of wine, forms part of our cultural capital and, subsequently, membership to particular social and cultural groups that share the same 'capital space'. Bourdieu (1987:231) identifies that individuals who possess similar levels of cultural capital and share the same capital space may 'have every chance of having similar dispositions and interests, and thus producing similar practices and adopting similar stances'. It is important to note that cultural capital is not just the preserve of elitist groups, but is important in defining membership and the individual's hierarchical in all forms cultural groupings, for example, people will express their knowledge of football, cars, fashion, music, food or even tattoos. As stated previously, within wine studies it is important to understand how different consumers amass their cultural capital or, in other words, gather knowledge, what levels of cultural capital various groups possess and what language is used and understood by each of these groups. This type of knowledge enables authors to pitch their books at the correct level, defines what information needs to be included on a wine label, and is also a means of segmenting wine consumers into different categories.

Cultural capital and taste

Knowledge can be seen as the most important aspect of cultural capital, as knowledge underpins how cultural capital outwardly manifests itself. One of these manifestations is the outward expression of cultural capital through the articulation of taste within individual consumption patterns. For example, the clothes we wear, the décor of our homes, the architectural style of our houses or the car we drive are all outward expressions of our taste that are expressed through consumption practices. However, deficiencies in cultural capital (wearing the wrong clothes to an event) may also generate conflicting effects by lessening a consumer's relative status within a group, which consequently may exclude them from membership of a group and removal from their 'capital space' and the social relationships that exist within the group. Consequently, individual expressions of cultural capital and taste can have substantial social impact for the consumer as cultural capital also directly translates into social capital.

It is important to recognise that the amassing of cultural capital and its relationship to social capital is often not a conscious activity, and that for many consumers their social positioning, community affiliation and group membership is just the way things are. That is, their cultural capital and outward expressions of lifestyle position them within a certain social group without their explicit knowledge, and indirectly this in itself becomes a means of distinction in its own right. Thus, if we are trying to understand the behaviour or consumption patterns of wine consumers we need to understand the relationship between wine and cultural capital. According to Tresidder and Hirst (2012), consumers buying behaviour or consumption pattern becomes a tripartite process. This process can be clearly illustrated through the consumption lifecycle of a bottle of wine, for example:

- When David decides to host a dinner party he expresses his level of cultural capital by choosing the right wine for the food. Although they may have sought advice, David has still used his cultural capital to source and interpret that wine for the guests and ensure that the consumption activity is successful.
- The meal, wine and the status of the guests also contributes to David's particular stock of cultural capital, and is reinforced by the communicative setting of the dinner party, for example, dress code, table setting, décor and in some cases evidence of previous consumption, including empty wine bottles or photographs of consumption occasions.
- The dinner party also provides a platform for David to express his other cultural capital endowments, that is, during the meal knowledge and experience is exchanged (e.g. I possess certain qualifications, belong to a particular club, have been to a particular vineyard, and so on). What this demonstrates is that the host possesses the knowledge of the world that surrounds the serious appreciation of wine, and that the wider knowledge of, and engagement in, the wine experience is an expression of David's cultural capital, and that by attending or consuming the experience the guests are also adding to David's bank of cultural capital.

The cultural capital that is gained at the dinner party will be later used as a means of distinction from other consumers or reinforcing membership to a group or class. In conclusion, the engagement in the appreciation of wine is a lifestyle marker by which the individual may express both their identity and cultural capital. As a consequence, wine may be seen as a means to express identity. In this section we have explored how the individual wine consumer may collect and exchange cultural capital in order to express their identity and status. The next section explores how membership to identified consumption groups reinforces the individual's identity and status.

Groups, segmentation and membership

The first section of this chapter introduced Spawton's (1991) classification of wine consumers. The categories he identified are then given or bestowed upon consumers – in short they become labelled. However, according to the French sociologist Pierre Bourdieu (1987), society is structured by individual lifestyles, cultural practices such as the appreciation of wine, and preferences such as 'trophy wines' as discussed in Chapter 3. These lifestyles, practices and preferences are also shared by a group of peers. Bourdieu went on to refer to these groups as forming a 'habitus'. One of the most significant aspects of this is that social mobility can be accessed by anyone. Allen and Anderson (1994:71) state that: 'One's class origin is not, therefore, a structural straight jacket that determines with certainty one's actions. But on the other hand, there is a certain probability that persons exposed to similar life experiences will display similar "lifestyles"'.

This is where wine and the appreciation of wine plays such a significant role in contemporary society as individual consumption patterns become a means to define yourself, membership of a particular habitus and your position within that habitus (Henry and Caudwell 2008). Habitus becomes a complex system of distinctions based on cultural capital and taste. This distinction acts as a group-distinctive framework of social cognition and interpretation that creates communities of a particular lifestyle (Izberk-Bilgin 2010). For Miles (1996:152) 'the "habitus" is the embodiment of the cultural dispositions and sensibilities of the group that structure group behavior, simultaneously allowing group members a mechanism for structuring their social experience'.

Thus, even if we look at the cultural attributes of societies and groups that contain connoisseurs of wine, all of the groups will have their own status within the oenological world and this status will depend upon their members' 'special knowledge of things' (Miles 1996:152).

It is also possible to think of a habitus as a consumption tribe whose membership and access is governed through individual consumption patterns and knowledge of the product's language and expected behaviours, and that the group utilise this to include and exclude individual consumers. According to Bruwer and Reid (2002:218) wine marks the 'move from work to relaxation, as well as acting as a marker of personal identity and of boundaries of inclusion and exclusion . . . Connoisseurship is a classic example of this, it marks the individual as well as the wine'.

However, just like the idea of class membership, membership of a particular habitus or tribe is also a fluid process whereby consumption patterns enable us to balance the need to express our individuality, while finding the comfort of being able to belong to a group, tribe or micro culture (Branch 2007), or a particular community of consumption who share consumption patterns, passion, emotion, values and knowledge. Cova and Cova (2002:599) maintain that consumer tribes have the following characteristics:

- *They are ephemeral and non-totalising groupings*: That is, they are dynamic, continually changing with the emergence of new trends and fashions.
- *A person can belong to several tribes at the same time*: Often defined by interests and different life roles; for example, many people will engage in activities at weekends that are very different for their normal week-time behaviours.
- *The boundaries of the tribe are conceptual*: Membership of a consumer tribe does not require that people attend meetings or events, but rather the relationship is virtual: often members will never meet.
- *The members of the tribe are related by shared feelings and re-appropriated signs*: Shared outlooks, perceptions of particular goods and experiences govern membership, and they share a language that consists of outward expressions of the tribe's identity. This is achieved through shared dress codes, magazine readership, music tastes and codes of behaviour.

Therefore, what we see is the emergence of new groups of consumers that have a continually shifting relationship to fashion, styles and taste. This is also very much the case within the area of wine. Cova and Cova (2002:602) further comment that:

> Of course, tribal groupings are not directly comparable with reference groups or psychographic segments. One the one hand they differ from reference groups in that they do not focus on normative influences of the group or of individual group members on one another. Instead tribes concentrate on the bonding or linking element that keeps individuals in the group. Tribes differ from psychographic segments by their short life span and their diversity. It is fair to say that postmodern neo-tribalism translates a need to belong not to one but to several groups simultaneously, and that tribal membership does not involve set personality traits or same values, but expresses a shared experience of maybe only some aspects of a person's personal history.

The cohesion that holds these groups together is their relationship to culture, lifestyle and taste. This is important because it is the opposite approach to the one taken by Spawton (1991) where classification is governed by the individual consumer and their consumption choices. For Thompson and Troester (2002), consumption tribes or a habitus cut across the traditional categories of gender, class, ethnicity and age. The practice of engaging in the appreciation of wine forms consumption spaces in which groups or tribes can share and build articulated social and cultural wine experiences. As membership to wine tribes is governed by shared experiences and meanings, the actual identification of members is difficult as members do not merely meet at wine society meetings or events and they are bound by behaviour, knowledge and values.

The degree to which we adhere to or immerse ourselves in a particular habitus or tribe is down to personal choice, and we may belong to more than one habitus, changing our identity according to social or cultural situations (Izberk-Bilgin 2010).

Consumption as personal identity

As stated previously, the appreciation of wine is one of the major means of expressing both individual identity and taste (Bourdieu 1987). Significantly, Holt (1998:4) argues that 'consumption is a particular status game that must be analyzed in isolation rather than lumped together with work, religion, education and politics'.

The significance of this for the individual is that 'we have now entered the era of the ordinary individual, that is to say an age in which any individual can – and must – take personal action, so as to produce and show one's own existence, one's own difference' (Cova and Cova 2002:596).

Consequently, the consumption, classification and appreciation of wine becomes a significant means of symbolically sending messages to others about our knowledge and identity, and is read by other consumers who then make assumptions about who we are. Thus, the consumption of wine is essentially a social activity that incorporates meanings within the culture in which we live. As Izberk-Bilgin (2010:307) states, consumers expertly use goods, in this case wine, to 'communicate, mark and classify social relations, it is a way of communicating individual taste, status, aspiration and even protest'.

Despite the recognition of the historical and cultural significance of wine (as discussed in Chapter 2), the role of wines has the additional contemporary attribute as marking identity. As Holt (1998:13) states, 'the pursuit of individuality through consumption is a central characteristic of advanced capitalist societies'. What is important to re-state here is that although at first the relationship between wine appreciation and identity can be viewed as a superficial one, it provides freedom for individuals to generate and form an identity consumers want, rather than having one inflicted upon us by the social category we were born in to. As Miles (1996:150) states:

> the evidence suggests that consumption performs the role of *solidifying* an individual's identity. In the context of cultural ramifications of peer relations amongst you people (sic), identities in a so called 'postmodern' world might well be argued to be far more stable than many commentators would be prepared to admit.

The appreciation and consumption of wine, in conjunction with its history and cultural embedding, elevates its significance and role in contemporary society and allocates the status of being an 'aesthetic object' (Crane 2007). This means that like art, music and architecture, wine becomes associated with a cultured, rarefied world where the appreciation and knowledge of 'aesthetic objects' are traded and exchanged both in financial and symbolic terms. There is a strict global hierarchal system that assigns value and taste that is dominated by certain consumption tribes and habitus. Membership and knowledge of these groups are used to reinforce individual identity projects; therefore the aroma, tasting notes and taste of the wine is only a small part of the consumption process.

Wine consumers: a summary

Wine is an important social and cultural article whose consumption leads to various definitions of the individual consumer and their identity.

The first section of this chapter examined how the wine industry and wine marketing bestowed characteristics and labels on consumers according to their consumer resources. It is an easy way in which to segment the market and to provide a generalised target market to whom service and goods can be offered. However, this approach makes assumptions that all wine consumers with the same financial resources, for example, will engage in the same consumption patterns. According to Lockshin and Corsi (2012) there is little new research being undertaken in this area within wine studies and that perhaps it has run its course.

It is becoming increasingly clear, as we saw in the second section of the chapter, that consumers are reflexive individuals who will often resist approaches to categorise them, and that through consumption and the adoption of consumption patterns, can express their own identity and gain membership to groups that share the same lifestyle and values. The means by which people express their identity in contemporary society is through the consumption of goods and experiences and the development of knowledge around particular products and lifestyles. In this world wine has become one of the most important products in expressing distinction, cultural capital and most importantly identity.

For discussion

1. Which of Spawton's categories do you see yourself belonging to?
2. Do you perceive wine buying as scary? What are the risks that concern you? How do you mediate risk when buying wine?
3. Place in order the consumer resources you feel are most important to understand for a wine merchant to be successful.
4. In assessing Mitchell and Greatorex's (1989) or Spawton's (1991) risk-reducing strategies, which do you think is most effective and can they be applied to all the categories of wine consumer?
5. How far is the notion of 'consumption tribes' helpful in understanding wine consumers? List the main tribes you can identify amongst the people you meet or the customers in an establishment that you know.
6. How do you express your identity through consumption practices?

Note

1 A standard shape of tasting glass prescribed by the International Standards Organisation designed for systematic comparison of wine samples taking account of the appearance, nose and palate.

References

Allen. D. and Anderson. F. (1994). Consumption and social stratification: Bourdieu's distinction. *Advances in Consumer Research*, 21, 70–4.

Arnould, E.J., Price, L.L. and Malshe, A. (2006). Toward a cultural resource-based theory of the consumer. In: R.F. Lusch and S.L. Vargo (eds), *The Service-dominant Logic of Marketing: Dialog, Debate, and Directions*, pp. 91–104 (London: Routledge).

Arnould, E.J., Price, L.L. and Tierney, P. (1998). Communicative staging of the wilderness servicescape. *Service Industries Journal*, 18(3), 90–115.

Atkin, T. and Thach, L. (2012). Millennial wine consumers: Risk perception and information search. *Wine Economics and Policy*, 1(1), 54–62.

Aurier, P., Fort, F. and Sirieix, L. (2005). Exploring terroir product meanings for the consumer. *Anthropology of Food* (online). Retrieved from http://aof.revues.org/187.

Belk, R.W. (2010) 6th July-last update, Benign Envy, Key Note; Academy of Marketing Conference. Available from: http://www.youtube.com/watch?v=IZwgznJwGno (accessed November 21, 2011).

Bitner M., Faranda, W., Hubbert, A. and Zeithaml, V. (1997). Customer contributions and roles in service delivery. *International Journal of Service Industry Management*, 8(3), 193–205.

Bourdieu, P. (1987). *Distinction: A Social Critique of the Judgment of Taste* (Nice, T., transl.) (Cambridge, MA: Harvard University Press).

Branch, J.D. (2007). Postmodern consumption and the high-fidelity audio microculture. *Research in Consumer Behavior*, 11, 79.

Brunner, T.A. and Siegrist, M. (2011). Lifestyle determinants of wine consumption and spending on wine. *International Journal of Wine Business Research*, 23, 210–20.

Bruwer, J. and Buller, C. (2012). Consumer behavior insights, consumption dynamics, and segmentation of the Japanese wine market. *Journal of International Consumer Marketing*, 24(5), 338–55.

Bruwer, J. Fong, M. and Saliba, A. (2013). Perceived risk, risk-reduction strategies (RRS) and consumption occasions: Roles in the wine consu'er's purchase decision. *Asia Pacific Journal of Marketing and Logistics*, 25(3), 369–90.

Bruwer, J., Li, E., Bastian, S. and Alant, K. (2005). Consumer household role structures and other influencing factors on wine-buying and consumption. *Australian & New Zealand Grapegrower and Winemaker*, December, 50–5.

Bruwer, J. and Reid, M. (2002). Segmentation of the Australian wine market using a wine related lifestyle approach. *Journal of Wine Research*, 13, 217–42.

Chronis, A., Arnould, E. and Hampton, R. (2012). Gettysburg re-imagined: The role of narrative imagination in consumption experience. *Consumption, Markets and Culture*, 15(3), 261–86.

Cova, B. (1997). Community and consumption: Towards a definition of the linking value of product or services. *European Journal of Marketing*, 31(3/4), 297–316.

Cova, B. and Cova, V. (2001). Tribal aspects of postmodern consumption research: The case of French in-line roller skaters. *Journal of Consumer Behavior*, 1(1), 67–76.

Cova. B. and Cova. V. (2002). Tribal marketing: The tribalisation of society and its impact on the conduct of marketing. *European Journal of Marketing*, 36(5/6), 595–620.

Cova, B. Kozinets, R.V. and Shankar, A. (eds) (2007). *Consumer Tribes* (New York: Butterworth-Heinemann).

Crane T. (2007). Wine as an aesthetic object. In: Smith, B.C. (ed.), *Questions of Taste: The Philosophy of Wine*, pp. 141–56 (Oxford: Oxford University Press).

Gluckman, R.L (1990). A consumer approach to branded wines. *International Journal of Wine Marketing*, 2(1), 27–46.

Henry, P. and Caldwell, M. (2008). Spinning the proverbial wheel? Social class and marketing. *Marketing Theory,* 8(4), 387–405.

Hoffman, C.A. (2004). When consumers buy wine, what factors decide the final purchase? *Wine Industry Journal*, 19(2), 82–91.

Hoffman, M. (2013). Ask a sommelier: What's the greatest wine you've ever tried? *Serious Eats* [online], available from http://drinks.seriouseats.com/2013/07/ask-a-sommelier-the-greatest-wine-in-the-world.html.

Hollebeek, L.D., Jaeger, S.R., Brodie, R.J. and Balemi, A. (2007). The influence of involvement on purchase intention for new world wine. *Food Quality and Preference*, 18, 1033–49.

Holt, D. (1998). Does cultural capital structure American consumption? *The Journal of Consumer Research*, 25(1), 1–25.

Izberk-Bilgin. E. (2010). An interdisciplinary review of resistance to consumption, some marketing implications, and future research suggestions. *Consumption Market & Culture*, 13(3), 299–323.

Kozinets, R.V. (1999). E-tribalized marketing? The strategic implications of virtual communities of consumption. *European Management Journal*, 17(3), 252–64.

Kozinets, R.V. (2010). *Netnography: Doing Ethnographic Research Online* (London: SAGE).

Kozinets, R.V., Iacobucci, D. and Mick, D. (2004). Ludic agency and retail spectacle. *Journal of Consumer Research*, 31(3), 658–72.

Lockshin, L., Jarvis, W., d'Hauteville, F. and Perrouty, J. (2006). Using simulations from discrete choice experiments to measure consumer sensitivity to brand, region, price, and awards in wine choice. *Food Quality and Preference*, 17, 166–178.

Lockshin L. and Corsi A.M. (2012). Consumer behaviour for wine 2.0: A review since 2003 and future directions. *Wine Economics and Policy*, 1, 2–23.

Miles. S. (1996). The cultural capital of consumption: Understanding 'postmodern' identities in a cultural context. *Culture & Psychology*, 2, 139–58.

Mitchell, V.W. and Greatorex, M., (1989). Risk reducing strategies used in the purchase of wine in the UK. *International Journal of Wine Marketing*, 1(2), 31–46.

Olsen, J.E, Thach, L and Nowak, L (2007). Wine for my generation: Exploring how US wine consumers are socialized to wine. *Journal of Wine Research*, 18, 1–18.

Peñaloza, L. (2000). The commodification of the American west: Market'rs' production of cultural meanings at the trade show. *Journal of Marketing*, 64(4), 82–109.

Ritchie, C. (2007). Beyond drinking: The role of wine in the life of the UK consumer. *International Journal of Consumer Studies* 31, 534–40.

Rubio, N., Oubiña, J. and Villaseñor, N. (2014). Brand awareness–Brand quality inference and consumer's risk perception in store brands of food products. *Food Quality and Preference*, 32, 289–98.

Somogyi, S., Li, E., Johnson, T., Bruwer, J. and Bastian, S. (2011). The underlying motivations of Chinese wine consumer behaviour. *Asia Pacific Journal of Marketing and Logistics*, 23(4), 473–85.

Spawton, T. (1991). Of wine and live asses: An introduction to the wine economy and state of wine marketing. *European Journal of Wine Marketing*, 25(3) 1–48.

Thompson, C.J. and Troester, M. (2002). Consumer value systems in the age of postmodern fragmentation: The case of the natural health microculture. *The Journal of Consumer Research*, 28(4), 550–71.

Tresidder, R. and Hirst, C. (2012). *Marketing in Food, Hospitality, Tourism and Events* (Oxford: Goodfellow Publishers).

Vargo, S.L. and Lusch, R.F. (2008). Service-dominant logic: continuing the evolution. *Journal of the Academy of Marketing Science*, 36(1), 1–10.

Winsted, K.F. (2000). Service behaviors that lead to satisfied customers. *European Journal of Marketing*, 34(3/4), 399–417.

5
TERROIR

Wine is fundamentally a product of a specific place. It is the result of grapes grown in a specific location, which (at least for quality wines in the European Union) the vinification must also take place close to where they are grown (see the definitions in Chapter 1). The French term *vigneron* (winegrower) implies that the grower also has a close involvement in the final wine.

This notion of wine as a product of a specific place – having a geographical identify – is fundamental to the understanding of wine in society. Although some entry-level wines are sold only with a brand name, or perhaps with a grape variety but no country of origin, the place of origin is extremely important for any wine that we may class as a 'fine wine' (see Chapter 3) and even for many wines below this. For the most exclusive wines, extremely small geographical identifications – often down to a particular château or vineyard – are almost always central to the status of the wine.

This linkage between a wine and its geographical origin is enshrined to a large extent in the French term terroir (although it is nowadays applied to wine regions throughout the world). But the term terroir means much more than just the territory from which a wine originates – it encompasses a huge range of factors, many with deep anthropological significance – by which wines are identified, marketed and consumed.

Vineyard location and wine quality – the technical origins of terroir

The vineyard location is absolutely critical to the quality of wine. The cheapest wines to produce are those grown on relatively fertile soils, with consistent, fairly warm weather during the growing seasons and reasonably generous water content in the soil. For economy of production a vineyard is preferred that is relatively flat or only moderately sloping, making it easy to use tractors and automated harvesters.

But these factors all work against quality. The best wines come from vines that have had to work hard to get the water and nutrients they need from the soils. The best vineyards are normally on stony or rocky soils with little nutrition available. Ideally the vineyard will be on a significant slope so that water tends to run away. All these factors force the vine to dig deep roots, which then bring complex flavours into the grapes they produce.

Also, the best sites are not the hottest – too much heat can lead to flabby wines where the grapes have high sugars, but possibly a jammy taste, often lacking in acidity and complexity. Better quality wines can be produced in regions with more moderate climates, especially those with good diurnal temperature variation (warm in the day and cool at night). But where vines are grown in regions that are not consistently warm, the precise angle of the vineyard to the sun can make a big difference. A vineyard on a good south-facing slope will get considerably more sun exposure than a vineyard in the same area on the flat. For the best wines, the grapes will usually be picked by hand – if the vineyard topography is complex there is no alternative to hand picking, but even where this is not the case, hand picking means much less damage to grapes before they reach the winery than if a mechanical harvester is used.

The precise soils are also extremely important. Certain grape varieties grow much better in terms of the structure and complexity of the wine if grown on the most appropriate soils. For example, Chardonnay and Pinot Noir are at their best on chalk or limestone soils, whereas Gamay does better on granite soils. In areas like Burgundy with complex geology, there can be significant variations between one vineyard and the next.

But even amongst high-quality sites there may be subtle differences. Where the vines catch the morning sun, the taste may be more floral; a little way round the hill where there is more afternoon sun, they may be slightly richer. One vineyard may give a delicate 'feminine' style of wine with great finesse; a vineyard a short distance away may yield wines that are more earthy and 'masculine'.

These issues are all part of the terroir of a particular site – the combination of soil, grape variety, weather conditions (sun, rain, wind) and the historical expertise of caring for the site. Over the years, experience has shown that certain regions of the world are particularly successful for certain types of wines and certain grape varieties. Within the major winegrowing regions, there may be much smaller areas – for example, around a particular town or village – that give certain expressions to the flavours of the wine. In some cases there may be significant variations between individual vineyards in one village.

Therefore the name of a wine in geographical terms – where it comes from in terms of the region, the town, or even the specific vineyard – is extremely important in the identity of the wine. Understandably, winegrowers in locations that are known for wines of a particular style wish to see the name of the location protected so that inferior wines from elsewhere cannot be sold under the same name. Much of the role of PDOs is to protect the use of particular geographical names on labels so that only wines that are truly representative of the local terroir (both in terms of where the grapes are grown and the style of wine produced) can be sold under the appellation concerned.

Wilson (1998) offers in-depth discussion of the technical aspects of terroir, but it is important to note that terroir is about much more than soil content or the weather. The rest of this chapter examines how the sense of terroir of a particular wine may be fundamental to its identity and hence its perception by wine consumers and those choosing wines for purchase.

Use of the term 'terroir'

Although the term terroir is French in origin, some have argued for extending the concept of terroir to encompass all wines wherever they are produced, on the grounds that wine is always a product of a specific place. However, within the field of critical wine studies they may be seen as controversial. For example, Mason and O'Mahony (2007) suggest that the concept of terroir has been adopted by the French wine industry as almost a brand in order to achieve definition of origin and quality for its products. They argue that wine defines a country's or region's image and is helped by 'the distinctions in character that are derived from geographical differences, or terroir, an oft-contested concept denoting the unique combination of topographic, soil, climate, and cultural particularities that impart a special character to the wines' (Mason and O'Mahony 2007:501).

This view is also explored by Barham who identifies that: 'This story of terroir is not unusual in its blending of human and environmental history, to the point that it is difficult to disentangle the two' (Barham 2001:19). Concepts of terroir are fundamental to protected designations of origin (see Chapter 1) – this would include, for example, the French *appellation d'origine contrôlée* (AOC) system as a marker of quality and pedigree of wine. Aurier, Fort and Sirieix (2005) also maintain that the idea of terroir should not just be applied to wine, but also to other locally produced products: 'The food product constitutes a relevant category to study the terroir concept due to its natural and strong link with the geological, climatic, cultural, sociological characteristics of the production area' (Aurier, Fort and Sirieix 2005:4). This is now possible under EU law, with PDOs adopted for many different alimentary products such as cheeses, olive oils and smoked fish. Aurier, Fort and Sirieix (2005:5) go on further to state:

> Thanks to 19th century anthropologists, we are aware of the strong relationship between what one eats and what he is or thinks to be, and we understand that when someone eats a 'terroir' product, he feels like if he incorporated the territory with the product.

As such, wine may be seen as a direct expression of a society and its way of life.

There is a great deal of discussion surrounding the concept of terroir. This is reflected in the work of authors such as Riley (2005) and Tikkanen (2007) who examine how the relationship between the local cuisine and culture is sustained and reinforced by local food festivals and a small number of highly visible chefs or specialist suppliers. López-Guzmán and Sánchez-Cañizares (2012) also link both food and wine within the same category and as such question the ownership of terroir by the AOC rules. They assert that:

> Food and wine form an integral part of a local life, and the history, the culture, the economy and the society of a given area, and have been shaped by history by local lifestyles. This intensifies the contrast between one locality and another, and between rural tradition and urban modernity (López-Guzmán and Sánchez-Cañizares 2012:64).

Alternatively Croce and Perri (2010) define terroir as the characteristics of landscape associated with wine production rather than adopting the wider notion of terroir.

The notion of wine is surrounded by history, stories and myths about the soil, the culture and significance of wine, and it forms an important part of the consumption process in differentiating it from other alcoholic drinks. The philosophical idea of terroir encapsulates all of these myths and stories linking the wine to the physical and cultural geography of the label. As such, through the physical consumption and appreciation of wine the body interacts with the environment and reflects embodied experiences through their immergence in what may be labelled 'sensescapes' (Trauer and Ryan 2005). In commenting on the notion of embodiment, Chronis, Arnould and Hampton (2012:263) maintain that:

> human perception privileges sensations felt through the body, they conceive imagination too as steeped in embodied perception. For them, perception is a synthetic experience. Consumers grasp the world directly through their multiple senses and by imaginary modes of embodiment.

The idea of terroir adds another experiential sensual characteristic to the consumption process that is far beyond just smell, touch, etc. It provides a link to something that is more real, authentic and representing a time that was simpler and more organic in nature. Thus the consumption of wine linked with the notion of terroir offers an experience that enables the consumer to explore their senses, and more significantly their sense of being within the world. As Marshall (2005:73) states, the consumption of food and wine is an 'authoritative act', that 'authenticates' our desired identity and position within the world, acting as a social marker of who we are and who we wish to be (see also Gillespie and Morrison 2001; Gvion and Trostler 2008; Brownlie, Hewer and Horne 2005), and who we do not want to be (Cronin, McCarthy and Collins 2012).

Geographical identity of wine

The significance and symbolism of wine is not only used by individuals to mark their own personal identity in contemporary society, it is also used by nations and regions to reinforce their social and cultural characteristics and their identity in an increasingly globalised world (Guy 2007). According to Mason and O'Mahony (2007:501), wine 'defines' a country or region's image and is helped by 'the distinctions in character that are derived from geographical differences, or *terroir*, an oft-contested concept denoting the unique combination of topographic, soil, climate, and cultural particularities that impart a special character to the wines'.

Even in the New World, there are examples of success in exploiting the 'marketability' of terroir and, as such, terroir continues to play an important role in risk reduction by consumers during the purchasing process (Easingwood, Lockshin and Spawton 2011). An example of this in New Zealand is the formation of the Gimblett Gravels Winegrowers Association. With no compulsory viticultural practices as in French wine regions, Gimblett Gravels is largely a marketing tool for a sub-region within the broader Hawke's Bay wine region (Turner and Creasy 2003:50). The notion of terroir is also explored by Barham (2001:19), who identifies that: 'This story of terroir is not unusual in its blending of human and environmental history, to the point that it is difficult to disentangle the two'.

As such, wine may be seen as a direct expression of a society and its way of life (see Boniface 2003). Terroir can be simply defined in environmental terms; however, the origins and significance of the phrase may be located within wider philosophical historical, social and cultural debates that define the soul of a particular locality or region. Douguet and O'Connor (2003:238) state that:

> terroir (an untranslatable word that connotes the local spaces and soils, and also symbolic relations of goods and services production), tend to identify features of their food, cuisine, buildings and wider habitats as 'critical' patrimony in view of their symbolic as well as functional significance.

Although there are various conflicting definitions of terroir there is a clear consensus that terroir links the wine to the earth from where it originated, as well as to the historical, social and cultural origins and influences that define the region.

Terroir in contemporary society

It is also possible to think about the idea of terroir as fulfilling another role in contemporary society. The concept of terroir provides another layer of meaning to the appreciation and consumption of wine. Terroir may be seen as a refuge from the modern world, as Houston and Meamber (2011:178) comment: 'Embedded within this notion of escape lies the implicit search for an "authentic" past; one that is unsullied by the contemporary cloak of commodification'. Resultantly, terroir is a response to what Douguet and O'Connor (2003:234) refer to as '*le revers du progrès*' (progress in reverse) by creating an environmental awareness that 'is not just a matter of people displaying, individually and collectively, *different forms of life*' (Douguet and O'Connor 2003:249). It offers a gateway into a more organic reflexive life. As such, terroir provides a conceptual and symbolic refuge from modern production systems and environmental degradation (Aurier, Fort and Sirieix 2005; Charters 2010). Douguet and O'Connor (2003:250), in reinforcing the significance of terroir, assert that for the French people there is a:

> strong preoccupation with maintaining integrity of their environmental space and ecosystems, where this is to be understood in the sense of the terroir, as the quality of food, as the identity and integrity of an organism, or the relation of oneself to one's origins and symbolic space.

In this vein of thought Trubek (2008:3) defines terroir as a 'foodview' that enables the concept to become naturalized and associated with a specific place or destination, and is underpinned by a particular set of production and consumption practices that are directly informed by local historical and social practices and is reinforced by institutions and practices that shape the ways that taste comes to define place and its people.

Terroir can be seen to provide an experiential link to the past. If we accept Jameson's (1991:1) definition of postmodernism as 'the cultural logic of late capitalism', we can identify cycles of food trends that reflect cultural movements that are linked to culture and the economy. Fonseca (2008) posits that food and wine is more than a unit of sustenance as it represents an important form of cultural expression; it links us back to a myth of the past. As Barham (2003:127) states, terroir is part of a 'biopolitics of food that relinks the local and global through an emphasis on place' and localization. For Trauer and Ryan (2005:482) this 'is part of a process of globalization, mobility and migration, of finding itself involved in political and economic agendas, yet also the creation of modern identities that have also entered political conflict on a personal level'.

As a reaction to this, wine and in particular the notion of terroir play a part in the reinvention of traditions and cultural memories (Chronis, Arnould and Hampton 2012) through the creation of communities (Beebe et al. 2013) and sometimes even to exclude outsiders through the creation of local consumption rules (Gibson and Weinberg 1980). Regional food and wine events (or what may be termed terroir events) also reinforce regional identity (see Hall and Sharples 2008) events such as the Bordeaux Wine Festival in France, the Virginia Annual Wine Festival in the USA, McLaren Vale Bank SA Sea and Vines Festival in Australia, etc., where wine and cultural traditions are conceived and reinvented by local people. In a way this is just another form of communicative staging of a servicescape in which wine plays a central role whereby place and wine become merged into the notion of terroir as a symbolic representation of place identity (Aurier, Fort and Sirieix 2005).

Terroir, identity, tourism and sensescapes

Apart from reinforcing place identity, a connection to a particular wine and its terroir also creates a sensual space that is accessed through wine tourism. Wine tourism is used not only as a significant marketing and branding tool and an additional income source in wine regions (Beverland 2006), but it also reinforces the individual identity of regions and wineries by presenting and preserving the unique authentic social, cultural, historical and geographical characteristics of wine-producing regions. Furthermore, wine tourism can play a significant role in wine education (see Chapter 9).

The significance of senses in contributing to the tourism experience is well charted (Pan and Ryan 2009; Low 2005; Law 2001). As Dann and Jacobsen (2003:19), in exploring the significance of senses for tourists, state: 'the successful tourist destination, which otherwise could be regarded as something of a hybrid and living anachronism, blending ancient with postmodern, now can be the winning formula, precisely because it does not rely on sight alone'.

Thus the essence of the terroir wine experience is that it creates a multi-sensory oenological experience in which the social, cultural, geographical, ecosystem and 'servicescapes' offer a unique sensual experience where all of the senses are engaged. Located in the terroir, wine tourism places the wine tourist within what Law (2001:265) identifies as the 'sensory geography' of tourism (or alternatively Low's (2005:398) notion of 'sensory landscapes'). Thus wine tourists do not merely metaphorically consume the landscape, they tangibly consume elements of the landscape and culture by drinking the wine at the site of production. As Carlsen and Dowling (1998:24) state:

> There is no more tangible, and therefore enduring, image than the sensation of experiencing wines and foods in the region where they were produced. It is this imagery which provides the attraction for wine tourists to experience not only the wines, but also the culture and natural attraction of wine regions.

Terroir and wine tourism also reinforce the identity of place while simultaneously increasing the cultural capital of tourists and resultantly the manifestation of their identity through the appreciation of wine. Visiting a vineyard as part of the tourism experience is a means to emerge yourself in the authentic communicative staging of wine. For many wine tourists visiting the famous wineries of France is akin to a pilgrimage, and during the experience they are immersing themselves in the terroir, thus adding another sense-based dimension of consumption and the appreciation of wine (Mason and O'Mahony 2007).

In exploring the complexity of senses and their linking to touch, smell, feel, etc., Sutton (2010:217) goes further by introducing the concept of 'synaesthesia'. This represents the idea that senses do not operate in isolation, but rather operate in relation with all of the other senses. The significance of this is important when attempting to define and comprehend the experience offered at tourism sites, and how it differs from more traditional wine consumption experiences. Sutton (2010:210) identifies that:

> Synesthesia ... blurs the objectivity and passivity of western sensory models by showing the ways that sensory experience is not simply passively registered but actively created between people. Synesthesia is a reminder of why food and the senses should be considered together.

This view of the senses has been explored in tourism studies. For instance, Pan and Ryan (2009) identify the multisensory nature of tourism and its significance to the contemporary tourist. Senses have always been an important part of tourism. We can chart this beginning with Baudelaire's (1863) notion of the *flâneur* and the idea of exploring the city through a heightened sensual awareness of the environment. According to Biehl-Missal (2013), we need to consider the impact senses have on our understanding of the world and how it influences our behaviour. She states, we gather 'aesthetic experiences through our five senses to create an embodied, tacit knowing that ... can influence behavior' (Biehl-Missal 2013:5). However, as a result of their New Zealand research Pan and Ryan (2009) found that although tourists utilised all of their senses, taste was privileged as the most significant sense experience within all of the sites investigated in New Zealand. This exploration of the senses is particularly reflected in wine tourism. According to López-Guzmán and Sánchez-Cañizares (2012:63), the exploration of the senses through the consumption of food and wine of the region is one of the major motivations for the tourist to engage in gastronomic tourism. This association between food, wine and sensory experiences is lucidly summed up by Sutton (2010:215), who comments on the significance of the relationship between food and the senses. He states that: 'food is central to cosmologies, worldviews, and ways of life' and is reflected in the term 'gustemology' as a means of understanding the spectrum of cultural issues that exist around taste and the sensory aspects of food and wine.

Intrinsically, the experience offered at wineries is an ontological journey that through the challenging of senses grounds the individual metaphysically within the terroir (see Brownlie, Hewer and Horne 2005). By challenging and stimulating the senses, the relationship between terroir and wine, and arguably food, provides a rupture or break from the everyday. According to Bruwer, Li, and Reid (2002:220), wine 'helps us to construct an idea world, one which is more "bearable" than the "painful chaos" which threatens us continually'. As such, the consumption of wine creates a purity of experience and a re-establishment of an awareness of the senses that have been dulled by the act of 'being' in a world dominated by mass production and the chemical enhancement of food and wine. In assessing the significance of the senses Levi-Strauss (1983:153, quoted in Sutton 2010:210) states:

> The senses ... are operators, which make it possible to convey the isomorphic character of all binary systems of contracts connected with the senses,

and therefore to express, as a totality, a set of equivalences connecting life and death, vegetable foods and cannibalism, putrefaction and imputrescibility, softness and hardness, silence and noise.

Thus, for Levi-Strauss (1983:164) senses are codes that transmit messages and the 'gustatory code' or 'oenological code' is privileged over other sensory codes, but most importantly he links the codes that surround the food and wine system to the 'social system' in which we live (Sutton 2010:210). This view is supported by Weismantel (2005:97), who ascertains that sensory aspects of taste change 'the social and economic structures that make consumption possible', therefore, although the production of 'sensescapes' within tourism provide us with place and space to explore the sensual side of life, we cannot remove or isolate them from social and economic structures.

Terroir: a summary

In the first five chapters of this book we have seen that wine fulfils many roles in contemporary society, and the understanding and knowledge of these roles is important when attempting to engage with wine consumers.

The classification of wine as an 'aesthetic object' places the cultural and social significance of wine in the same category as art, architecture and other aesthetic categories or pastimes. The appreciation of 'aesthetic objects' requires specific forms of knowledge and experience that are manifested in the membership requirements in terms of behaviours, knowledge and other consumer resources.

In this chapter we seen that wine has become an important means of protecting and revitalising regional identities, expressed most profoundly in the notion of terroir. Terroir is inextricably linked to the cultural, social and geographical heritage of a region and has become materially revealed in the produce itself, whether that be food or wine.

Wine symbolises a form of simplicity or authenticity that is opposite to the fast-food culture of the contemporary world. Wine provides an expression of regional identity that transcends globalisation and the homogenization of society, and perhaps this is the biggest contribution to culture that the notion of terroir makes. It is this authenticity, identity and sensual experience that attracts millions of wine tourists to France, the Napa Valley and to the leading regions of Spain and Italy, in search of experiences that will also express their identities.

For discussion

1. How far does the terroir affect the taste of a wine? Is it worth paying more for a wine from a particular terroir?
2. The term terroir originates from France, but how far can it be used in other countries?

3   Even in France, does the term terroir have a greater significance in (say) Burgundy as compared to Languedoc? Or is it equally significant in all regions?
4   Why is geographical identity so important with wine? In particular, is it more important with wine than other food and drink products?
5   Is it meaningful to describe wines as 'masculine' or 'feminine'? How does this link to the understanding of terroir?
6   Does terroir only matter to wine connoisseurs, or does it have wider relevance? What do you feel about wines sold with no geographical identity – should they be classed as 'plonk'?
7   Can terroir be 'experienced' by visiting a wine region? Do wine tourists gain more from visiting regions with a strong sense of terroir?

References

Aurier, P., Fort, F. and Sirieix, L. (2005). Exploring terroir product meanings for the consumer. *Anthropology of Food* (online), available from: https://aof.revues.org/187?lang=en, accessed 4 May 2005.

Barham, E. (2001). Translating 'Terroir': Social Movement Appropriation of a French Concept. Paper presented at the *International Perspectives on Alternative Agro-Food Networks, Quality, Embeddedness, and Bio-Politics*, University of California, Santa Cruz, 12–13 October.

Barham, E. (2003). Translating terroir: The global challenge of French AOC labeling. *Journal of Rural Studies*, 19, 127–38.

Baudelaire, C. 1964[1863]. *The Painter of Modern Life* (New York: Da Capo Press. Orig. published in *Le Figaro*.

Beebe, C., Haque, F., Jarvis, C., Kenney, M. and Patton, D. (2013). Identity creation and cluster construction: The case of the Paso Robles wine region. *Journal of Economic Geography*, 13(5), 711–40.

Beverland, M. (2006). The 'real thing': Branding authenticity in the luxury wine trade. *Journal of Business Research*, 59(2), 251–8.

Biehl-Missal, B. (2013). The atmosphere of the image: An aesthetic concept for visual analysis. *Consumption, Markets and Culture*, 16(4), 1–12.

Boniface, P. (2003). *Tasting Tourism: Travelling for Food and Drink* (Farnham: Ashgate Publishing Ltd).

Brownlie, D., Hewer, P. and Horne, S. (2005). Culinary tourism: An exploratory reading of contemporary representations of cooking. *Consumption, Markets and Culture*, 8(1), 7–26.

Bruwer, J., Li, E. and Reid, M. (2002). Segmentation of the Australian wine market using a wine-related lifestyle approach. *Journal of Wine Research*, 13(3), 217–42.

Carlsen, J. and Dowling, R. (1998). Wine tourism marketing issues in Australia. *International Journal of Wine Marketing*, 10(3), 23–32.

Charters, S. (2010). Marketing terroir: A conceptual approach. Paper presented at *5th International Academy of Wine Business Research Conference*, Auckland, New Zealand, 8–10 February.

Chronis, A., Arnould, E. and Hampton, R. (2012). Gettysburg re-imagined: The role of narrative imagination in consumption experience. *Consumption, Markets and Culture*, 15(3), 261–286.

Cronin, J., McCarthy, M. and Collins, A. (2012). Covert distinction: How hipsters practice food-based resistance strategies in the production of identity. *Consumption, Markets and Culture*, 15(1), 1–27.

Croce, E. and Perri, G. (2010). *Food and Wine Tourism: Integrating Food, Travel and Territory* (Oxfordshire: CABI Tourism Texts).

Dann, G. and Jacobsen, J. (2003). Tourism smellscapes. *Tourism Geographies*, 5(1), 3–25.

Douguet, J.-M. and O'Connor, M. (2003). Maintaining the integrity of the French terroir: A study of critical natural capital in its cultural context. *Ecological Economics*, 44, 233–54.

Easingwood, C., Lockshin, L. and Spawton, A. (2011). The drivers of wine regionality. *Journal of wine research*, 22(1), 19–33.

Fonseca, M. (2008). Understanding consumer culture: The role of food as an important cultural category. In: Acevedo, R. (ed.), *Latin Advances in Consumer Research*, volume 2, pp. 28–33 (Duluth, MN: Association for Consumer Research).

Gibson, J.A. and Weinberg, D. (1980). In vino communitas: Wine and identity in a Swiss Alpine village. *Anthropological Quarterly*, 53(2), 111–21.

Gillespie, C. and Morrison, A. (2001). Commercial hospitality consumption as live marketing communication system. *International Journal of Contemporary Hospitality Management*, 13(4), 183–8.

Gvion, L. and Trostler, N. (2008). From spaghetti and meatballs through Hawaiian pizza to sushi: The changing nature of ethnicity in American restaurants. *The Journal of Popular Culture*, 41(6), 950–74.

Guy, K.M. (2007). *When Champagne became French: Wine and the Making of a National Identity* (JHU Press).

Hall, C. M. and Sharples, L. (eds) (2008). *Food and Wine Festivals and Events around the World: Development, Management and Markets* (London: Routledge).

Houston, H. and Meamber, L. (2011). Consuming the world: Reflexivity, aesthetics, and authenticity at Disney World's EPCOT Centre. *Consumption, Markets and Culture*, 14(2), 177–91.

Jameson, F. (1991). *Postmodernism, or, The Cultural Logic of Late Capitalism* (New York: Verso).

Law, L. (2001). Home cooking: Filipino women and geographies of the senses in Hong Kong. *Ecumene*, 8, 264–83.

Levi-Strauss, C. (1983). *The Raw and the Cooked: Mythologiques*, volume 1 (Weightman, J., transl.) (Chicago, IL: Chicago University Press).

López-Guzmán, T. and Sánchez-Cañizares, S. (2012). Gastronomy, tourism and destination differentiation: A case study in Spain. *Review of Economics and Finance*, 1, 63–72.

Low, K. (2005). Ruminations on smell as a sociocultural phenomenon. *Current Sociology*, 53(3), 397–417.

Marshall, D. (2005). Food as ritual, routine or convention. *Consumption, Markets and Culture*, 8(1), 69–85.

Mason, R. and O'Mahony, P. (2007). On the trail of food and wine: The tourist search for meaningful experience. *Annals of Leisure Research*, 10(3/4), 498–517.

Pan, S. and Ryan, C. (2009). Tourism sense-making: The role of the senses and travel journalism. *Journal of Travel and Tourism Marketing*, 26, 625–39.

Riley, M. (2005). Food and beverage management. A review of change. *International Journal of Contemporary Hospitality Management*, 17(1), 88–93.

Sutton, D. (2010). Food and the senses. *Annual Review of Anthropology*, 39, 209–23.

Tikkanen, I. (2007). Maslow's hierarchy and food tourist in Finland: Five cases. *British Food Journal*, 109(9), 721–34.

Trubek. A. (2008). *The Taste of Place: A Cultural Journey into Terroir* (Berkeley, CA: University California Press).

Trauer, B. and Ryan, C. (2005). Destination image, romance and place experience – an application of intimacy theory in tourism. *Tourism Management*, 26, 481–91.

Turner, P. and Creasy, G.L. (2003). Terroir: competing definitions and applications. *Australian and New Zealand Wine Industry Journal*, 18(6), 48–55.

Weismantel, M. (2005). Tasty meals and bitter gifts. In: Korsmeyer, C. (ed.), *The Taste Culture Reader*, pp. 87–99 (Oxford: Berg).

Wilson, J.E. (1998). *Terroir: The Role of Geology, Climate and Culture on the Making of French Wines* (London: Mitchell Beazley).

6
WINE AT HOME

Wine can be consumed in a huge range of contexts, but it is helpful to distinguish between domestic settings as opposed to bars, restaurants and similar hospitality settings. This distinction is linked to widely used terminology in countries that require licences for the sale of wine (see Chapter 7 for more on licensing law). It is normal to distinguish the fundamentally different sales channels corresponding to these settings as:

- 'On-trade' – where wine is sold for consumption on the premises where it is sold, so bottles are opened for consumption at the venue concerned.
- 'Off-trade' – where wine is sold for consumption off the premises, away from where it is sold, most commonly for consumption at home (with strict rules that bottles must not be opened at the venue where they are sold).

This chapter focuses on a number of social and cultural issues related to the consumption of wine at home – normally wine purchased through the off-trade. In other chapters we have considered the on-trade service of wine in restaurants and bars.

In households directly involved in wine production the wine consumed at home may be largely the production of the farm, domain or estate where the family resides. It has not been purchased through either the on-trade or off-trade. But for the purpose of this chapter, we look at wine that has been bought from an external source and brought into the consumer's home.

Getting wine into homes: off-trade channels

Wine for domestic consumption is normally purchased through the off-trade. This includes, for example, purchases made through wine shops, mail-order wine merchants, through supermarkets and other retailers that sell wine alongside other goods, and in some cases through direct purchases from wine producers.

Each of these suppliers will have particular marketing techniques: many retailers offer a huge choice of wines from many countries whereas others specialise in wines from specific countries or regions. Some focus on value for money, whereas others stress the offering of exclusive wines that are not widely available. Some will only sell wine by the case (usually this means at least 12 bottles at one time, although occasionally a case means six bottles) but most are happy to cater for the casual purchaser just wanting one bottle.

In countries with little or no domestic wine production, any wine purchased directly from producers will usually involve 'imports of wine for personal consumption'. For some wine connoisseurs, being able to serve wine that they have personally bought from a particular wine-producing country gives the wine a special mystique – in the sense that the host has personally met the producer and seen the vineyards or the cellars where the wine is made. The laws on personal imports vary from country to country: where duty rates differ it is sometimes possible to purchase wine at prices well below the domestic price by travelling abroad. In the European Union (EU) there is no formal limit on the amount of wine a private individual can bring in from another country if it is genuinely for the personal consumption of the purchaser and their family or friends (i.e. if it will not be resold), although in practice customs authorities will require explanations from those importing very large quantities.

For more on the broader issues in the marketing wine, see Chapter 8. This chapter focuses on what happens to the wine once it reaches the purchaser's home.

Storing wine in the home

Once wine arrives at someone's home, either following a shopping trip or a delivery from a wine supplier, the first question is: where is it put? How people choose to store wine at home (if at all – in some cases it may be consumed immediately) tells us much about their consumer resources (as seen in Chapter 4) and about their understanding and relationship with wine.

Possible actions include:

- opening a bottle for immediate consumption when getting home after shopping;
- opening a bottle later that day, perhaps with a meal;
- putting the wine to one side for a short period and then taking it elsewhere – for example, as a gift to friends;
- putting the wine in the refrigerator (particularly for whites, rosés and sparkling wines) for consumption in due course;
- putting the bottle alongside other bottles in a convenient storage location, possibly on a wine rack, perhaps in the kitchen or under the stairs;

Wine at home

FIGURE 6.1 A typical temperature-controlled cabinet for wine storage in the home. (Courtesy of Eurocave Importers Ltd.)

- putting the wine in a specialist part of the house set aside as a 'wine cellar'; or
- putting the wine in a temperature-controlled wine storage cabinet such as a 'Eurocave' (see Figure 6.1).

Immediate consumption

Retailers commonly report that a high proportion of wine is bought for consumption within 24 hours of purchase. In such cases, storage is not a major issue. Indeed, many retailers offer selections of white, rosé and sparkling wines in chiller units (adopting practices from the on-trade) for those wishing to buy chilled wine ready to take to a party or to open at home, probably within an hour of purchase.

Home wine cellars

At the other extreme is the wine lover with a home wine cellar, in some cases able to take thousands of bottles – usually with some bottles in racks, making them easily accessible, but also with ample space for full cases of wine.

Whether the wines are left in cases or placed on racks, all wines with cork closures will be stored horizontally so that the wine remains in contact with the cork to prevent it drying out. Every attempt is made to maintain a reasonably constant temperature – generally around 12°C is considered ideal – with little or no light, and little vibration so that wines can develop gently over time. Quality red wines and Ports will usually deposit a sediment in bottle, so if the bottles can be left undisturbed for several years the sediment will be gently deposited along one side of the bottle. It can then be gently decanted when ready to be served.

A wine cellar can take many forms – it has sometimes been assumed that a 'wine cellar' must be underground, but the term can be used for any kind of wine storage area. Traditionally, the best wine cellars are underground in order to benefit from the relatively constant temperatures of the surrounding earth, but a wine cellar can be created in a suitable room above ground if it has no heating or windows. However, in the warmer regions of the world an above-ground cellar needs to be constructed with a high standard of insulation and a cooling system in order to maintain a suitable temperature for long-term storage.

For houses with no basement, wine cellars are sometimes specially constructed by digging out below the floor of an existing room or garage, often in a circular layout with access from above by means of a spiral staircase. In some cases no expense is spared in creating a prestigious space with special lighting and expensive materials so honoured guests can be invited to visit the cellar (Figure 6.2).

For the connoisseur with a wine cellar, wines are likely to be bought months or years before their intended consumption, usually in full cases (12 bottles) and often acquired under the *en primeur* system (see Chapter 3) in order to secure

FIGURE 6.2 A specially constructed home wine cellar. (Courtesy of Carter Jonas LLP.)

wines in limited supply. Certainly a committed wine lover will avoid as far as possible wines that have been traded between many merchants and stored in uncertain conditions. Buying en primeur usually means that the wine is shipped directly from the château or estate where it is produced, to a specialist wine warehouse in the country of the buyer, and then in due course to the cellar of the purchaser, so the subsequent ageing of the wine is under the purchaser's control.

The best wines that are likely to be stored for many years are almost always shipped by the producer in wooden cases to facilitate this (cardboard cases can fall apart after a few years, especially if there is any dampness). Medium-priced wines will come in card cases with 12 bottles in two horizontal layers of six (rather than retail boxes where the bottles may be upright).

For those looking to age wine for several years in a personal cellar the total space needed may be considerable. Consider the example of 'Andrew' – a wine lover who mainly buys red Bordeaux and who takes the view that *on average* the wines should be kept for 12 years before drinking. If the household typically consumes around two bottles of red Bordeaux a week, this amounts to an average of 100 bottles per year. So Andrew will need space to store *at least* 1,200 bottles (100 bottles × 12 years) to cover his expected future needs for red Bordeaux. In addition he will want space to store other wines for shorter periods – but even with white wines, he may well buy a case that is only consumed gradually over five years. He may also have some very special bottles or vintage Ports that will be kept for considerably more than 12 years. So he probably needs a cellar with capacity for at least 2,000 bottles – perhaps 500 on racks to allow easy access to specific bottles and a further 1,500 bottles stored in cases.

However, some wine lovers also buy for investment purposes, which they plan to resell at a later date. Others may be regularly hosting large parties and will be consuming wine in much larger quantities than Andrew. In these cases, if all the wine is to be stored in a home cellar, the space requirements can be huge.

Storage with a wine merchant 'in bond'

An alternative to a large personal wine cellar is to store wine with a wine merchant. Almost all wine merchants who provide en primeur sales offer the facility to keep wines in a temperature-controlled warehouse under the merchant's control. In such cases, where the national laws impose duties on wine, there is usually a choice of storing the wine 'duty paid' (where taxes are paid at the outset) or keeping the wine 'in bond' so that duty and other taxes such as VAT do not have to be paid until the wine is withdrawn. Keeping the wine in bond is particularly useful for wine investors if the wine may subsequently be exported.

However, storing wine on this basis will involve an annual fee for each case stored, usually with additions for insurance, and most wine warehouses will only hold full cases of wine. So careful decisions are needed about when to withdraw wines for consumption, and unless the owner plans to consume a full case of expensive wine within a few weeks or months of withdrawing it from the warehouse, good facilities are still needed to hold bottles in the home.

These examples show that the costs of storing wine for a long time before consumption are considerable, and it is not surprising that in the on-trade only the most exclusive restaurants can afford to maintain quality red wines in store for a sufficient length of time so that they are ready for drinking when they appear on the restaurant's wine list.

Ad hoc *storage arrangements*

Many wine-drinking households have some arrangement that falls between the extremes of always buying wine for immediate consumption or a full-scale home wine cellar.

It is common for wine consumers to keep a few bottles in a kitchen cupboard, or perhaps in a cupboard elsewhere in the house, such as under the stairs (in most cases this is a fairly stable unheated area and is often the best option in the majority of homes with no wine cellar). In many cases a small wine rack may be used.

For example, 'Bethany' likes to have around 10 to 15 bottles of wine in the house, so she has a choice of what to open when serving a meal. When she was having her kitchen refitted she arranged for a 15-bottle wine rack to be incorporated at the end of the cupboards. Although a kitchen is not the ideal place to store wine due to the variations of temperatures when cooking, her wine rack is well away from the cooker and she rarely keeps any bottle more than two or three months, so any deterioration will be modest. By contrast, 'Charlotte' likes to have a bit more wine available and sometimes keeps bottles for up to two years. She has a 36-bottle wine rack under the stairs and also has room to store a couple of 12-bottle boxes. For 'Denise' who only drinks white and rosé wines, space for three to four bottles in the refrigerator is sufficient for her needs. Although she drinks wine most evenings, she normally only buys a couple of branded wines that she knows she likes, so she does not need to keep many bottles in stock.

For the serious wine collector wanting top storage conditions for wine in the home without the need for a purpose-built cellar, a temperature-controlled wine storage cabinet such as a 'Eurocave' (see Figure 6.1) may be a solution.

Sizes and packaging of wine for home consumption

Although the 750ml bottle is the most common size for the sale of wines, consumers are increasingly buying wine in other kinds of containers – see Figure 6.3 for some of the bottle sizes available.

But aside from normal bottles, wine boxes ('bag-in-box') have long been popular. They are convenient for domestic parties where just one or two standard wines are offered. They are also popular with those who like an occasional glass of wine, but who would not generally finish a bottle and are happy to have just

FIGURE 6.3 Various sizes of wine bottles. The bottles shown in the picture range from 100ml, 250ml, 375ml (half bottle), 750ml (bottle), 1,500ml (magnum), 3,000ml (double magnum), 5,000l (jeroboam) to 6,000ml (imperiale).

a choice of one or two wines (perhaps a white wine box kept in the refrigerator and a red wine box on the kitchen worktop). The most common size is a three litre wine box with a plastic tap. As the wine is withdrawn the bag inside collapses, so that little or no air comes into contact with the wine. Larger bottles, usually one litre, and normally with screwcap closures, are also popular for entry-level wines served at parties where the status of the wine is unimportant.

At the other end of the scale, mini-bottles (sometimes call 'airline-sized' bottles) are now widely available from supermarkets and convenience stores with caps that just have to be twisted to open. They are popular with consumers who just want a modest quantity of wine – a glass or two – to drink on a single occasion. This can be a way for an individual to justify opening wine on their own without the sense of guilt that may be implicit in opening a full bottle for personal consumption (even though the full bottle would possibly be consumed across several days). For those who might be tempted to drink more than they intend if a full bottle were opened, it has the effect of restricting one's consumption to the specific volume in the mini-bottle. Although originally developed for use in the on-trade (particular in bars that do not wish to keep open wine bottles and for travellers on trains and planes), these bottles are now widely available for domestic purchase. The usual sizes are 187ml or 250ml (although buying wine in mini-bottles is proportionally more expensive than in normal 750ml bottles, due to the higher bottling and distributions costs). Small-serve quantities of wine are also sold in cans and cartons.

As well as these special types of container, leading wine producers will often supply wines in conventional glass bottles with cork closures in a range of sizes, including half bottles (375ml) and magnums (1,500ml) and when wine is bought by mail order or en primeur the purchaser may well be offered a choice of size. Half bottles are sometimes chosen by those wishing to limit their wine consumption – especially those who live alone or with someone who does not drink wine. They are also popular for dessert wines where smaller quantities are the norm. On the other hand, to serve a wine from a magnum can create a sense of atmosphere at a large dinner party. Moreover, a red wine that is being kept for some years will age more slowly in a larger bottle as the ratio of surface area to volume is lower, so for some wine connoisseurs who plan to store wines for many years, the magnum is the preferred size.

Sometimes wines are released in double magnums (three litres – equivalent to four bottles), in jeroboams (five litres in Bordeaux, though in Burgundy a jeroboam is the same as a double magnum), or imperiales (six litres in Bordeaux – equivalent to eight bottles). Occasionally even larger sizes are used, especially with Champagne. These *large format* bottles are usually more expensive than the same quantity of wine in normal bottles, and they can be expensive in terms of carriage and difficult to handle, but for the serious wine lover hosting a large event, they can create a powerful sense of occasion with great symbolism. (The use of large formats can also sometimes be helpful to a wine producer trying to promote sales of wine from a less successful vintage.)

When to drink the wine

In some cases, people buy wine with little intention of consuming it. Sometimes this is because wine is deliberately purchased as an investment with the intention of subsequent resale (though in that case storing the wine at home would be rare: serious investors will generally leave wine with a merchant 'in bond' as mentioned above). Alternatively, a committed wine collector may buy special bottles in the same way that a collector of coins or rare books might do: solely with the intention of interacting with them as objects in a collection. In that case the wine will probably be brought into the home, but only to be brought out on occasion for admiration by others and with no expectation that the wine will actually be consumed.

However, these patterns of behaviour are the exception to the norm. Most people buying wine to store at home intend that it will be consumed at some point. The next sections of this chapter explore a range of domestic circumstances where wine may be consumed.

For a connoisseur who is deliberately buying wine with the intention of storing it for some time, there is always a key question: when should a particular wine be drunk? This is particularly important with fine wines (see Chapter 3).

Most wines, especially quality red wines, develop in bottle, and for someone with an extensive wine cellar there may be major considerations of when a particular wine will be ready to drink. Generally a top red wine from a region such as Bordeaux will have very high tannins when young, making it quite harsh to drink (and likely to give the drinker a headache). Also, in a young wine the fruit flavours may be too dominant and not yet in harmony with other elements such as the vanilla notes or spicy character that may have been picked up from ageing the wine in oak – with the result that it does not really complement savoury foods.

To a lesser extent, white wines can also benefit from some ageing, especially if they have high levels of acidity or if the wine has been vinified in oak, as time is needed for the oak flavours to marry with the acids and polyphenols in the wine. (See pp. 23–4 and pp. 77–8 for more on vintages and ageing.)

A quality wine is often more enjoyable, particularly if it is to be served with food. After a number of years' development in bottle when the tannins have softened, the young fruits are less astringent, the acidity may be slightly less, and the overall flavours have become more complex due to the long slow chemical reactions taking place in bottle. During this time, red wines especially may throw a sediment, which may necessitate decanting the bottle when it is opened (see p. 129).

So the dimension of time is an incredibly important element in the esteem afforded to wine. Exploring this is easier for a purchaser who has bought a case (12 bottles) of a wine, as the bottles can be opened over a period of time to see how the wine is developing (although this only works if the owner is prepared to make some kind of tasting note when each bottle is opened). For a wine connoisseur who has invested in a single very expensive bottle, knowing the optimum time to open it is a real challenge and there is a considerable demand for guidance on this. Whole books such as Broadbent (1991) and nowadays websites such as www.jancisrobinson.com and more informal sites such as www.wineanorak.com are devoted to publishing notes on each vintage from major producers. Robinson (1989) presented a book of time charts, with graphs seeking to show how perceived wine quality varies against time for a wide range of vintages from major producers in different parts of the world.

Because of the uncertainty of when a wine will be at its best for drinking, specialist wine merchants often seek to help with such decisions by publishing tables showing the state of vintages. This is particularly important for those keeping wines in store with the merchant, as mentioned above. For example, a table may list various vintages of wines from different regions with symbols (often using bottles shown horizontally, diagonally and vertically) to indicate a wine's readiness to drink. For example, the famous London wine merchants, Berry Brothers & Rudd (BBR) publish a chart on their website that at the time of writing shows vintages from 2013 back to 1978. In early 2015, for recent vintages of red Bordeaux they showed:

- to indicate those years that BBR considered should still be 'laid down' – in other words, left to mature further: in early 2015 they applied this indicator to the vintages 2013, 2012, 2011, 2010, 2009, 2008, 2006, and 2005;

- to identify those years that BBR considered to be suitable for current drinking but also capable of further development: this applied to the 2004, 2002, 2001 and 2000 vintages; and
- to show those vintages that BBR suggested are now suitable for 'drinking up' rather than further storage: in early 2015 they showed the 2007, 2003 and 1999 vintages of red Bordeaux in this category (Berry Bros & Rudd 2015).

BBR also gave a rating for the quality of each vintage on a 1 to 10 scale – though they stress that such ratings can only be used as generalisations as there will be significant variations from one château to another, even within the same region.

However, there is a further problem that people's tastes vary – as one would expect. Some wine consumers prefer wines young and fruity even if they may still be somewhat tannic, whereas others prefer the complexity of age. It is also commonly suggested that there are differences in palate between different nationalities, with the French generally enjoying their wines younger than traditional wine connoisseurs in the UK, and Americans somewhere in the middle (Robinson 1989:17). However, there are also generational differences and many other factors at play. Sometimes a wine lover will find ecstatic pleasure in tasting a really old bottle, whereas others drinking the same wine at the same time may find it positively unpleasant. There is a particular debate with the red wines of Burgundy that can sometimes develop a 'farmyard' nose when mature, with hints of rotting hay or even a slight sense of manure. Some argue that a small note of 'farmyard' is a good sign of complexity in well-aged wines, but other experts insist that this is a fault due to contamination of the wine with a non-spore forming acidogenic yeast called *Brettanomyces*.

Whatever one's drinking preferences, storing wine is expensive, especially if it is to be kept for many years in an environment with a controlled temperature. It also requires a great deal of organisation and record-keeping to maintain a home wine cellar where bottles are kept for many years. So even those who enjoy drinking fine wines may not wish to commit to long-term storage arrangements. For all these reasons, it is widely reckoned that most quality red wines (and also many whites) are drunk well before their peak. Economic pressures are very significant: wine producers and distributors want to convert their stocks into cash, and individuals often lack the storage facilities or the will-power to postpone opening wines for several years.

However, there is also a converse phenomenon of wines that are kept for much longer than intended – this is typically due to wine lovers buying wines well in excess of what they can reasonably hope to consume. It is easy for such individuals, especially if relatively affluent, to be tempted by *en primeur* offers of wines that may never be available again, or to find themselves agreeing to place orders from suppliers offering cases of fine wines at attractive prices. The result is that even for wine connoisseurs with specially created wine storage spaces, the over-full cellar is a common problem! Also, wine lovers will often speak of having very special bottles in their cellar but finding there is never a sufficiently special occasion to justify opening the ultimate bottle in their collection. The result may be that as wine lovers get older, especially if their health deteriorates, they may be left with extensive wine collections that they will never drink. Sometimes wine collections are specifically left to children or other relatives when a wine lover dies, but often the children may lack the same interest in wine or may have no means of storing it. Many wines sold at auctions thus arise from the disposal of the contents of wine cellars from a deceased wine lover.

Opening and serving wine at home

The ways in which wine is served in the home tell us perhaps more than anything else about the 'cultural capital invested in the ritual of wine consumption' (Ulin 2013:79).

For some it is a simple matter of grabbing the first available bottle of wine from the shelf or refrigerator, opening it as quickly as possible and possibly even pouring it into a tumbler or a mug rather than a wine glass. But for the serious wine lover a complex series of steps may be involved, for example:

- selecting the wine from some kind of index or cellar record;
- retrieving the relevant bottle from the cellar or store (in some cases this may even involve 'breaking open' a wooden case when the first bottle in the case is retrieved);
- placing the bottle on to a suitable support and carefully removing the cork without disturbing the sediment;
- where appropriate (see p. 129–30) pouring the wine from the bottle into an elegant glass decanter, taking care not to transfer the sediment (usually with the aid of a light or candle to spot the sediment through the neck of the bottle);
- bringing the bottle or decanter to the relevant temperature for service – perhaps by bringing it into the room where it will be served (for a red) or chilling it in the refrigerator (for a white wine);
- choosing appropriate glasses in which to serve the wine (a serious wine lover may well have different wine glasses for different styles of wine);
- perhaps tasting a small sample (as in a restaurant) before offering the wine to others;
- pouring the wine into glasses for each person who will drink it (but rarely filling more than one-third to one-half of each person's glass, so that there is ample room to swirl the wine and appreciate the aromas); and
- subsequently topping up glasses as the wine is drunk (although in the case of a very special wine, the total quantity served to each person may be considerably less than usual glass sizes in the on-trade).

There are many possibilities between these extremes. Many people drinking wine at home will take care to choose a wine that they believe will complement the food being served, will use wine glasses of some kind, and will chill a white wine before serving, even if they do not engage in all the ritual stages above.

When serving wine to guests, the theatre of opening the bottle (assuming it was not pre-decanted) may be very significant. Whilst consumers in many countries are increasingly willing to accept wines with screwcaps, particularly for white and rosé wines, there is no doubt that some hosts like the symbolism of opening a bottle by extracting the cork with a corkscrew.

With Champagne and other sparkling wines, there can be great significance in the ritual of removing the foil covering, then the wire cage protecting the cork, and then releasing the cork with the sound of a distinctive 'pop', and then pouring the wine into glasses with a great deal of mousse (froth) – although serious wine lovers insist that the cork should be released as gently as possible with no large 'pop'.

Decanting

For the serious wine lover, the question of whether to decant a wine (and if so, when) is central to the process of serving wine in the home.

In most cases a red wine, especially a robust red with significant tannins, will slowly throw a sediment in the bottle. Technically this is due to some of the smaller organic molecules in the wine polymerising into longer molecules that are too large to remain dissolved, so that they are precipitated as solids at the bottom of the bottle (along the edge if the bottle is stored horizontally). This is rarely a problem with young wines, but a red wine that has been stored for several years may have a significant sediment. A wine connoisseur will take great care with opening such a bottle and decanting the wine into a jug or carafe leaving the sediment behind (see Figure 6.4). The result is a mature wine that is delicate and enjoyable to drink, with increased complexity from the years of development in bottle but without the excessive tannins or excessive young fruit flavours that may have been present when it was much younger.

The need for decanting varies with the style of wine. Most high-volume branded wines are filtered before bottling to reduce the chances of throwing a sediment in bottle, as the producers are targeting the majority of consumers who do not want the complications of having to decant a wine. In any case, such wines are usually bottled to be suitable for immediate drinking so they are rarely laid down for longer periods. Also, as white wines contain very little tannin it is rare for them to need decanting (although occasionally there can be a deposit of tartrate crystals – see p. 10). Amongst fine red wines, lighter styles of wine such as red Burgundies usually only throw a very light deposit so decanting may not be necessary even with a bottle that has been aged for some years. Rather more sediment is likely with claret (red Bordeaux), wines from the Rhone, and some of the unfiltered wines from leading producers in the New World. Decanting is usually desirable with any quality red wines from these regions drunk more than about five to eight years after the vintage date. Vintage Port needs ageing in

FIGURE 6.4 Decanting a bottle of wine to be served in the home.

bottle for a very long period – normally at least 15 years – and throws a huge amount of sediment so decanting is essential. Drinking an undecanted vintage Port is a very unpleasant experience (but many other styles of Port are available that do not need decanting).

Sometimes even young wines are decanted – not so much to separate the wine from the sediment, but more in order to provide additional aeration of the wine, as contact with oxygen has a natural effect of softening harsh tannins.

Even if a wine is not decanted, some people serving wine at home place emphasis on removing the cork some time in advance so that the wine has 'time to breathe'. However, the small surface area of the wine that is then in contact with the air in the neck of the bottle is not sufficient to achieve any significant level of oxidation: where a good deal of oxidation is intended, it is more effective to decant the wine.

Storing partly drunk bottles of wine

Some domestic consumers will always finish a bottle of wine on the day it is opened, but regularly drinking a whole 750ml bottle in one evening is highly unwise for a single person. Even if it is shared between two people, it will generally exceed recommended safe drinking limits (see Chapter 7). Given that wine is a relatively expensive product, only the very affluent will throw away the remains of half-drunk bottles, so it is not unusual in a domestic situation to have partly drunk bottles that need to be stored for another day. Also some consumers like to have more than one wine on the go at any one time to suit different foods (typically a white and a red) or to suit the preferences of different family members.

This issue may be solved by purchasing wine in smaller bottles or relying on bag-in-box wines (see p. 123) but choices are more limited, so for most consumers some approach is needed to store partly drunk bottles from day-to-day. The approach to such storage is a further indication of attitudes to wine as an object.

The simplest approach is to buy wines with screwcap closures – if the bottle is partly drunk, the cap is screwed back on and the wine will keep without serious deterioration for a couple of days (especially if refrigerated). However, for a bottle with a cork closure, it is relatively difficult to reinsert the cork, and a wide range of temporary bottle stoppers are sold as gifts for wine lovers for this situation.

But simply replacing a screwcap or inserting a temporary stopper still leaves the wine in contact with a considerable volume of air, and for a wine connoisseur this is a cause for concern as the wine can deteriorate due to oxidation. Indeed, even the less serious drinker wanting to keep an open bottle for a week or more needs a mean of excluding the air. Various accessories are sold to wine drinkers to assist with this problem – one of the most common is the 'Vacuvin' (see Figure 6.5) where rubber bottle stoppers incorporating an air valve are provided together with a simple hand-operated air pump that makes it possible

FIGURE 6.5 A 'Vacuvin' wine saver. (Courtesy of International Innovation Company BV.)

to remove much of the air from a bottle of wine, greatly reducing the oxygen contact and thus increasing the period of time for which the wine can be stored without deterioration. However, this does not work for sparkling wines due to the high volumes of dissolved carbon dioxide: attempting to remove all the air with a pump would eventually lead to all the fizz being removed from the wine! Other systems designed for domestic use rely on spraying an inert gas such as nitrogen into the bottle in order to displace the oxygen before inserting a stopper.

Domestic settings for wine consumption

Drinking wine alone

Wine drinking is often seen as a social event – for example, the famous anthropologist Mary Douglas (1987:4) describes it as an 'essentially social act, performed in a recognised social context'.

However, in many societies the number of people living on their own is on the increase, and even in multi-person households individuals will often find themselves alone and may well wish to drink wine either with a meal or as a means of relaxation.

In some cases, drinking wine alone can lead to excess alcohol consumption especially for those who find it difficult to take a glass or two and put the rest of the bottle aside for another day, so much health education work is directed towards discouraging drinking alone. But in other cases it can be an act with positive social meaning with some sense of esteem – for example, a widow who opens a special bottle from time to time and drinks a glass to her late husband's memory, remembering the wines they shared together.

Wine in the family

Family meals are a traditional context for serving wine, at least to the adults present.

Even in households where wine is only drunk on special occasions, the wine shared at a special birthday or similar celebration may be hugely symbolic: it serves to differentiate the celebration meal from a more everyday meal (for further discussion see Chapter 2). For other households, wine may be drunk at a particular meal each week even though not on other occasions – for example, at the Saturday night dinner or Sunday lunch. In a Jewish household, the sharing of wine in the Shabbat meal on a Friday night, after saying *Kiddush* prayer of blessing, is a deep expression of faith and identity. The act of drinking wine together in a collective setting is a profound symbol of bonding in many societies.

Many households consume wine more regularly. In the UK, 11% of the adults report drinking alcohol on five or more days in the previous week, increasing to 18% of those over 65 (ONS 2013), and whilst this encompasses a wide range of alcoholic drinks, it certainly includes a significant number of households that have wine with their meals on most days.

However, formal family meals are becoming less common in many Western countries: indeed the density of accommodation means that many households do not possess a table where the whole family can sit down for a meal together. Even where there is a dining table of some kind, the complex interplay of different commitments by adults and children means that meals where the whole family eat together may be infrequent.

But if the rare occasions when the family eats together are marked by serving wine, this can add to the significance of the event. In particular, it is often suggested that it is beneficial to future drinking habits if children learn the pattern from their parents of drinking wine in moderation with a meal (see Chapter 9 for research on this issue and the role of family meals as means of wine education).

Entertaining with wine in the home

Where the service of wine in the home shows its greatest cultural significance may be when guests are present. This could range from inviting friends round for an informal evening – sharing a bottle of wine with little or no food alongside – to a formal dinner party when the service of wine to match the food may be a powerful symbol of hospitality or even a means of demonstrating the host's cultural capital, status and esteem.

For many wine lovers, inviting others into their home to share a meal, and then to open some special bottles to share with their guests, may be the central act in their relationship with wine. As explored in Chapter 4, being able to present special wines from prestigious châteaux or appellations that their guests are unlikely to have drunk elsewhere, or where they can speak from first-hand about how the wine is produced, can be a hugely significant marker of esteem. In some cases the guests may be other wine specialists, in which case the main purpose of the meal may be to discuss the wines in detail – though in any gathering of wine connoisseurs there may be some element of competition (Douglas 1987:9).

Many wine connoisseurs are also gourmands who enjoy eating in fine restaurants. However, for someone with an extensive personal wine cellar assembled over many years, the range and quality of wines they are able to serve at home is likely to exceed the wine lists even of top restaurants. In such cases, dining at home with the finest wines from a personal cellar is likely to be a more significant act than any kind of restaurant meal.

Domestic parties

Depending on the size of the home, many households will from time to time host a party of some kind where wine is served to a range of guests. This can range to an informal gathering in an apartment where guests are expected to go into the kitchen and pour their own wines, to sophisticated parties marking special events in a large house with extensive gardens. For some people, the scope to host high-status parties where wine is served to honoured guests may be an important consideration in deciding their choice of home.

A party may simply be an occasion for meeting up with friends or family members, but will often be held to mark a special birthday, initiation of children (through christening or similar religious rights), a family wedding, or maybe a gathering following a funeral, sometimes called a 'wake'. At a party, wine is often much more than simply a drink offered with food: it will frequently play a central role in the cultural identity of the event. Sparkling wines (Champagne, in particular) are often used to mark a special celebration.

It is very likely that guests will be invited to 'drink a toast' to the cause of the celebration, which typically means a ritual of glasses being raised together by all those present, often with a process of 'chinking' where each person's glass is deliberately touched on the glasses of those nearby, and then everyone takes a sip of wine at the same time. In most European countries (and elsewhere) there are common phrases said in unison on such occasions such as 'Cheers' in the UK, 'Santé' in France, 'Sláinte' in Ireland, 'Prost!' in Germany or 'Salute' in Italy (Europe is not Dead 2013). These phrases are usually an expression of good health or well-being to others present – or guests may collectively name the person or couple to whom the toast is directed. At a formal gathering such as a wedding reception, wine is likely to be served at various stages – for example, an aperitif as guests arrive, white and red wines may be offered with different courses of the meal, and then Champagne to toast the couple following speeches. Such communal bonding rituals using food or drink are observed in ethnographic studies of almost all societies.

At a large party with a wide cross-section of guests, wine connoisseurs are unlikely to serve their most valuable wines, whatever the occasion, due to the risks of wasting expensive wine on guests who do not appreciate it. The top wines are more likely to be reserved for smaller gatherings and dinners with guests whose palates are sufficiently refined to appreciate the very best wines. Nevertheless, even at a large party there will be some guests with an appreciation of wine, and no wine connoisseur wishes to find themselves hosting an event where the wines are criticised. So a mid-range wine will normally be offered on such occasions.

However, there are exceptions – for example, at a winter event where 'mulled wine' is to be served (wine heated with spices, sugar and sometimes fruit – also known as *vin chaud* or *glühwein*) even the most conscientious wine-loving host is likely to feel that an ordinary red wine is sufficient to use as the base. Likewise, at an event where 'Buck's fizz' (sparkling wine and orange juice) is offered as an aperitif, no one would insist on using a prestigious Champagne to blend with the orange juice, except perhaps a millionaire who was keen to flaunt their wealth with no concern for any sense of value for money.

Domestic consumption away from the home

We should, of course, note that not all domestic wine consumption literally takes place in the home. Increasingly people choose to take wine on a wide range of outings.

Picnic meals are an obvious example where wine may be consumed in a relaxed setting in the open area – perhaps by a river or in a spot with an attractive view or at an evening picnic possibly linked to an open-air concert or event. As with other settings, the choice of wine on such occasions tells us much about the cultural significance that is given to wine.

At an evening picnic linked to a concert in a stately home, where participants may be taking chairs, tables and tablecloths, the wine may be an important focus. Equally, a daytime outing for a couple may involve a wine specially chosen for a sense of romance – perhaps a sparkling wine or a bottle of rosé. When different members of extended families meet up for a barbeque at an external location, wine will often be on offer for the adults in the group. However, patterns of wine consumption at picnics will often be moderated if one member of the party will have to drive home afterwards.

Other methods of travel thus have particular attractions for wine picnickers. It is becoming more common to see groups of friends travelling by train for a special day out where picnic foods are accompanied by generous supplies of wine (often Champagne or other sparkling wines). Sometimes this is with a deliberate intention for the participants to achieve a measure of inebriation, but it is more likely that wine is simply a symbol of joy and friendship and happiness, clearly identifying the occasion as a 'day off' from normal commitments.

Wine at home: a summary

The home space is widely accepted by ethnographers and sociologists as the most important context for expression of personal identity. It is not surprising, therefore, that understanding how people choose to engage with wine when at home is perhaps the single most important environment for understanding the place of wine in society.

We have seen that 'wine at home' can range from the occasional glass consumed by a solo drinker to lavish dinners where the finest wines are served. We have also noted that the home environment presents one of the greatest risks for excessive alcohol consumption, not least because few people accurately measure the quantities they are drinking in a home situation. But the home environment – particularly for the connoisseur with a significant wine collection – may well be the primary place where personal esteem is sought through the service of fine wines to honoured guests.

For discussion

1 If you go into a home, what can you learn from observing the way in which any wine is stored?
2 What motivates people to buy expensive wines for use at home?
3 To what extent would you expect to find gender differences in terms of the relationship with wine in the home? Does this vary between different countries and social groups?

4   How important are wine-related objects in understanding people's attitudes to wine (e.g. corkscrews, wine glasses, decanters, arrangements for storage of opened and unopened bottles)?
5   For problem drinkers, is the consumption of wine at home likely to be a significant pattern in their behaviour, and if so why?
6   How far does society's changing habits with regard to meals in the home affect people's relationship with wine?

References

Berry Bros & Rudd (2015). *Vintage Chart* [online] at www.bbr.com/vintage-chart.
Broadbent, M. (1991). *The Great Vintage Wine Book II* (London: Mitchell Beazley).
Douglas, M. (1987). A distinct anthropological perspective. In: Douglas, M. (ed.), *Constructive Drinking: Perspectives on Drink from Anthropology* (Cambridge, UK: Cambridge University Press, republished 2003 by Routledge).
Europe is not Dead (2013). *European Toasts* [online] at europeisnotdead.com/disco/words-of-europe/european-toasts/.
ONS (Office for National Statistics) (2013). *Drinking Habits Amongst Adults 2012* [Online] at www.ons.gov.uk.
Robinson, J. (1989). *Vintage Timecharts* (London: Mitchell Beazley).
Ulin, R.C. (2013). Terroir and locality: An anthropological perspective. In: Black, R.E. and Ulin, R.C. (eds), *Vine and Culture: Vineyard to Glass*, pp. 3–15 (London: Bloomsbury).

7
LICENSING LAW, DUTY AND THE ETHICS OF ALCOHOL

Checking the consumption of wine

The dangers of alcohol have been known since the dawn of humanity. In one of the earliest written accounts of wine growing, the book of Genesis in the Bible tells us: 'Noah, a man of the soil, was the first to plant a vineyard. He drank some of the wine and became drunk' (Genesis 9:20–1). This story is set around the year 3000 BC.

Every society that produces wine (or other alcoholic drinks) has to devise a framework to balance the joys, pleasures and status of wine with the risks of over-consumption. In modern societies these balances typically take three forms:

- Education on responsible drinking (or, in some cultures and religions, requiring complete abstinence from consumption of alcohol).
- Restricting the sale of alcohol, typically through a licensing system that controls where alcoholic drinks can be purchased.
- The imposition of taxes or other price controls that restrict consumption by increasing the price of alcoholic drinks (and they can also generate worthwhile revenue for the state, or the body that collects the tax); taxes that are linked directly to specific products such as a bottle of wine are generally described as 'duties'.

The place and meaning of wine in society is linked to these issues, just as much as it is to the metaphors of joy, hedonism and social esteem. We cannot understand the nature of wine as a social symbol without a sound appreciation of checks and balances that society uses to limit or control its consumption.

Each of these checks is discussed in a separate section of this chapter. However, legislation varies enormously from one country to another, and it is impossible in a book of this size to give detailed accounts of the various controls in relation to numerous countries. So, in each of the later sections we focus on England and Wales as an example of a jurisdiction that is rated internationally as having a 'medium level' of strictness with regard to alcohol controls (see below for the assessment of this). But first we look at general principles regarding legislation on the sale and consumption of alcohol and draw some broad international comparisons.

Legal controls on alcohol – general principles

In modern societies, issues of licensing and duties are built into the relevant local or national laws. Many countries also have legal restrictions on the marketing of wine so that it can only be sold in such a way that messages about responsible drinking are included. Much of this chapter is concerned with legal issues.

The European Union

Of the various regions of the world, the European Union (EU) has the highest levels of alcohol consumption per head at 27g per day on average per adult (Anderson *et al.* 2013:1) – this amounts to almost three units per person per day (see p. 141 regarding 'units' of alcohol). Some health researchers such as Anderson and his colleagues estimate that as many as 55 million Europeans drink at levels that could actually be classed as dangerous (AMPHORA Project 2013) – this amounts to more than 10% of the EU population.

However, within the EU the approach to alcohol controls varies hugely between (say) Italy and Sweden (for comparative tables, see Anderson and Baumberg 2006:381–91). In Italy, wine is seen as a normal agricultural product, part of everyday life, and there is an assumption that most people understand how to consume wine responsibly so the legal controls are relatively modest. Wine can generally be bought by anyone aged 16 or over. By contrast, in Sweden, alcohol is seen as much more dangerous: as in many northern countries the local production is primarily distilled spirits (mainly vodka) rather than wine. The country has a history of alcohol abuse, and there is a strong temperance movement. Alcoholic drinks can be sold in bars and restaurants to those over 18, but bottles for home consumption can only be purchased by those aged 20 or over from the '*systembolaget*' – a state monopoly with a nationwide retail network of 418 stores. This system is said to enjoy widespread support in Sweden (Regeringskansliet 2013).

Various scales have been used to measure the relative strictness of alcohol control regimes in different counties – for example, Karlsson and Österberg (2007) describe their 'Bridging the Gap' scale that considers seven factors. Rating 30 European countries (including some non-EU members), out of a potential score of 40 for the strictest possible regime, their scores range from 37.5 for Norway to 4.5 for Luxembourg. They divide the countries into four groups:

- countries in the Nordic area with the strictest policies (Norway, Sweden, Finland);
- countries with medium levels of control such as the UK, Ireland, Denmark, France, and Poland;
- central-European countries with lighter controls where beer is generally drunk more than wine, such as Germany, Austria and the Czech Republic; and
- countries mostly in the Mediterranean with the lightest controls, such as Greece, Italy, Spain and Portugal – although Luxembourg, the most affluent country in Europe, also has very light controls.

However, Karlsson and Österberg stress that their scale only considers *legal* controls: they point out that informal alcohol control tends to operate in Mediterranean countries. The different regulatory approaches are also possibly linked to religious traditions: most of Europe has a Christian heritage, but predominantly Catholic countries in Southern Europe tend to have lighter controls than predominantly Protestant countries. For example, in the UK and in Scandinavia, the temperance movement historically had strong links to Methodist, Baptist and Lutheran Christianity.

Other regions

In other parts of the world, legislation various enormously. In the United States, the famous prohibition years (1920 to 1933) made the sale of all alcoholic beverages illegal except for religious use (such as wine for the Christian Eucharist or Jewish Passover). Even once prohibition was abandoned, the transport of alcohol has continued to be tightly regulated, especially the import from one state to another. The legislation is complex with major variations from state to state, and even within specific local communities. In almost all states the national minimum drinking age is 21 and there are strict time limits during which alcohol can be sold. Some 33 states still have local cities and counties that remain 'dry' (Wikipedia 2015). The structure of alcohol legislation makes it particularly difficult for producers and wine societies or clubs that post or ship wine to members or customers as the alcohol laws vary so widely across states (Sheridan, Cazier and May 2009).

In many Muslim-majority countries the sale of alcohol is prohibited entirely or extremely limited. For example, in Saudi Arabia and Iran only non-alcoholic and low-alcohol beer can be sold; the sale of any other alcoholic beverage carries severe penalties. However, many other countries such as Egypt, Malaysia and Lebanon permit alcohol to be traded by non-Muslims for their own consumption.

Alcohol and driving

Nearly all countries where alcohol is available have restrictions on the consumption of alcohol where it would lead to danger. The focus is typically on the risks of 'drinking and driving' – consuming alcohol before driving a motor vehicle (although similar risks apply to operating any kind of equipment that could lead to injury).

Driving whilst drunk is manifestly extremely dangerous, but even moderate levels of alcohol can lead to impaired judgement and delayed response times while driving, which greatly increase the risk of an accident. However, it is worth noting that other factors such as driving whilst tired (due to lack of sleep or heavy eating) and driving while unwell or under the influence of drugs (even if legally prescribed) can carry similar risks – alcohol is not the only cause of impaired attention by drivers.

As it is notoriously difficult to define the point at which someone is 'drunk' or at least whether their actions are impaired due to alcohol, most legislation is based on 'blood alcohol content' (BAC). This can be measured in grams of alcohol per litre of blood (g/l), or sometimes in milligrams of alcohol per 100 millilitres of blood (mg/100ml), or (especially in the US) it may be shown as a percentage based on grams of alcohol per 100 millilitres of blood (that is a direct measure of the proportion of the person's blood that is in the form of alcohol, if we ignore the fact the alcohol is slightly less dense than water). Care is therefore needed to check the measure when comparing rules. Also, many countries rely on breath testing to avoid the need to take blood samples, so limits can also be expressed in terms of micrograms of alcohol per 100 millilitres of air in the person's breath.

In the EU, most countries prohibit anyone from driving with more than 0.5g/l BAC, although at the time of writing a higher limit of 0.8g/l applies in England and Wales (though in 2014, Scotland reduced the limit to 0.5g/l, following a similar reduction in 2011 in the Republic of Ireland). Some countries (the Czech Republic, Hungary, the Slovak Republic and Romania) have limits of zero, though these can be difficult to enforce, as someone could have a very small level of blood alcohol due to factors such as consuming food products that had started to ferment naturally or due to traces of alcohol consumed a long time previously. A number of countries have lower limits for new drivers and for those driving professionally.

Distinguishing beers, wine and spirits

In many countries, legislation on the sale and taxation of alcohol draws a distinction between three main categories of alcoholic beverages: generally described as beers, wines, and spirits.

- Beers and ciders rarely have more than 6% abv and are seen in many countries as a normal beverage, subject only to limited controls. Although heavy consumption of beer can be harmful, and can certainly lead to dangerous driving, a considerable amount of water has to be consumed with the alcohol that has a dilution effect.

- Wines will typically have between 8.5% and 15% abv – as we saw in Chapter 1 – so there is a greater risk than with beer, in that smaller volumes of the products can lead to inebriation. Nevertheless, wine is still regarded as a normal beverage in many countries, especially when served with food.
- Spirits (primarily brandy, whisky, gin, and vodka) are often treated separately from other alcoholic drinks because of their much higher alcohol content – most spirits are sold at around 40% abv, though some specialist spirits are sold close to their distillation strength, well above this. A beverage with more than around 17% abv is impossible to achieve purely by the fermentation of sugars through the action of yeasts, but by distillation of an alcohol-containing liquid such as beer, wine, or fermented grain or potatoes, a concentrated spirit can be produced. However, it is very easy for someone to get seriously drunk from relatively modest quantities of spirits, and large quantities of spirits can be lethal. The high concentration of alcohol makes spirits attractive for taxation.

Many countries therefore place much tighter controls on the production and sale of spirits than on beers and wines. Certain outlets may be allowed to sell beers and wines, but are not allowed to sell spirits, or the minimum age to purchase spirits may be higher. Indeed, whilst many countries allow people to produce beer and wine freely for personal use (so long as it is not sold), that is not usually the case with spirits. Even to possess a distillation still without an excise licence is an offence.

In some countries there is also a differentiation between the permission needed to sell beer and wine, with greater relaxation in selling beer.

Units of alcohol

Because consumers find it difficult to relate measures such as abv to what they are actually drinking, health education initiatives in many countries now encourage notion of the 'unit of alcohol' and encourage clear labelling of the number of units of alcohol in a particular product in typical glass sizes.

A unit of alcohol is defined as 10ml of pure alcohol. So, for example:

- A small glass (125ml) of wine with an abv of 11% contains 13.75ml of alcohol (125 × 11%) – or about 1.4 units.
- A large glass (250ml) of wine with an abv of 14% contains 35ml of alcohol – or 3.5 units.
- A single serving of spirits (25ml) with an abv of 40% contains 10ml of alcohol – or 1 unit.
- A small glass (50ml) of a fortified wine with an abv of 20% contains 10ml of alcohol or 1 unit.
- A full bottle (750ml) of wine at a typical 13% abv contains 97.5ml of alcohol – almost 10 units – so if two people share a bottle they will consume an average of 5 units each.

Advice on responsible drinking typically focuses on the number of units of alcohol consumed per day or per week. This raises problems of generalisation as the resultant levels of blood alcohol (BAC) that a person will develop from drinking a given number of units will vary considerably depending on the person's body weight and the rate at which each person's body metabolises alcohol and whether the alcohol is consumed with food (which slows down absorption) or on an empty stomach. Nevertheless all alcohol consumed, whilst providing a source of calorific energy, must ultimately be broken down by the liver.

It is widely agreed by clinicians that responsible limits for alcohol consumption are lower for women than men due to a combination of lower average body weight and longer timescales for alcohol to break down. The current recommendations from the UK Department of Health are that adult males should not consume on average more than 3–4 units per day (21–28 units a week) and adult females not more than 2–3 units per day (14–21 units per week) – though with a clear recommendation to have at least one or two alcohol-free days per week (Change4Life 2015; NHS Choices 2015). Alcohol can be particularly damaging for children while their bodies are still growing, and medical advice stresses avoiding alcohol completely except perhaps for those approaching adulthood drinking small quantities under supervision.

Promotion of responsible drinking

The dangers of excessive alcohol consumption are well known. In the short term it can lead to impaired judgement, danger to oneself or others, sexual promiscuity, anti-social behaviour, fights, violence and sexual assaults. In countries such as the UK where alcohol abuse is a common social problem, the short-term consequences of excessive drinking create huge demands on police and others responsible for law and order, and on healthcare services.

Alcohol and health

In the longer term, excessive use of alcohol leads to a wide range of serious health conditions (both mental and physical) and ultimately to premature death. Alcohol dependency – where an individual is physically or psychologically dependent upon drinking alcohol – can lead to problems in the workplace, breakdown of family relationships, domestic violence, crime, and homelessness. Where the dependency becomes compulsive it is described as alcohol addiction.

Government research at household level shows that only 58% of UK adults (aged 16 or over) report that they have drunk alcohol in the previous week (64% of men; 52% of women) (ONS 2013c). These figures have been falling slightly over time, possibly explained by increases in the proportion of people from ethnic and religious minorities who do not drink alcohol at all (the proportion who drink alcohol is considerably higher amongst the white population than amongst people of other ethnicities).

However, the proportion of people drinking heavily is substantial, particularly amongst young adults. The ONS study (2013c) found no less than 35% of female drinkers aged 16–24 had drunk *more than 9 units on one day* in the previous week, and 43% of male drinkers in the same age group had drunk *more than 12 units on one day*.[1] The proportions drinking heavily on one day are smaller amongst older age groups – they are more likely to spread their drinking – so although 'binge drinking' is rarer, the *frequency* of drinking is higher. For example, in the 65+ age group, 23% of men and 14% of women reported drinking alcohol on at least five out of the previous seven days (ONS 2013c).

In England it has been estimated that 35% of admissions to accident and emergency (A&E) departments of hospitals are alcohol-related, rising to 70% at weekends (Campbell 2010). Spending on the treatments of such cases has been estimated at £3.5bn (Health and Social Care Information Centre 2014) – amounting to more than 3% of *all* expenditure by the National Health Service (NHS). In 2012 it was reported that there were 8,367 deaths *directly* related to alcohol in UK – around 1.5% of all deaths that year (ONS 2013a, 2013b). Around 1.6 million people in England – around 3% of the population – are believed to be alcohol-dependent (Alcohol Concern 2014) – although the numbers with some degree of alcohol dependency may be much higher.

Nevertheless, heavy drinking is by no means centred on wine. The ONS (2013c) study found that beers, lager and cider were the most popular drink for males in all age groups (consumed by 59% of male drinkers compared to just 30% who had drunk wine in the previous week). For females, wine is more likely to be the drink of choice (64% of female drinkers had drunk wine or sparkling wine in the previous week) – but even amongst women, spirits are more popular than wine in the 16–24 age group.

But although there is wide consensus on the dangers of excessive drinking, especially by young people, habits vary substantially between countries. Binge drinking by young people is sometimes seen to be an issue centred on the UK. In the USA, for example, where the legal age of drinking is 21, one study found that parents have a major influence on wine-drinking preferences by those aged 21–35, a group that accounts for 30% of the American wine-drinking population (Halstead 2014).

Whilst the consequences of excessive alcohol consumption are clear in all cultures, it does not necessarily follow that alcohol is always harmful. Many studies suggest that moderate consumption has few adverse effects and, in some respects, may even be beneficial. For example, moderate amounts of alcohol can lead people to relax, which can reduce stress, which may in turn alleviate a wide range of stress-related conditions. Indeed, much of this book explores ways in which wine can have a positive social value.

The ONS (2013c) study asked respondents about their perceptions of their own health: it found that those who consumed alcohol on three days per week had the highest perception of their health (88% regarded their health as good or very good) as compared to those who did not drink at all or those who drank on seven days a week (for both the non-drinkers and seven-day drinkers only 74% considered themselves healthy). Nevertheless, such statistics do not amount to proof of a causal relationship – those who do not drink at all are often poorer than the rest of the population and those who drink seven days a week are also more likely to smoke regularly – so in both cases their poorer health experience *may* be due to other factors.

However, the possible health benefits of moderate drinking lead to a highly contested field of research, as headline statistics regarding the beneficial effect of alcohol on one aspect of life or on one medical condition may be outweighed by increased risk in relation to other conditions. Beardsmore (2010) discusses a range of research in this field in order to argue that 'a diet including wine, beer and spirits in moderation is *not* bad for your health'. In particular, he refers to a J-curve suggested by some researchers that modest amounts of alcohol consumption may lead to health benefits, but this is reversed as consumption increases.

Whatever the precise conclusions on this issue, for the most part health professionals agree that promoting responsible drinking is more likely to be effective than encouraging complete abstinence.

The drinks industry perspective

At one time the drinks industry was heavily opposed to publicity warnings of the risks of alcohol, viewing such messages as unnecessary and leading to potential loss of sales. However, towards the end of the twentieth century, and certainly in the twenty-first century, that position has changed dramatically, with most wine producers – and the producers of many other alcoholic drinks – keen to embrace the responsible drinking message.

In the UK, the Portman Group was established as long ago as 1989 as the 'responsibility body for drinks producers in the UK'. It is funded by 11 major producers of alcoholic beverages that together account for more than 50% of the UK market. The Group has developed various voluntary codes on the labelling and marketing of alcoholic drinks and provides a forum for liaison with government on responsible drinking practice and legislation. In 2004 the Group developed the website www.drinkaware.co.uk to provide advice to consumers (now operated by an independent charity, to separate it from the industry). They report that over time 'the UK's drinks producers have delivered a series of substantive pledges to improve labelling, cut units, fund alcohol education, and support community schemes to tackle alcohol harms' (Portman Group 2014).

All alcohol advertising in the UK must now carry a responsible drinking message – many producers will say 'Enjoy [name of product] responsibly' or 'in moderation' – and a reference is usually given to the Drinkaware website.

Moreover, in 2012, 34 leading producers and retailers of alcoholic drinks signed up to a pledge proposed by government to remove a billion units of alcohol from the UK market by 2015. With total sales amounting to around 52 billion units per year, this would mean a reduction of around 2% in total alcohol consumption. The reduction was to be achieved primarily by reducing the alcoholic content of drinks sold, and by making low-alcohol drinks more widely available – although other measures such as encouraging consumers to 'drink less but better' (see p. 152), a message that is particularly relevant for wine drinkers, may also have helped. An interim report (Department of Health 2014) found that in just two years, between 2011 and 2013, the total alcohol on the UK market had dropped by 1.9 billion units – almost double the target – although changes to the alcohol content of beers contributed much more than wine to this reduction. Of this total reduction, 0.6 billion units were attributed to reduced sales (which could in part be due to pressures on consumer spending at a time of recession rather than a permanent change in patterns of consumption). But the government estimated that 1.3 billion units of the reduction was directly due to industry initiatives to reduce alcohol content.

Similar initiatives have been developed internationally – in particular an EU-wide scheme 'Wine in Moderation' (WIM) is supported primarily by major companies in the wine trade. Based in Brussels, WIM has board members drawn from a range of EU countries, although it is also supporting responsible drinking initiatives in other regions such as South America. Its website www.wineinmoderation.eu uses the French strapline 'Art de vivre' and seeks to promote a 'culture of moderation' (specifically in relation to wine). WIM make strong use of the J-curve argument (see p. 144) and suggest that:

> Wine is ... integral to European life and culture. Each wine is a natural, unique product ... If consumed in accordance with the recommended guidelines, moderate wine consumption by adults, as part of a balanced diet, is compatible with a healthy lifestyle (Wine in Moderation 2011).

Some commentators, including a number of academic researchers, are dismissive of such initiatives, suggesting that the drinks industry is only prepared to embrace responsible drinking 'in order to create regulatory environments conducive to corporate interests' (Drinks Business 2015:3). But for producers of premium alcoholic drinks that focus on issues such as aesthetic quality – which includes most wine producers – the responsible drinking message fits well with other messages. No producer or retailer of fine wines wishes to see their products associated with 'binge drinking'.

Moreover, the message of responsible drinking can encourage trading up – in other words, consumers may be led to drinking smaller quantities of a more expensive product. This is beneficial both in health terms (less alcohol consumed) and in the consumer's aesthetic experience if it leads to enjoyment of a wine with greater length and more complexity than a cheaper alternative.

Legal controls on the sale of alcohol

Because of the risks associated with excessive and inappropriate consumption of alcohol almost all countries place controls on how and when it can be sold – though as noted at the start of this chapter, there is a broad spectrum between those with strict controls and those where the rules are much lighter.

England and Wales is an example of a jurisdiction considered to have a 'medium level' of control (Karlsson and Österberg 2007). It should be noted that within the UK, alcohol licensing is a devolved matter so it is not possible to speak of a single UK regime: slightly different legislation applies in Scotland and Northern Ireland.

The sale of alcohol in England and Wales is governed by the Licensing Act 2003 and by various statutory instruments and codes of practice made under the Act. The Act is not solely concerned with the sale of alcohol: it also deals with activities such as 'the provision of late night refreshment' (hot food takeaway providers) and 'regulated entertainment' (for example, theatre and dance) that are not relevant here. In relation to alcohol it deals with sales in the on- and off-trades and also the supply of alcohol in clubs, because it is not technically a sale when a club provides something to a person who is a member of the club even though the member makes a payment. (But for simplicity the discussion below does not include clubs.)

The Act sets out four 'licensing objectives'[2] that underpin all its provisions:

1 The prevention of crime and disorder.
2 Public safety.
3 The prevention of public nuisance.
4 The protection of children from harm.

On a day-to-day basis, licensing decisions are taken by the relevant licensing authority, which in most cases is the local council. Licensing is considered both at an individual level and in terms of premises. In general, alcohol can only be sold under the supervision of an individual who holds a personal licence under the Act, and from a venue that holds a premises licence and in compliance with the conditions laid down in the premises licence. The venue could be a shop, bar, restaurant, hotel, nightclub, theatre, conference centre, sports venue, college, university or any location at all where alcohol is to be provided. A mail-order wine merchant needs a premises licence to cover the premises from which the wines are dispatched, even if customers will never visit that location. Special arrangements apply to sales from vehicles or trains.

Personal licences

To become a personal licence holder a person must be aged 18 or over, hold a relevant qualification showing understanding of licensing law, and be free of relevant convictions. Many colleges offer a one-day course including a multiple-choice examination at the end leading to one of the permitted qualifications. An application is then made to the licensing authority to issue the personal licence. This involves a one-off fee, currently £37, and following the Deregulation Act 2015 a personal licence lasts indefinitely.

A venue wishing to sell alcohol – whether for consumption on or off the premises – first needs a personal licence holder who will be the 'designated premises supervisor' (DPS) for the venue. Many people in managerial roles in the wine and hospitality trades are thus required, as a condition of their job, to be personal licence holders.

Premises licences

An application for a premises licence involves submitting detailed plans of the premises, the name of the DPS, and an 'operating schedule' explaining how alcohol is to be sold, the hours of opening, and steps that will be taken to promote the licensing objectives – for example, security arrangements and arrangements to ensure alcohol is not sold to children. For venues seen as high risk in terms of the potential for alcohol-related disorder, the operating schedule may be the subject of detailed negotiation with the licensing authority with input from the police and environmental health. Applications for premises licences are published allowing others to object. There is an application fee and if the premises licence is agreed an annual fee is payable – these fees are dependent on the size of the venue and the number of people accommodated. For very smallest venues the annual fee is £70, but for the largest sports venues able to hold tens of thousands of people, the annual fee could be over £30,000.

There are no set hours for the sale of alcohol: the hours are determined by the operating schedule. In the case of a residential venue such as a hotel a 24-hour licence is not seen as problematic if night sales are restricted to hotel guests, but there is considerable controversy regarding bars and clubs holding 24-hour licences and many prefer to apply for a premises licence with more limited hours. Where 24-hour licensing is agreed, the authority will impose strict conditions, because of the risks of alcohol-related disorder.

Temporary event notices

For venues only wishing to sell alcohol at occasional social or fundraising events (e.g. community centres, churches and schools) it is possible to submit a 'temporary event notice' (TEN) to the licensing authority at a one-off fee of £21, which replaces the need for a premises licence. It should be noted that if tickets are sold for an event where alcohol is included in the price (e.g. a wine tasting or a fundraising dinner with wine) this means that alcohol is sold and a TEN is required if the venue does not have a premises licence. The TEN can also be used for people running occasional supper clubs in their homes and similar domestic events where wine is provided and a charge is made.

The individual applying for the TEN is treated as the premises supervisor, but does not have to hold a personal licence if no more than five TENs are obtained per year; however, by becoming a PLH this increases to a maximum of 50 TENs per year. Most TENs are for short events, but a TEN can, if necessary, cover an event lasting up to a week. However, the maximum number of people on the premises cannot exceed 499 (so large festivals need a premises licence even if they are one-off events).

Offences

The Act allows significant penalties to be imposed for any breaches of these terms. For example, selling alcohol outside the circumstances permitted by a premises licence or TEN is a serious offence that could potentially lead to a fine of up to £20,000 and six months' imprisonment for anyone responsible.[3] Even having alcohol on display, or held with the intention of selling on an unlicensed basis, is an offence.

There are also serious penalties for selling alcohol to persons under 18,[4] or allowing others to do so, which can lead to fines of up to £5,000. To avoid uncertainty with young people who appear to be over 18 but who are actually younger, most venues insist on evidence of age for anyone who appears to be under 25. Many retailers have suffered penalties because of occasional incidents where a member of staff failed to check the age of a customer – both the DPS (usually the manager) and the member of staff concerned can be penalised. It is also an offence for a young person under 18 to attempt to buy alcohol and a more serious offence for someone to buy alcohol on behalf of a person aged under 18 or knowingly delivering alcohol to a person under 18.[5] Those under 18 are not allowed to sell alcohol even if the customer is older, so in supermarkets, checkout staff aged under 18 must call a supervisor to authorise the sale whenever a customer is buying wine or other alcohol.[6]

A limited exception allows beer or wine (but not spirits) to be served to 16 or 17 year olds with a meal served at a table with at least one person aged 18 or over (though the drinks must be ordered and paid for by the adult). This is intended to allow families dining together to share beer or wine with young people approaching adulthood. However, many restaurants are unfamiliar with this rule and because of the risk of penalties when the Act is breached, they may refuse to serve alcohol of any kind to a person who is clearly under 18, even in this situation.

The Act also imposes serious penalties for selling alcohol to a person who is drunk, or to anyone attempting to buy alcohol for someone who is drunk.[7] There are also specific offences for disorderly conduct on licensed premises or when a person who is drunk refuses to leave the premises when requested to do so.[8]

Effectiveness of the licensing regime

The Licensing Act 2003 was intended by the government of the time to bring in a fresh modern approach to the sale of alcohol, without restrictions such as fixed licensing hours, in the hope of transforming England and Wales into a more 'café culture' where alcohol consumption was a natural social activity linked to responsible drinking.

Following implementation of the Act from 2005 there was much media criticism, especially on the idea of 'all-night drinking' and there were attempts to highlight increased instances of binge drinking and drunken behaviour allegedly as a result of the Act. However, the Act considerably strengthened the powers of licensing authorities and the police, and a number of studies a few years after its implementation found little or no evidence of increased disorder. One academic study, which examined the views of two-thirds of licensing authorities, reported:

> The findings from this survey – in agreement with other research – have not found a consistent picture across the country regarding the effects of licensing change on alcohol-related harms; but reports indicate that, overall, there has been little change for the better or for the worse (Foster et al. 2007).

However, licensing law is a blunt instrument for managing and encouraging the responsible use of alcohol. Binge drinking and anti-social behaviour by young people who have consumed excessive alcohol continues to be a problem in many English towns and cities, and the media report increasing instances of rapes and sexual assault linked to high levels of alcohol consumption. Some suggest that the Act is not properly applied and enforced – in particular, it is rumoured that there are many instances in pubs and clubs where a customer who is already drunk is supplied with further alcohol (in breach of the Act) but no action is taken to prevent this.

But instances of drink driving have fallen considerably and controls on the sale of alcohol to those under 18 are manifestly much stronger than in the past. Overall levels of alcohol consumption are falling as more people shun alcohol entirely. So the picture remains mixed. It must also be noted that most studies on licensing issues do not distinguish wine consumption from other alcoholic drinks: the most serious instances of drunkenness often involve consumption of spirits.

Duties and price controls on the sale of alcohol

One of the simplest ways in which governments can influence the consumption of alcohol is by imposing duties or other taxes that serve to increase the price. The simple argument is that if a bottle of wine costs more, fewer people will buy, and those who do so may reduce the number of bottles bought. This will tend to reduce the overall consumption.

The imposition of government duties and taxes on the sale of particular products is also a very effective means of generating revenue that can be used for other government expenditure – for example, on the provision of a free health service. So, whilst taxes on wine are unpopular with consumers, their imposition can lead to a double win in terms of government policies.

However, if this argument is taken too far, little wine will be sold and the government will lose out in terms of revenue and it will destroy jobs in wine and hospitality trades. It may also be politically unacceptable if wine drinkers are tempted to vote for another political party.

Collecting duties

Duties are one of the oldest forms of taxation as they are relatively simple to collect. The tax collector finds a suitable physical location through which merchants have to pass with the goods they wish to sell, and refuses to let them pass without paying the duty. Traditionally, duties were collected at key bridges across rivers or gates into a city as farmers brought their goods for sale. At that stage no one can be sure whether the goods will sell or what price they will attract, so duties have traditionally been collected at a fixed rate according to the weight or volume of goods (rather than being based on the retail price as with more modern sales taxes like VAT or GST, which can only be collected after the goods are sold). In the case of wine, duties were traditionally charged as a price per barrel – nowadays expressed as a price per hectolitre of the product – which converts to a fixed price per bottle.

In the case of a country like the UK where the vast majority of wine is imported, duties have been traditionally collected at seaports where shipments of wine arrive. This is relatively straightforward, although smugglers have always looked for ways to get round the system! For a country that for many years produced little or no wine, a significant duty on wine was also attractive because it imposes a significant price increase on goods from abroad that could be taxed as luxury products with damaging local industry. However, EU member states are not allowed to set duties in a way that discriminates between products from different member states, so the rising quantity of English wines are subject to the same duties as those from abroad.

However, countries where most wines are produced and sold locally have found it much less attractive to impose high duties on wine, as to do so damages local winegrowers by making it harder to sell their wines. In practice, too, it is hard to collect duties efficiently if much of the trade is very local.

There is a wide range in rates of duties between different countries. One analyst reports that 'the global average import duty rate for wine is 0.5%, with a minimum of 0% and a maximum of 3000%' (Duty Calculator 2015).

Tables published by the European Commission (2015) show a huge range even within the EU member states. Some 16 EU countries impose no duty at all on still wine – these include Germany, Austria, Spain, Italy, Luxembourg, Hungary, the Czech Republic, Greece, Bulgaria and Romania. Of the 13 countries that do levy some kind of duty, the rates (expressed in euro for 750ml bottle at a typical abv between 8.5% and 15%) range from €0.03 per bottle in France to €3.19 per bottle in Ireland. The UK is the second highest country, charging the equivalent €2.63 per bottle (£2.05 in sterling) and the third highest is Sweden with duty at the equivalent of €2.08 per bottle.

Many countries charge higher rates of duty on sparkling wines and on products over 15% abv (which will usually be fortified wines). Again the highest EU rate is in Ireland, where the duty on sparkling wine is €6.37 a bottle (plus a further 23% VAT).

Whether or not duty is charged, all EU countries charge VAT on the sale of wine (and where duty applies, the VAT is calculated on the total price *including* duty – so even the duty is subject to VAT in addition). The rates of VAT vary between 13% in Portugal and 25% in Denmark, Sweden and Croatia (20% in the UK).

Using duties and sales taxes to manage the price of wine

The imposition of increased duties and taxes is often seen as effective in curbing consumption of an undesirable product – certainly in the case of cigarettes, the increase in rates of taxation are widely believed to have contributed to a reduction in smoking.

But in the case of wine, the argument is more complex as most health experts argue for the consumption of wine in moderation rather than complete abstinence. Even in countries such as the UK with modest wine production, the sale and distribution of wine, and its role in the hospitality trade creates viable industries that contribute significantly to the economy.

It is self-evident that increasing the price of wine through the imposition of duties hits the poor much more than the rich, but problems of excess consumption are present across all social classes.

Duties also have the effect of simply adding a fixed price to each bottle. As we saw in Chapter 3, this means the duty may amount to a very significant element in the cost of a cheap wine, but only a fraction of the total cost of a very expensive wine. So those buying cheaper wines – who are likely to be poorer – end up spending a much higher proportion on duty than those buying more expensive wines, which is a socially regressive taxation policy.

It is also worth noting that the duty is the same whether wine is sold for consumption on or off the premises, but since prices are normally much higher in the on-trade, the duty forms a smaller proportion of the total price.

It is perhaps fairer to tax wine as a proportion of the sale price, using VAT rather than duty. But few governments wish to take the unpopular step of setting a VAT rate on alcohol that is higher than that charged on other consumer goods.

Moreover, excessively high rates of duty and tax can encourage substantial levels of cross-border shopping from other countries, which may harm the domestic market and lead to loss of tax revenues.

Minimum pricing

As an alternative to increasing prices through duties and taxes, there has been considerable debate in some countries (especially the UK) on the idea of 'minimum pricing'. The idea is that a minimum price is set per unit of alcohol, applicable to all alcoholic beverages, such that it would be illegal to sell to consumers below that price. A figure of £0.50 per unit has been suggested – so, for example, the minimum legal selling price for a bottle of wine containing ten units of alcohol would be £5 – though the effect would be more dramatic on spirits, as the minimum price for a 700ml bottle of spirits at 40% abv would be £14 – a significant increase on the current prices of supermarkets' own label spirits.

The charity Alcohol Concern (2015) has been campaigning for some time to introduce minimum pricing. They say: 'This campaign targets high strength alcoholic drinks that [are] sold very cheaply – drinks that are often consumed by the heaviest drinkers, as well as by younger drinkers. Moderate drinkers will feel little effect from minimum pricing'.

There has been a particular concern about supermarkets selling multi-packs of beers and ciders at very low prices, in some cases at a loss, in order to encourage shoppers into their stores. The very cheap prices of these products lead to excessive consumption, it is argued. The proposal is supported by the four Chief Medical Officers in the UK (NHS Health Scotland 2015) and research undertaken at the University of Sheffield (Brennan et al. 2014) is widely quoted in demonstrating the health benefits of minimum pricing.

In Scotland a minimum price of £0.50 per unit has been enacted in the Alcohol (Minimum Pricing) (Scotland) Act 2012, though at the time of writing it has not yet been implemented pending an appeal to the European Court of Justice referred by the Scottish Court of Session on the application of the Scotch Whisky Association.

Critics of minimum pricing point out, however, that by setting a minimum price it removes competition and allows retailers to make much larger profits, typically at the expense of those at the poorer end of society who are forced to pay more for their alcohol. The alternative of increasing duties means that the additional revenue would go to the Exchequer.

In the meantime, an 'alcohol floor price' has been established in England and Wales by means of a mandatory licensing condition linked to all premises licences under the Licensing Act 2003. This makes it illegal to sell alcohol at less than the price of the duty pus VAT, which at the present time creates a floor price of £2.46 for a 750ml bottle of wine (Home Office 2014).

Drink better but less

The effect of increased duties (or minimum pricing) serves to make wine more expensive at the lower end of the price scale, but it also makes it proportionately more attractive for consumers to spend more on a bottle of wine, as a smaller proportion of the price is spent in duty and more is spent on the wine, as we saw in Chapter 3.

A number of initiatives in various countries have focused on encouraging wine consumers to 'drink better but less' (see Lyons 2014 for an American example) – often promoted by wine writers rather than government agencies. In other words, consumers are encouraged to spend the money they would allocate to buying wine on a smaller quantity of higher quality wines. This is likely to lead to increased pleasure for the consumer as well as health benefits – indeed most wine connoisseurs would naturally choose their wines on this basis. It is also popular in the wine trade, because more expensive wines are often sold with larger margins, and shipping fewer bottles to achieve the same turnover means substantial savings in logistics.

Some see the message of responsible drinking as being in opposition to the enjoyment of wine, but this need not be the case. The concept of 'drinking better but less' is an appropriate note on which to end this chapter, as it brings the issues of responsible drinking in line with the priorities of those seeking greater aesthetic pleasure in wine drinking – a theme that has been at the centre of many other chapters of this book.

For discussion

1. What are the main causes of excessive consumption by wine drinkers?
2. How far can the risks of excess wine consumption be addressed through voluntary changes of policy by (a) wine retailers and (b) pubs, bars and clubs?
3. What do the changing patterns of alcohol consumption across different age groups imply for future alcohol policy?
4. How far would you agree that the drinks industry is only prepared to embrace responsible drinking 'in order to create regulatory environments conducive to corporate interests'?
5. Is alcohol an 'easy target' for taxation?
6. To what extent do you consider the following measures help to promote a society where wine is consumed safely and responsibly: (a) licensing law; (b) duty and taxation; (c) minimum pricing; (d) publicity campaigns supported largely by the trade such as Drinkaware.co.uk or WineinModeration.eu; (e) publicity campaigns run by Government health departments?
7. Is the message 'drink better but less' likely to promote significant changes in behaviour?

Notes

1. It should be noted that in England, under the Licensing Act 2003, 16 and 17 year olds cannot legally purchase alcohol, nor can others buy alcohol on their behalf apart from a limited exception in relation to restaurant meals (see pp. 145–8). So any drinking reported in surveys by those aged 16/17 (if they are complying with the law) should only have taken place in restaurants when dining with an adult or in domestic settings where someone aged 18+ has purchased alcohol originally intended for adults but then decides (after the time of purchase) to share it with the young person(s) concerned.

2   Licensing Act 2003, s. 4.
3   Licensing Act 2003, ss. 136–138.
4   Licensing Act 2003, ss. 146–147.
5   Licensing Act 2003, ss. 149, 151.
6   Licensing Act 2003, s. 153.
7   Licensing Act 2003, ss. 141–142.
8   Licensing Act 2003, ss. 140, 143.

References

Alcohol Concern (2014). *Statistics on Alcohol* [online] at www.alcoholconcern.org.uk/help-and-advice/statistics-on-alcohol/.

Alcohol Concern (2015). *Minimum Unit Pricing* [online] at www.alcoholconcern.org.uk/what-we-do/campaigns/minimum-unit-pricing/.

AMPHORA Project (2013). *10 Main Findings from AMPHORA* [Online] at www.amphoraproject.net

Anderson, P. and Baumberg, B. (2006). *Alcohol in Europe: A Public Health Perspective* (London: Institute of Alcohol Studies).

Anderson, P., Braddick, F., Reynolds, J. and Gual, A. (eds) (2013). *Alcohol Policy in Europe: Evidence from AMPHORA*, 2nd edn (Barcelona: The AMPHORA project) [Online] at www.amphoraproject.net.

Beardsmore, R. (2010). *Guilt-Free Drinking* (Birmingham: Vinifera).

Brennan, A., Meng, Y., Holmes, J., Hill-McManus, D. and Meier, P. (2014). Potential benefits of minimum unit pricing for alcohol versus a ban on below cost selling in England 2014: Modelling study. *British Medical Journal*, 349:g5452.

Campbell, D. (2010). Alcohol questions in A&E could cut £2.7bn NHS bill, say doctors. *Guardian*, 20 March.

Change4Life (2015). *Alcohol Units and Guidelines: The Lower Risk Daily Guidelines* [online] at www.nhs.uk/change4life/Pages/alcohol-lower-risk-guidelines-units.aspx.

Department of Health, UK (2014). *Responsibility Deal: Monitoring the Number of Units of Alcohol Sold – Second Interim Report, 2013 Data* [Online] at www.gov.uk/government/statistics/units-of-alcohol-sold.

Drinks Business (2015). Trade's 'sway on policy' slammed. *Drinks Business*, January, p. 16.

Duty Calculator (2015). *HS Tariff Codes, Import Duty & Taxes for Wine* [online] at www.dutycalculator.com/popular-import-items/import-duty-and-taxes-for-wine/.

European Commission (2015). *Excise Duty Tables – Part I Alcoholic Beverages* [online] at http://ec.europa.eu/taxation_customs/resources/documents/taxation/excise_duties/alcoholic_beverages/rates/excise_duties-part_i_alcohol_en.pdf.

Foster, J., Herring, R., Waller, S. and Thom, B. (2007). *Implementation of the Licensing Act 2003: A National Survey – Report to the Alcohol Education and Research Council* [online] at www.alcoholresearchuk.org/downloads/finalReports/AERC_FinalReport_0054.pdf

Halstead, L. (2014). Interview as reported in 'parents guide to millennials' drinking' in *Drinks Business*, 146(Nov), p. 16.

Health and Social Care Information Centre (2014). *Statistics on Alcohol England 2014* [Online] at www.hscic.gov.uk/catalogue/PUB14184/alc-eng-2014-rep.pdf.

Home Office (2014). *Guidance on Banning the Sale of Alcohol Below the Cost of Duty Plus VAT* [online] at www.gov.uk/government/uploads/system/uploads/attachment_data/file/311735/Guidance_on_BBCS_3.pdf.

Karlsson, T. and Österberg, E. (2007). Scaling alcohol control policies across Europe. *Drugs: Education, Prevention, and Policy*, 14(6), 499–511.

Lyons, W. (2014). How to drink less but better. *Wall Street Journal*, 4 September [online] at www.wsj.com/articles/how-to-drink-less-but-better-1409258589.

NHS Choices (2015). *Alcohol Units* [online] at www.nhs.uk/Livewell/alcohol/Pages/alcohol-units.aspx.

NHS Health Scotland (2015). *Alcohol Minimum Pricing* [online] at www.healthscotland.com/topics/health/alcohol/MinimumPricing.aspx.

ONS (Office for National Statistics) (2013a). *Deaths in the UK* [Online] at www.ons.gov.uk.

ONS (2013b). *Alcohol-Related Deaths in the United Kingdom, Registered in 2012* and *Deaths in the UK* [Online] at www.ons.gov.uk.

ONS (2013c). *Drinking Habits Amongst Adults 2012* [Online] at www.ons.gov.uk.

Portman Group (2014). *Portman Group Leading Responsible Alcohol Standards* [Online] at www.portmangroup.org.uk/home.

Regeringskansliet (2013) [Government offices of Sweden]. *Information seminar on Sweden's Alcohol Policy and the Role of Systembolaget* [Online] at www.government.se/sb/d/16138/a/208532.

Sheridan, M., Cazier, J.A. and May, D.B. (2009) Leisure, wine and the internet: Exploring the factors that impact the purchase of wine online. *International Journal of Electronic Marketing and Retailing*, 2, 284–297.

Wikipedia (2015). *List of Dry Communities by U.S. State* [Online] at http://en.wikipedia.org/wiki/List_of_dry_communities_by_U.S._state.

Wine in Moderation (2011). *WineinModeration.eu – Stakeholder Brochure* (Brussels: Wine in Moderation).

8
MARKETING OF THE WINE EXPERIENCE

This chapter explores the complexity that surrounds the marketing of wine. At one level wine is merely a product to be bought and sold; however, to achieve this it is important to understand the complexity within the marketing of wine. Kotler (2008:12) states that 'Marketing is the social process by which individuals and groups obtain what they need and want through creating and exchanging products and value with others'.

Within the wine sector the role of sales and marketing is undertaken by many different people in different contexts, for example, marketing may be seen to be undertaken by a salesperson in a supermarket or wine shop, specialist wine dealers, a waiter, a sommelier or marketing executive. Each of them plays a role in the marketing process and all of them undertake within their roles the creation of the wine experience: the creation of value and exchange in some form or another.

As such this chapter explores the various aspects of marketing that form the contemporary landscape of the wine market and the various themes and issues this raises for the marketeer. In addition the various notions of value, values and value creation are examined within the context of the consumption and appreciation of wine, the ethics of marketing and the ethical consumer.

But before turning to the mechanisms of marketing it is important to understand the nature and landscape of the themes that create and underpin the contemporary landscape of wine marketing.

The contemporary landscape of wine marketing

In a recent paper Lockshin and Corsi (2012:4) undertook a review of academic literature that focused on the marketing of wine between 2004 and 2012. The analysis below follows their approach in identifying three thematic areas of interest within the marketing of wine.

Theme 1: context and location of purchase

Under this theme, we consider the actual locations where wine is purchased by consumers: the retail environment (off-sales), online purchasing (also called off-sales), and the purchase of wine in bars and restaurants for on-premises consumption (on-trade). We also consider the role of social media as a trigger for purchase.

Retail wine purchasing: The major focus here is on how consumers purchase wine in stores. Most research in this area attempts to understand purchasing within the context of supermarkets, where generally customers are classified as 'low-involvement' customers (see Chapter 4 for discussion) and buy wine like any of their other groceries. The important marketing themes are generally focused on measuring intended purchasing, as influenced by the sensory characteristics of wine, personal characteristics in terms of the consumers' involvement in the wine culture, and purchasing contexts in which consumer choices were made. In addition there is a heavy focus on the more traditional characteristics of marketing, including the influence of price on consumers' behaviour (Hollebeek *et al.* 2007; Ritchie 2007) and the role of promotions (Lockshin and Knott 2009) or tastings (Orth and Bourrain 2005) on consumer choice.

Different levels of retail outlets cater for different levels of consumer purchase, as discussed in Chapter 3. The higher the status of the wine, the more planning will go into the purchase and the greater the need to use a specialist wine merchant. In particular, with fine wines the purchase may well be made under the en primeur system, where there may be a delay of months or years between placing the ordering and receiving the wine.

Online wine purchasing: The research undertaken on online wine purchasing concentrated on purchasing behaviour of consumers, identification of the different behaviours adopted by different segments, or the barriers found in purchasing online. From the research undertaken in this area, price and convenience were the major factors for the use of online-platforms. According to Lockshin and Corsi (2012:5) the online market now represents about 5% of the total wine market in the developed world. However, there are still a number of barriers, the first being the issue around trust: trust of the website and payment methods and trust in the wine as it is not possible to taste it or even hold prior to purchasing. However, probably the major barrier concerns the technological knowledge resource of customers. Even within clearly identified demographic groups, IT literacy and engagement can differ greatly. Additionally, the selling of wine online also creates different legal considerations for sellers (as discussed in Chapter 7): in particular, as the buyer is largely anonymous it is difficult to guarantee whether the customer is of legal age to purchase wine. Sheridan, Cazier and May (2009) identified this issue as a particular cause of concern in markets such as America, as the laws relating to alcohol varies greatly from state to state. Thus it may be legal in the wine seller's or producer's state to sell alcohol to someone that is 18, but illegal in another state.

On-premise purchasing: This sector was dominated by the consumption behaviour and preferences of customers in restaurants, pubs, clubs and cafés. Lockshin and Corsi (2012) identify that this area is significantly under-researched; however, research has shown that customers are generally less confident with wine in a restaurant compared to a retail context. In pubs and clubs there is little choice; wine is usually sold in generic terms, purely by grape variety or brand name, as noted in Chapter 1. Thus distinguishing characteristics such as vintage, producer or even country of origin are not disseminated. So in short, consumer choice is governed by the fact that there is no choice. However, a limited number of high-end bars specialise in offering a wide range of wine by the glass (using appropriate storage systems to prevent deterioration) often with extensive background information to assist the consumer to choose.

It is clear that within the context of restaurants or even cafés (where licensed for the sale of alcohol) many consumers rely heavily on recommendations from the sommelier or waiter. If this advice is not possible they search back in their memory to attempt to remember a wine they last enjoyed. In addition to the availability of advice, the communicative staging is also important, as the information given on wine menus, displays of easily identifiable brands or regions' wines, or even tasting notes on walls, all reduce barriers to consumption and perceptions of risk.

Social media: The use of social media within contemporary marketing practices continues to proliferate. As such there is much research being undertaken about the use and effects of social media on consumer wine preference and behaviour. The impact of social media within wine studies has been largely undeveloped, but there is much evidence that with certain generations social media is key to increasing consumption and building relationships with customers. However, even if social media is employed to create awareness of particular wine products, the consumer must generally be directed to one of the channels above in order to make a purchase.

Nevertheless, in the marketing of wine the impulse purchasing driven by social media may not necessarily be the type of behaviour the drinks industry wishes to develop. In fact there are many ethical concerns about the use of social media in wine and alcohol marketing as it can be seen to be promoting unhealthy and excessive drinking patterns (see Chapter 7 for more on these issues). The role of social media in wine marketing is still in its infancy; however, the industry will have to think wisely about how it is used in the marketing process.

Theme 2: people, places and culture

This area of research considers factors such as the segmentation of consumers, and the relationship between wine marketing and consumer lifestyles – see Chapter 4 for a broader discussion of these issues.

Segmentation: This largely involves the classification of different types of consumers, and their subsequent purchasing behaviour based upon their attitudes and demographic profile, such as age, gender, ethnicity, income, education, etc. According to Lockshin and Corsi (2012) there is little research being undertaken in the area of the impact of traditional segmentation, and that the use of models developed by Spawton (1991) still dominate the approach to segmentation in the industry. However, there has been a gradual shift towards a more lifestyle approach of marketing, as discussed in Chapter 4.

Wine lifestyle: Much of the analysis focuses on measuring or grouping consumers into those who have a lifestyle/activities related to wine versus those who do not. This research also focuses heavily on the idea that it is possible to identify particular 'consumption tribes' (Cova and Cova 2001) or a habitus (Bourdieu 1987) that are formed around knowledge and lifestyle choices (see Chapter 4). Such groups generate and gather cultural capital from their engagement in the consumption and appreciation of wine. Although this may be seen as a subset of segmentation, it uses broader cultural and social classifications than traditional approaches to segmentation.

Values and social psychology: Various articles on wine marketing explore the influence of personal values and social psychological constructs on consumer wine preference or choice. This area of research is largely under-developed in wine studies with the blurring of the boundaries between this category and lifestyle research. For example, Orth and Kahle (2008) explored that social or cultural benefits gained from hosting friends was more important than value for money. However, in contemporary marketing the idea of values and values-driven marketing is one of the most important developments in recent years. There is the recognition that many customers are becoming more values driven, and as such issues like the ethical production of wine or the sustainability credentials of their produce is important, as is the organic authenticity of the wine. This area will be further explored later in this chapter.

Generational comparisons: Research in this area often focuses on the way in which age/generational factors influence buying decisions and also how taste changes with age and knowledge: it is very much part of traditional segmentation studies.

Country-specific surveys: In many cases research only attempts to understand wine-purchasing patterns in one country, drawing from many of the categories discussed above. Usually the focus is on understanding the basics of consumer behaviour within that country, the use of wine to reinforce regional identity and the impacts of country of origin in both positive and negative terms.

Cross-national studies: The contents of these papers are similar in nature to country-specific studies, but compare more than one country.

Region: This mainly concerns articles that focus on the effect of region, some with other attributes included such as country of origin on wine preference and choice. For many consumers, region is one of the major drivers for purchase and consumption of wine (Perrouty, D'hauteville and Lockshin 2006) and is used as one of the risk-reduction strategies adopted by consumers (see Chapter 4 for discussion).

Theme 3: packaging, senses and servicescapes

This field of research includes areas of interest such as the package and presentation of wine, the role of sensory studies, and the importance of environment issues to wine consumers.

Packaging and labelling: There is much interest in the effects of packaging design and the affect that the information contained on the external packaging and labelling has upon on consumer preference and choice. Often this is also tied into debates that surround the semiotics of wine that will be explored in some depth in Chapter 10.

Sensory studies: Sometimes sensory studies are also linked to wine labelling in relation to the environment where wine is consumed. However, the research aims of the studies are to examine the effect of taste on consumer preference and choice. The role of human senses in the appreciation of wine has been widely examined by marketeers and leads to the creation of what may be defined as the 'sensescapes' of wine. The role of the senses has been discussed throughout this book: see in particular the discussion of wine quality in Chapter 1, the sensorial expectations of consumers in Chapters 2 and 4, and the role of wine education in developing the sensory appreciation of wine in Chapter 9.

Environment and sustainability: There is a clear link here with the ideas of consumer values. Research in this area focuses on the effect that environmental sustainability claims and certification, such as the organic or biodynamic credentials, have on consumer preference and choice. As stated previously in this section, consumers have many concerns about the environment and sustainability of the products they purchase and consume. This also directly links to the values and social psychology elements involved in the consumption process.

Actors in wine marketing

As can be seen, the marketing of wine covers a wide range of interests and approaches that are far beyond the realms of this book; however, some of the aspects and influences that underpin the contemporary marketing of wine are considered in more detail in other chapters of this book. For example, the labelling and packaging of wine is explored in Chapter 10, whereas issues surrounding lifestyles, identity and elements of social psychology are examined in Chapter 4.

However, before we explore some of the other areas identified above, it is important to think about what is actually the role of marketing in contemporary wine studies. All of the categories explored above involve one of the four fundamental aspects of marketing (i.e. Price, People, Place and Product).

In the context of wine, the marketeer is often not someone who is seated in an office, but can also be other 'gatekeepers' such as the sommelier, sales people, wine merchants and wine clubs, marketing and sales, and is not merely important in terms of creating awareness, but it also involves developing the marketing offer and leading the consumer through to the purchase stage. Before we turn to the mechanistic elements of the role of the marketeer in wine marketing it is important to add a new category to the themes identified by Lockshin and Corsi (2012), and that is the role of 'values' and the idea of ethical marketing.

Values, ethics and marketing

Although ethical issues in the use of wine are explored in some detail in Chapter 7, this section considers how ethical behaviour and sustainable practices can inform the marketing of wine. This has been explored by Orth and Kahle (2008) and by Barber (2012) who found that there was a small segment of environmentally knowledgeable wine consumers who were directly influenced by the values and ethical characteristics of the wine.

However, in the field of wine studies and the wine industry in general, there has been a lack of incorporation of the 'green' or ethical credentials of wine brands or producers into the marketing process. The significance of this for the marketing of goods has been successfully recognised and utilised by other sectors for some time.

All consumers have a different value system: this may be seen as a cognitive or mental activity that locates the product within a value system; the consumer will explore whether there is a synchronicity between the values of the product or brand and their own personal value system. In fact, the interpretation of every marketing communication is informed by the consumer's value system. These personal values have been developed from various individual experiences and the knowledge we have collected over our lifetime, from sources such as our social and cultural background, religious beliefs, ethnic background, education, habitus, peers or philosophical worldview. There are a number of value judgements we make during the purchasing and consumption process and we need to understand how the consumer relates to our product or experiences.

In exploring the role of values on the consumers' decision-making processes, Holbrook (1996, 1999) identified that value can be generated either through extrinsic consumption, in the sense that the consumption of a product or service is a means to another end, for example the choice and consumption of a particular wine is used as a means to impress your boss or to cement membership to a habitus, or through intrinsic consumption implying that something is consumed as an end in itself, for example to enjoy a glass of wine just because the consumer likes that wine even if it has low cultural capital or prestige. Consumer values can be 'self-orientated values', where decisions are taken for the individual in response to their own values, or they may be 'other-orientated values', where decisions are pursued either for the sake of or in response to the reactions and responses it gets from others.

Types of values

Although Holbrook (1999) identifies a number of values-based judgements that are informed by efficiency, excellence, status, esteem, play, aesthetics or spirituality, for the purposes of this chapter the role of ethical consumption as an expression of a person's value system is of particular importance. In most parts of the industry, this has yet to be integrated into the marketing of wine and wine experiences.

In assessing ethical and organic wines at The Decanter World Wine Awards, Tastings Director Christelle Guibert stated that:

> Organic wine can be hard to find ... but there is more and more of it available on the shelves. More winemakers are today using less pesticide, fertilizers and fungicides in order to increase the natural balance of the soil. They are taking organic and bio-dynamic much more seriously resulting in better quality wines (*Independent* 2009).

It can be argued that the green credentials and providence of wines is becoming increasingly recognised both by wine consumers and the industry. This trend is reflected in consumer websites such as www.ethicalconsumer.org (Ethical Consumer 2015), which provides ethical ratings of 115 different wines by judging wines against four categories in terms of ethical traits including: ethical and sustainable approaches to the environment, animals, people, politics and product sustainability. In some cases the wine was ethical but the score was reduced as a result of other practices undertaken by the organisation or parent company. Using this criteria they give a wine a score out of 20, with 20 out of 20 being the highest possible score. Of the wines they considered, Stellar Organics Wine received the highest score with 17.5/20, whereas the worst performing wine was an Asda supermarket wine with a score of 1/20.

Using similar principles, it becomes possible to rank other wines according to their green and ethical credentials. For example, Ethical Consumer (2015) awarded the following scores to leading Champagne producers:

Charles Heidsiek Champagne	13/20
Piper Heidsiek Champagne	13/20
Mumm Champagne	8.5/20
Perrier-Jouet Champagne	8.5/20
Dom Perignon Champagne	5.5/20
Krug Champagne	5.5/20
Mercier Champagne	5.5/20
Moët & Chandon Champagne	5.5/20
Ruinart Champagne	5.5/20
Veuve Clicquot	5.5/20

As can be seen there is a great deal of variation in the green credentials of Champagne producers based on this scale – although it should be noted that all scoring systems of this kind depend on certain assumptions about methods of production, and in any case, scores can vary substantially from year to year as producers change methods.

Many leading wine producers have adopted measures to reduce their carbon emissions: for example, changing methods of viticulture to reduce the number of tractor movements up and down the rows of a vineyard can lead to very substantial reductions in total CO_2 emissions, as can the use of naturally cool underground cellars to keeps wines cool. But in the case of regions like Champagne where most Champagne houses are buying grapes from a large number of growers, it is very difficult to track the actual CO_2 emissions and assumptions have to be made. Other measures such as shipping wines in bulk and bottling in the country of final distribution can also lead to significant CO_2 savings, but this is not possible for bottle-fermented sparkling wines like Champagne.

However, CO_2 emissions are only one issue. Ethical consumers are also interested in issues such as the use of pesticides, the protection of the terroir in physical terms, the sourcing of oak for barrels, and the fair treatment of workers in developing countries – as witnessed by the growth in demand for 'Fairtrade' wines from countries such as Chile and South Africa.

At the current time, such charts and measurements are not a significant element in wine marketing, but if the wine industry follows the same path as other sectors the ethical categorisation of wine will become extremely important as it allows consumers to express their ethical values, moral duty or obligation, even though this may be an extrinsic factor.

The importance of such issues varies between consumers, but those who are drawn to ethical products will often boycott the purchase of unethical products as an expression of their value systems, habitus and identity.

Green marketing and the process of greenwashing

The inclusions of a company's green credentials within their marketing campaigns, their mission and values statements are becoming increasingly common. These are often utilised as a means to differentiate their product from others. This is also increasingly the case in the contemporary wine industry, with many vineyards making statements about the organic nature of the wine or using the certification of 'Fairtrade' as a marker of their ethics. Although many companies make claims about their ethical or sustainable practices, often there is little proof, yet consumers are often willing to accept these claims. However, does the fact that a wine is labelled as organic or 'Fairtrade' actually mean it is ethical? For Alves (2009:3): 'Green marketing is the tactical instrument by which companies derive value from Corporate Social Responsibility (CSR): hyping their green credentials in a poorly regulated environment where most claims cannot be corroborated'.

Claims of being green or ethical are often overstated and in certain cases just untrue. Greenpeace define greenwashing as 'the act of misleading consumers regarding the environmental practices of a company or the environmental benefits of a product or service' (Gallicano 2011:1).

The concept of greenwashing appeared as pressure groups and individuals began to identify inconsistencies between companies' claims and their actual behaviour. In returning to the ethical ratings of wine by www.ethicalconsumer.org, 'Sainsbury's So Organic' wine and their 'Fairtrade wine' only receives a score of 3/20, whereas their 'So Organic Fairtrade' wine receives a score of 5/20. The 'Co-Op Organic Fairtrade' wine receives a 7/20, but a small producer such as Moonlight Organics receives a 17/20. In order to be sustainable and ethical it means more than just being organic, 'Fairtrade' or vegetarian. It is a matter of companies adopting a holistic approach to all of their practices. Thus, what many companies do in their marketing is to attempt to greenwash consumers by exaggerating their green credentials.

Alves (2009:5) identifies that there are six common sins of greenwashing and green marketing that inform contemporary marketing practices, these include the:

- *Sin of the hidden trade-off*: For example, a wine may make claims that it is organic and environmentally friendly, but they may be exploiting workers by paying very low wages and providing poor working conditions. Thus, they may be environmentally friendly, but their business practices may not be ethical.
- *Sin of no proof*: Often companies will make green claims in their marketing and packaging without them ever being substantiated by a third party. For example, there are many companies claiming their foods are produced in an ethical and sustainable manner, but this is not supported by any evidence; as consumers we are often likely to accept their word for it.
- *Sin of vagueness*: Often phrases such as 'produced in a biodynamic' or 'ethical manner', or 'made from organic grapes', or a produced in 'sustainable environment' are used in marketing campaigns and on packaging. Such phrases are extremely vague and intimate but do not definitively state what these claims mean.
- *Sin of irrelevance*: Companies will forward attributes such as the product being biodegradable, yet the product may never have been harmful in the first place. A similar example is the claim that the packaging is CFC free, yet in many countries it has been illegal to produce such packaging since the 1970s.
- *Sin of lesser of two evils*: A good example of the lesser of two evils is where companies may claim that they are carbon friendly, that they use solar and wind power to produce energy, but they then generate substantial emissions in the use of transporting the wine in heavy glass bottles from Australia to the USA.
- *Sin of fibbing*: Finally some companies just lie about their green credentials.

Alves identifies that in research undertaken by TerraChoice Environmental Marketing in 2007, 1,017 out of 1,018 green-marketed products from a wide range of sectors committed at least one of these sins, with over 50% of the products committing the sin of the hidden trade-off. There remains a concern that green practices are motivated by saving money (Bivins 2009; Gallicano 2011), increased brand values as a result of being seen as ethical rather than actually having a concern about the planet. Although the use of ethical claims is an effective means to increase the values of the product or brand, if companies are found to be greenwashing the consumer and committing one of the sins it can have a devastating effect upon the values that have been built legitimately.

Marketing, wine and the exchange and generation of value

Traditionally marketing theory, including wine marketing, has been dominated by the exchange perspective (this is sometimes labelled 'goods dominant logic') (Vargo and Lusch, 2004, 2008).

The principle of exchange is fundamental to every sale of purchase in a society where trading takes place. In every exchange two or more parties come together – for example, the wine producer and the supermarket buyer – where they enter into a relationship involving the exchange of wine for money. This applies equally to consumer purchases at the retail level.

All wine marketing is linked in some way to this principle – for example, by seeking to add value or status to wine so that purchasers will pay more, or simply by seeking to create demand so the purchasers will choose the wines of one supplier rather than another.

However, marketing in wine is complex and unlike many other industries there is a significant experiential element to it. As we have seen in Chapters 3, 4, 5 and 10, there are numerous symbolic and semiotic processes that underpin the appreciation of wine and perceptions of the value of wine. We have noted that different categories of consumer or members of consumption tribes will be searching for different experiences. Thus, 'value' is exchanged at the physical level (i.e. in obtaining wine to drinking), but 'value' is also exchanged in the form of the symbolic significance of wine (i.e. the cultural capital associated with the appellation, the vintage or the producers).

The role of marketing is not just to sell products, but it is also about adding symbolic value to them. This is achieved through fairly complex forms of exchange. For example, in Moët & Chandon's sponsorship of the 34th America's Cup in Newport in the USA, there is a value exchanged in the marketing relationship between the two organisations. The America's Cup has taken place for nearly 160 years and is the oldest trophy in international sport, so there is heritage and tradition: sailing at this level is expensive and requires high levels of knowledge and resources – in short it is an elitist pastime. Moët & Chandon offers a similar significance in terms of the heritage and brand values of the company, so as a result both Moët & Chandon and the America's cup exchange history, heritage and values within the exchange process, thus increasing the symbolic and cultural capital of both organisations. Marketing in the form of sponsorship has added value to both products by association with each other, which then equates to higher levels of cultural and social capital and ultimately value for the Moët & Chandon customer.

Marketing of wine as interaction and service

There are a number of ways of exploring the role of marketing wine. The discipline has been largely dominated by the exchange-of-value approach as discussed above, but there exists a more fluid understanding of marketing that can be better elucidated by the concepts of interaction and the exchange of service.

Vargo and Lusch (2004, 2008) see this as an adjustment from a 'goods dominant logic' to a 'service-dominant logic', that is particularly appropriate for the context of wine. Simply, service-dominant logic involves the restructuring of the characteristics and roles of market actors (consumers, sellers, producers, marketeers, etc.) and moves the idea of value creation from being envisaged as a purely management practice, to a 'co-constitutive' or reciprocal interaction amongst consumers, organisations and their stakeholders. What this approach achieves is to recognise that it is not only the marketeer that generates value, but that they also act as a facilitator in the value-creation process.

For example, in the case of service-dominant logic the marketeer may organise a wine event as part of the marketing and launch of a new vintage, but rather than those invited to the event being merely sales targets of marketeer-created value, the guests become active players and co-creators of personalised value. Value creation can be explored, as either a co-constitutive or reciprocal and negotiated practice that takes place between two parties. A good example of this is the role of the sommelier as a marketeer and the restaurant customer: the two parties may engage in a reciprocal relationship where through interaction the value of the wine and the wine experience is co-created. However, the customer may choose not to engage with the sommelier and just order a wine she wishes to try. In that case, the value of the wine and the wine experience has been solely generated by the consumer herself.

Consequently, marketing cannot be purely conceived from the perspective of value only being exchanged through transaction, but rather value is created and negotiated through the communications made between the marketeer and the consumer, or exclusively by a consumer in the form of an interaction with marketing resources or suggestions provided by the marketeer. Alternatively, for Grönroos (2011), it is sometimes a combination of the two approaches. As such, the first stage of the marketing process involves the practice of constructing the marketing offer, which involves practical elements such as finding distribution routes, but significantly it is ultimately about generating value.

Constructing the marketing offer

The marketing offer can best be thought of in term of the process by which marketeers design, generate value and symbolise wine within the marketplace.

As seen in previous chapters, the appreciation and consumption of wine is a complex multifaceted process. Consequently, the marketing of wine has to reflect this complexity. The construction of the marketing offer can be seen to consist of four elements, which can be identified in order as:

1. *Configuration*: The first stage involves the configuration and design of the product in marketing terms. This means identifying the particular features or characteristics of the wine including taste, vineyard and country of origin, vintage, etc., and from this its possible market positioning in terms of price, competition, consumers and type of sales outlets. Additionally, it includes exploring the benefits, promotions activities and performances that are most likely to stimulate a desired response from the intended audience. Configuration also includes creating the means to differentiate the wine from its competitors by instilling notions of superior quality, value and value systems into the marketing offer. It is important to note that the configuration stage also includes the standard marketing mix of Product, Price, Promotion and Place (4Ps) (McCarthy 1964) or even Lauterborn's (1990) Consumer, Cost, Communication and Convenience (4 Cs). In the case of on-premise purchasing the configurations of the marketing offer also includes the communicative staging of the 'servicescape' (Bitner 1992) in order to fully engage customers in the wine-buying process, whether this be the construction of a wine menu or a glass-fronted wine cellar that displays the breadth of choice, but most importantly staff taking on the role of service staff acting as gatekeepers to the wine experience.
2. *Valuation*: This is an important element in wine marketing and it differs from other sectors as customers in the wine sector are often price sensitive. However, as seen in Chapter 4, in the research undertaken by Mitchell and Greatorex (1989), there was a perceived link between the price of wine and its quality. In fact the fifth most popular strategy for reducing risk in wine buying is that consumers are willing to pay more than a reasonable price for wine. However, the significance of price varies according to the type of consumer: in an assessment of purchase intention of wine consumers based upon the influence of price, price discount and region, Hollebeek *et al.* (2007) found that region was more important for high-involvement consumers and price more important for a low-involvement consumer. Thus, when constructing and apportioning a valuation to a wine it is important to understand the nature of the target market and the value that purchasers are looking to get from a given wine, whether it is cultural or financial capital based.
3. *Symbolisation of the wine experience*: This stage of constructing the marketing offer explores how the values of the wine, its history, heritage, its terroir and social and cultural significance will be represented and communicated within the marketing process to the end consumer. It is about creating a biography for the wine that articulates the additional aspects or additional value the consumer may gain from the purchasing and consumption of that wine.

In short, at this stage it is not about selling the wine, but the idea of the wine and it significance. All of this symbolic activity is communicated to the consumer through what may be termed 'the semiotic language of wine'. The wine industry and wine marketing use a set of codes in the form of words and images that come to represent the nature, designation and quality of a wine. This language is contained in marketing communications, wine labels and packaging (see Chapter 10 for a more in-depth exploration of the semiotics language of wine).

4 *Facilitation*: Finally, the marketing offer focuses on how value can be added by ensuring that the delivery, access or even the performance in delivering the wine is in place. Again this varies according to the context in which the wine is purchased. For example, in the instance of delivery, for many people who sign up to so-called 'wine clubs' operated by retailers to order regular cases of wine, perceive extra value coming from the wine being delivered directly to them, especially if the wine merchant is believed to have special expertise in the selection of the wines. This value element is increased even more if it is delivered free of charge (though in practice delivery charges are absorbed in the prices set).

Access to what is defined as 'backstage areas' can also add value to the marketing offer: this includes tours of wineries or cellars prior to purchase or invitations to events organised by the seller or producer. Finally, the idea of performance may be central to the marketing offer. Throughout this book we have talked about the rituals that surround the consumption and appreciation of wine. It follows that the ability to attend specialist tastings and to be involved in mechanisms of connoisseurship or the formal process of choosing a wine, having it brought to the consumers and presented formally, all add value in terms of performance and communicative staging.

In the appreciation and consumption of wine, sometimes easy access to the product or convenience does not add value. The scarcity of a wine and the process of searching for it also often adds value – for example, you may have to attend several auctions to acquire a wine that is within your financial boundaries, having been outbid several times. The process of waiting often adds a significant amount of value to the appreciation and collection of wine.

Once the offer has been fully developed by the marketeer it is then possible to enter the product into the market place. This requires the development of a strategy that moves the product, in this case wine, through the various stages that take the wine from general awareness to its purchasing and consumption. This process consists of three clear steps:

1 *Create awareness of the wine product*: This involves informing potential wine consumers about the wine, identifying the consumer tribe or segment you wish to engage with, identifying the right semiotic and cultural code to interact with them according to their consumer resources, knowledge and levels of

cultural capital and finally, finding the most appropriate communication channels. For some groups social media is the best method; for others it may be adverts in *Country Life* or *Forbes* magazines. The purchasing of wine is sometimes an intimate process and it is also the responsibility of the sommelier or salesperson to help identify options for the consumer.

2   *Help potential customers evaluate your wine*: At this stage the marketeer's role is about implementing a strategy that reduces as many of the risk factors and barriers to consumption as possible. For example, it is important that marketeers ensure the label, the colour and shape of the bottle, the images used on the packaging, the colour palette used on the label, and the use of various semiotic languages of wine (see Chapter 10) are appropriate for the target market and communicate the right messages about the wine. However, it must be recognised that this strategy will differ according to the intended target market or individual consumer's knowledge, values and cultural capital. For example, the green or ethical credentials of the wine can form an important part of the marketing offer as can the sponsorship of events, or claims as to the history and heritage of the wine brand. All of these elements help reduce risk factors for customers and ultimately will contribute to the removal of barriers to purchase.

3   *The purchase phase*: By this point the role of marketeer is largely done; however, in order to turn evaluation into purchase other incentives may be needed such as 'buy one get one free' (BOGOFF) or other promotions such as free credits or bottles of wine if you subscribe to a wine club.[1] The opportunity to open an account with a wine merchant, to attend tastings, and the ability for consumers to get their money refunded if they do not like the wine offered can all be attractive measures prior to purchase. The final reassurance provided by the salesperson may be very important to a purchaser who has taken the risk of buying a special bottle.

However, as wine is seen as an 'aesthetic object' or a luxury product, it is also the role of the marketeer (again in the widest terms) to create additional layers of value and utility to the process of purchasing wine, the consumption of wine and post-consumption including the concept of service recovery. The idea of creating additional value for the consumer can be seen as an essential component to the successful marketing of wine in contemporary society.

Marketing as a cultural process and practice

One of the original motivations for this book was to explore the different aspects of theory and practice that underpin contemporary wine studies, in particular, the social and cultural significance of wine.

The marketing of wine can sometimes be seen as a mechanical process whereby facts and figures in the form of demographical data is gathered, profit and sales margins are set and then wine is distributed and put on the shelves of shops and supermarkets. However, as can be seen from various chapters in this book, the consumption and appreciation of wine is a significant social and cultural activity, and as such, any effective marketing of wine needs to reflect this.

For many authors, such as McCracken (1986) and Moisander and Valtonen (2006), marketing is understood as a cultural process and rests upon the supposition that we live in a culturally constituted world whereby the cultural world is constructed by and made understandable to various actors and stakeholders through various recognisable cultural codes, narratives and discourses. In the context of this book, the actors are the various individuals and organisations involved in the production and marketing of wine, knowledge generators such as critics and educators of wine, and finally consumers, all of whom participate in the production of cultural codes and are represented in the semiotic language of wine, the rituals that surround its consumption and appreciation and the knowledge required to participate. As a result, marketing can be seen as a cultural practice in which marketeers engage in a process of (re) or (de)constructing and (re)circulating systems and units of meaning to consumers or other targets of their activity, such as their shareholders or internal audiences. Put succinctly, marketeers are conceived as cultural intermediaries (Moisander and Valtonen 2006) or tastemakers, whose role it is to award products and servicescapes with significance and values that are attractive and meaningful to consumers in terms of their potential use as cultural resources for the accomplishment of individual goals and projects.

These goals and projects can include supplying, supporting and protecting consumers' independent and collective identities (Arsel and Thompson 2011). In the case of wine and identity, this may be applied to the connoisseur or aspirational drinker who uses wine as a cultural resource in which to reinforce their identity or to attain and construct specific lifestyles (Holt 1997) or membership of a consumption tribe or other life projects. But while the world and marketplace may be understood culturally, it is important to recognise that all consumers do not all interpret products and servicescapes in the same way.

However, it is clear that the idea of the exchange perspective in marketing, whereby marketeers construct the meanings of their products, which are then transferred to and accepted by consumers at the moment of purchasing, is not always appropriate for understanding the contemporary marketing of wine. Whilst some wine purchases are spontaneous, many involve an extended period of deliberation, especially where the buyer is seeking a 'wine experience' rather than just a beverage. So, consumers looking for wines will find different meanings, feelings and experiences that are not imposed on them, rather, they either co-create or find their own meanings from the wine-marketing process.

Wine marketing: a summary

The marketing of wine is a complex process that involves not just the selling of a product, but also the selling of experience and generating value. The marketing of wine is further complicated by the different contexts within which it is purchased or consumed. For example, the same brand of wine may be sold in retail, on-premise and online contexts, but the way in which that wine is marketed will differ in each context, as will the needs and wants of consumers, the perceived risk and the correct marketing strategy to adopt.

The complexity increases when we place the different types of consumer within the equation. Whether those consumers have been identified and segmented according to lifestyle or demographics, they are individuals, each possessing their own motivations for purchasing the wine, each with different life projects, personalities, value systems and identities to explore.

Also, as we saw in Chapters 3 and 4, the consumption and appreciation of wine acts as a social marker. Wine choices may enable consumers to define the type of person they are, or who they wish to be seen as. The role of the marketeer, whether they be a salesperson in a supermarket, specialist wine dealer, waiter, sommelier or marketing executive, remains the same: that is, the creation of value for the customer, whether that be price based, experiential or symbolical value.

For discussion

1. There are many different type and categories of wine marketeers. Develop a definitive list of these and identify which environment they operate in, for example, on-premise or retail, etc.
2. How do you see marketeers adding value to the wine product or experience?
3. How do you see consumers adding value to the wine product or experience?
4. Is wine harder or easier to market than other food and beverage products? What are the particular challenges that differentiate wine marketing from the marketing of other products?
5. Do you think that sustainable or green marketing will further develop within the wine sector?

Note

1. It should be noted that such promotions are illegal in some jurisdictions such as Scotland, on the grounds that they are likely to promote irresponsible purchasing and excessive consumption.

References

Alves. I. (2009). Green spin everywhere: How greenwashing reveals the limits of the CSR paradigm. *Journal of Global Change and Governance*, II(I), 1–26.

Arsel, Z. and Thompson, C.J. (2011). Demythologizing consumption practices: How consumers protect their field-dependent identity investments from devaluing marketplace myths. *Journal of Consumer Research*, 37(5), 791–806.

Barber, N. (2012). Consumers' intention to purchase environmentally friendly wines: a segmentation approach. *International Journal of Hospitality and Tourism Administration*, 13, 26–47.

Bitner, M.J. (1992). Servicescapes: The impact of physical surroundings on customers and employees. *Journal of Marketing*, 56(2), 57–71.

Bivins. T. (2009). *Mixed Media: Moral Distinctions in Advertising, Public Relations and Journalism*, 2nd edn (New York: Routledge).

Bourdieu, P. (1987). *Distinction: A Social Critique of the Judgement of Taste* (Nice, R., transl.) (Boston, MA: Harvard University Press).

Cova, B. and Cova, V. (2001). Tribal aspects of postmodern consumption research: The case of French in-line roller skaters. *Journal of Consumer Behaviour*, 1(1), 67–76.

Ethical Consumer (2015). *Ethical Guide to Wine* [online]. Available from: http://www.ethicalconsumer.org/buyersguides/drink/wine.aspx.

Gallicano, T. (2011). A critical analysis of greenwashing claims. *Public Relations Journal*, 5(3), 1–21.

Grönroos, C. (2011). Value co-creation in service logic: A critical analysis. *Marketing Theory*, 11(3), 279–301.

Holbrook, M.B. (1996). Special session summary customer value: A framework for analysis and research. *Advances in Consumer Research*, 23, 138–45.

Holbrook, M.B. (1999). *Consumer Value: A Framework for Analysis and Research* (London: Routledge).

Hollebeek, L.D., Jaeger, S.R., Brodie, R.J. and Balemi, A. (2007). The influence of involvement on purchase intention for new world wine. *Food Quality and Preference*, 18, 1033–49.

Holt, D.B. (1997). Distinction in America? Recovering Bourdieu's theory of tastes from its critics. *Poetics*, 25(2–3), 93–120.

Kotler, P. (2008). *Principles of Marketing* (Harlow: Pearson Education).

Lauterborn, R. (1990). New Marketing Litany: 4Ps passé; 4Cs take over. *Advertising Age*, Oct. 1:26 edn.

Lockshin, L. and Corsi, A. (2012). Consumer behaviour for wine 2.0: A review since 2003 and future directions. *Wine Economics and Policy*, 1, 2–23.

Lockshin, L. and Knott, D. (2009). Boozing or branding? Measuring the effects of free wine tastings at wine shops. *International Journal of Wine Business Research*, 21, 312–24.

McCarthy, E.J. (1964). *Basic Marketing: A Managerial Approach* (Homewood, IL: Richard D. Irwin).

McCracken, G. (1986). Culture and consumption: A theoretical account of the structure and movement of the cultural meaning of consumer goods. *Journal of Consumer Research*, 13(1), 71–84.

Mitchell, V.W. and Greatorex, M. (1989). Risk reducing strategies used in the purchase of wine in the UK. *International Journal of Wine Marketing*, 1(2), 31–46.

Moisander, J. and Valtonen, A. (2006). *Qualitative Marketing Research: A Cultural Approach* (London: Sage).

Orth, U.R. and Bourrain, A. (2005). Ambient scent and consumer exploratory behaviour: A causal analysis. *Journal of Wine Research*, 16, 137–50.

Orth, U.R. and Kahle, L.R. (2008). Intrapersonal variation in consumer susceptibility to normative influence: Toward a better understanding of brand choice decisions. *The Journal of Social Psychology*, 148, 423–48.

Ritchie, C. (2007). Beyond drinking: The role of wine in the life of the UK consumer. *International Journal of Consumer Studies*, 31, 534–40.

Sheridan, M. Cazier, J.A. and May, D.B. (2009). Leisure, wine and the internet: Exploring the factors that impact the purchase of wine online. *International Journal of Electronic Marketing and Retailing*, 2, 284–97.

Spawton, T. (1991). Marketing planning for wine. *European Journal of Marketing*, 25, 6–48.

The Independent (2009). The 10 Best Ethical Wines; 3/10/2009; Available from: http://www.independent.co.uk/extras/indybest/food-drink/the-ten-best-ethical-wines-1781196.html.

Perrouty, J.P., D'hauteville, F. and Lockshin, L. (2006). The influence of wine attributes on region of origin equity: An analysis of the moderating effect of consumer's perceived expertise. *Agribusiness*, 22, 323–41.

Vargo, S.L. and Lusch, R.F. (2004). Service-dominant logic: Continuing the evolution. *Journal of the Academy of Marketing Science*, 36(1), 1–10.

Vargo, S.L. and Lusch, R.F. (2008). Why service? *Journal of the Academy of Marketing Science*, 36(1), 25–38.

9
WINE SOCIETIES AND WINE EDUCATION

Why learn about wine?

In the earlier chapters we have explored various elements of wine in contemporary society: especially its cultural significance and the ways in which the sale and labelling of wine is protected by law.

But how do consumers gain the knowledge to choose wines? How does a retail purchaser judge whether a particular bottle of wine is worth £25 a bottle, when there are other bottles on sale for £5? How do diners in restaurants make an informed choice on the wine or wines to order which will be shared with the guests at their table?

In part, such purchases are guided by marketing information (see Chapters 8 and 10), for example, by back labels on wine bottles, point-of-sale information in stores, or information in brochures or websites aimed at those ordering wine for delivery. When ordering wine in a restaurant, the descriptions provided on wine lists can be important.

But increasingly people want to learn about wine in order to have their own understanding to draw upon. Sometimes this is because knowledge of wines is an essential requirement of their occupation. Anyone serving in a wine store needs at least some understanding of the products in order to advise customers. This ability to give advice is often central in enabling specialist wine shops to differentiate their offering from supermarkets, but it is only possible with suitably trained staff. In a restaurant, staff should to be able to offer meaningful guidance regarding wines on the wine list and offer advice on wines to match with food. Ideally, a specific staff member is designated as the sommelier to offer detailed guidance and first-class wine service. For anyone involved in buying wine and compiling wine lists, whether for a retail outlet or an on-trade venue, extensive wine knowledge is needed – not just at a technical level, but also in terms of understanding consumer preferences and current trends.

However, there are also many people wishing to learn about wine in order to enhance their engagement with wine for their own interest as consumers or as a means to add to their reservoir of cultural capital so that it may be exchanged at a later date. It is by learning about wine (usually with a good deal of tasting as part of the process) that someone may move from the simple enjoyment of wine to becoming a wine connoisseur.

The reasons for wanting more understanding of wine are varied and complex. Almost any aesthetic experience can be enhanced by greater knowledge: whether it is an enjoyment of works of art, music, theatre or historic buildings. Wine is no different: someone who understands how the final taste of a wine is affected by the choice of grape variety, the location of the vineyards and the techniques used, the fermentation process or the selection of barrels for ageing the wine can engage with the wines they drink in much more depth and with a greater appreciation than someone without such knowledge. People may also wish to learn about wine in order to impress others, perhaps to demonstrate social standing (as explored in Chapter 4).

In this chapter we explore the world of wine education: ranging from informal wine-tasting events to serious courses leading to examinations and qualifications.

Informal wine tastings

Attending a wine tasting is probably the most significant act by which an individual gives a meaning to wine and is able to recognise that a particular wine has some unique properties that make it more than a simple beverage. Even the most basic wine tasting involves comparing one wine with another, and hence a recognition of wine differentiation. Moreover, given that the consumption of wine is widely seen as pleasurable, a wine tasting offers a hedonistic experience in the comparison of alternative pleasures.

However, a 'wine tasting' can mean many different things in practice.

At its simplest, it could just involve some friends meeting socially, opening two or more bottles of wine and comparing how they taste. Even if those involved know little or nothing about the wines they are tasting, and even if the main purpose of the gathering is social rather than educational, the mere process of comparing one wine with another can develop some basic wine-appreciation skills.

At this level the discussion might be focused simply on asking, 'Which wine do you prefer – A or B?' But even engaging at this level means participants are challenged to make some kind of sensorial assessment of the wines, or an 'organoleptic assessment' to use the terminology of wine law applicable in most protected designation of origins (see Chapter 1). People may decide they prefer one wine rather than another because they perceive that it is more fruity, or because it exudes more freshness or crispness (acidity); or because it seems sweeter or drier, or because it tastes richer (more concentrated); or because they feel it has more structure (tannins); or because they feel it has more body (higher alcohol). Many other characteristics could be raised, but even the most basic discussion on these lines is causing people to reflect on the nature of wine.

Of course, such differentiation may contribute little to someone's learning about wine unless they have some memory of which wines they were drinking. But if they leave the gathering remembering that they generally prefer wines of brand A rather than brand B, or from grape variety P rather than Q, or from region X rather than region Y, they have started to gain some elementary wine knowledge.

Informal tastings can go much further than this: for example, where six people each bring a bottle, there are many more comparisons to be made – though unless participants make some kind of notes, they may find it hard to remember in retrospect which wines they preferred.

Rather than just comparing a random selection of bottles, much more meaningful comparisons can be made where a number of wines are selected on a common theme: for example, six wines from a particular country or six wines made from the same grape variety but produced in different parts of the world. By controlling one variable such as the region or grape variety, the other differences are more easily observed. However, once a group starts to organise regular tastings on these lines, it is probably better described as a wine society of some kind (see p. 177) rather than simply an informal gathering.

Matching wine and food

Many wine tastings focus on assessing wines in their own right, and there is no doubt that for formal assessment of wines it is best to avoid food. At serious tastings it is normal to have no more than dry biscuits or bread to clear the palate (at least during the formal tasting – other food may be served at the end). But as we have seen in earlier chapters, the cultural context for wine drinking is often alongside food, and in practice many people will build their knowledge of wine from drinking wines with food.

The combination of wine and food creates endless opportunities for tasting wines in terms of their ability to complement specific foods. Someone may ask: 'Does the wine taste better with the meat or with the cheese?' or 'Can we find a wine to go with the pudding?'

There are important scientific questions (outside the scope of this book) about how the human nose and palate responds to such combinations, but learning how different wines complement different foods is, for many people, the traditional way of learning about wine. In households where wine is served at family meals, children and young people may be allowed a small taste of the wine: over the course of time a great deal of wine knowledge can emerge from such experiences. Moreover, if children only have small sips and tastes, some research suggests that this may help them develop moderate drinking behaviours as they learn to differentiate one wine from another (see, for example, Donovan and Molina 2008). Certainly this is the traditional context for learning about styles of wine in many wine-producing regions.

Much can be learned by presenting more than one wine at a meal, so participants can discuss which wine better complements a given dish. At the very least it is helpful to present a different wine with each course (typically a white wine with the starter and a red wine with the main course). However, observations in restaurants suggest that few customers order wine in this way, even when there are clearly enough diners to justify ordering more than one bottle.

Beyond this, some wine merchants and wine societies (see p. 180) organise special meals as part of their activities, often with multiple courses and several wines with each course, with the explicit purpose of tasting different exclusive wines against food dishes prepared by a top chef.

Aside from formal meals, there are many informal opportunities to match wine with food. One of the most common formats in the UK (popular since the 1970s, though now in decline) is a 'cheese and wine' tasting where participants taste a number of different cheeses alongside a selection of wines. Often these are pure social events, or arranged as charity fundraising evenings, but they can be educational if participants are encouraged to make notes. However, often the problem is an impossibly large number of matches to assess: for example, if there are six wines and four cheeses each participant has 24 possible food and wine combinations to consider. Some wine educators overcome this by organising tastings with a single carefully chosen canapé to match each individual wine.

Wine societies and tutored tastings

Once someone begins to gain an interest in wine beyond the sharing of bottles with friends or exploring different wines with a meal, the next step is often to join a wine society of some kind, or perhaps to attend an informal wine class.

Groups for those interested in wine, or 'wine circles' as they are often called, appear from informal evidence to be growing in many countries where wine is seen as a premium product, conveying a measure of social esteem – for example, in the UK, USA, China, Singapore and Malaysia (see Chapter 4 for more on wine and social esteem). Such groups are less common in major wine-producing countries, where production of wine may be seen to be a normal day-to-day occupation – but even in a country such as France there have been reports of younger professionals in major cities forming groups to learn more about wine.

The tutored tasting format

Many wine-interest groups use the format of a 'tutored tasting' where a number of wines are presented in a predetermined sequence, introduced by a specialist who will say something about the characteristics of each wine – typically some information about where the grapes were grown and the methods of vinification and maturation – before participants taste each wine. It is usual to taste a number of wines with a common theme such as a country, region, or style of wine, allowing meaningful comparisons, though most wine groups will offer a variety of topics from meeting to meeting.

Depending on the experience of the tasters or the level of guidance offered by the tutor, participants will typically take some time assessing each wine, considering first its appearance (colour, transparency, viscosity), then its aroma or bouquet (possibly distinguishing primary and secondary aromas and different 'notes' within these) and finally its taste on the palate (qualities such as fruit, acidity, sweetness, alcohol, minerality, tannins, woody or spicy flavours, length or concentration, overall balance). On formal courses (see pp. 187–90) much emphasis is placed on systematic tasting techniques, but even in informal groups many participants will make some kind of tasting notes, or at least will seek to record their enjoyment of each wine using a personal scoring system.

The wines (typically five to ten over the course of an evening) are presented at intervals so that after the tutor has introduced each wine, participants have time to make observations on each wine, discuss with their immediate neighbours or with the group as a whole, and make notes if relevant. The tutor will usually provide a list of wines being tasted, sometimes with considerable background details such as the precise balance of grape varieties, the alcohol level as shown on the label, the site where the grapes were grown, or the specific type of barrels used for ageing the wine (see example in Table 9.1). Maps or other supporting information may also be provided. In some cases the tutor may use slides or other visual aids to support the presentation. Allowing time for questions to the tutor or comments by participants, such a tasting will usually take at least an hour – possibly much longer.

Some groups have specialist procedures, equipment and rituals at their events – for example, professional ISO tasting glasses may be provided (the shape recommended by the International Standards Organisation designed to allow careful examination of a sample of wine with ample space for the aromas). Serious groups will use a separate glass for each wine, to eliminate the residual drops of one wine affecting the next one so that wines can be compared over the course of a tasting. Sometimes members bring their own sets of tasting glasses. For a tutored tasting it is common to provide a sample of around 50ml of wine per person (this amounts to 15 tasting samples per 750ml bottle). But a participant tasting eight wines over the course of an evening may not wish to consume 400ml of wine (which could typically add up to around 5 units of alcohol) so it is essential to have a means for participants to dispose of wine that they do not wish to consume.

Organisers of wine tastings in formal groups will normally provide spittoons. Professionals tasting large numbers of wines will always first observe the colour and aromas and then taste the wine simply by taking it into their mouth, assessing the flavours in each part of the mouth then spitting as much of the sample as possible (see p. 183, 'Trade tasting events'). In amateur groups, spittoons are more likely to be used simply to dispose of unwanted samples of wine left in participants'

TABLE 9.1 Extract from a list of wines at a tutored tasting

Typically, the tasting sheet will include space for participants to make notes on each wine.

[Name of organisation and date]
BORDEAUX TASTING

<u>Whites</u>

(1) **Gaston Tureau 2013**   11.5%
AOC Bordeaux (Négociant blend)

(2) **Vieux Château Gaubert 2011**   13%
AOC Graves
Grapes: Sauvignon Blanc (50%), Sémillon (50%)
Fermentation in oak, 35% new. 9 months élevage with regular battonage

<u>Reds</u>

(3) **Château Lamothe-Vincent 2005** 'Heritage'   12.5%
AOC Bordeaux Supérieur
Grapes: Cabernet Sauvignon + Merlot. Oak aged

(4) **Château les Ricards 2007**   13%
AOC Premières Cotes de Blaye
Grapes: Merlot (70%), Cabernet Sauvignon (20%), Malbec (10%). 16mths in oak.

(5) **Château Beaumont 2004**   12.5%
AOC Haut-Médoc: Cru Bourgeois Supérieur
Grapes: Cabernet Sauvignon (46%), Merlot (48%), Cabernet Franc (4%), Petit Verdot (2%)

(6) **Château la Mouleyre 1999**   12%
AOC St Émilion Grand Cru
Grapes: Merlot (65%), Cabernet Franc (23%), Cabernet Sauvignon (12%)

---

glasses as it takes a measure of confidence to spit in front of others, and for many the actual consumption of the wine may be part of the pleasure of the tasting. Nevertheless, getting to the point of being comfortable with spitting wines at a tasting can be an important transition ritual between the casual drinker on the one hand and, on the other, the serious connoisseur engaging with wine at a semi-professional level.

The 'tutor'

The person presenting the wine at a tutored tasting can come from various backgrounds.

- The simplest (and least expensive) option is where an ordinary member of the group who has taken the time to read a little about the wines acts as the tutor introducing each wine. Sometimes wine groups have a number of experienced members they can call upon in this way, who may have a great deal of knowledge of particular wine regions. In other cases, being asked to lead a tasting may encourage the speaker to research an area, country or style of wine that he or she may not previously have known much about. Being invited to present the wines at a meeting of a wine society can be an important step on the road to being recognised by fellow wine lovers as a wine connoisseur. However, there is also a danger of choosing a 'tutor' who is simply an individual who enjoys speaking! Sometimes there are reciprocal arrangements with experienced members from other nearby wine groups.

- Some groups regularly invite wine merchants to present a selection of wines from their range and a number of independent wine merchants specialise in this: indeed some run their own wine clubs. However, the merchant is usually hoping to collect some orders at the end of the evening, so it can be impossible to present the wines from a truly independent perspective. Newly formed wine groups sometimes hope that wine merchants will give up their time and their wines to present promotional tastings of this kind free of charge, but that is rarely cost effective: few wine merchants can offer such events without charging for the wine samples provided. In fact, unless a good volume of sales is anticipated, wine merchants may also need to charge for other costs such as their time and travel.
- Groups may also rely on wine educators (see p. 191): professionals who have studied wine – often holding advanced qualifications, who teach about wine for a living (rather than working in the wine trade). This is never a cheap option as of necessity the wine educator will need a fee for his or her time in addition to the cost of wines presented, but for wine societies whose members are seriously keen to learn about wines, this can be very rewarding. For the most special events, a wine society may even invite a Master of Wine (see p. 190) as a speaker – see Figure 9.1.
- Occasionally wine producers visiting other countries are willing to speak to local wine societies in order to present their wines and talk about their properties. Sometimes wine merchants organise special tastings or dinners with visiting winemakers. Hearing first-hand from a winemaker is often the ultimate event for a wine society, but many wine producers find it hard to justify their limited time abroad in speaking to amateur groups.

Within all these categories there are many different styles of presentation: some tutors focus on presenting the region or topic in a clear educational manner whereas others focus more on 'fun' wine events, with extensive use of humour and anecdotes.

The focus of the society

Wine societies vary enormously between those explicitly focused on learning about wine, and those that are primarily social – with all possibilities in between.

Wine societies and wine education

FIGURE 9.1 A wine society tasting presented by a Master of Wine (Peter Carr MW speaking to the Yorkshire Guild of Sommeliers in York, UK).

In some cases there may be tensions between members of a group who have differing views on the social/educational focus.

Membership of a wine society can be a significant symbol of identity of status for those who enjoy wine. Some long-established societies have complex customs and procedures established over many years regarding the format of events, the choice of speakers and venue, and even over who pours the wines. Taking on a formal office in such a society – especially in a major role such as chair, president, or tastings co-ordinator – can be a very significant mark of esteem for a wine connoisseur – it is not unusual for the holder of such roles to have a ceremonial chain to wear or similar artefacts that are passed on from one office-holder to the next. There may well be a sense of hierarchy as people work their way up the ranks to the more senior roles.

Other wine societies are more informal groups of professionals who work together, or operate simply as networks linked to an individual with better than average wine knowledge, or with an impressive personal cellar.

So the motives for joining a wine society can range between those primarily wishing to learn more about wine, those for whom the society is more an opportunity for social interaction where the wine is secondary, and those for whom involvement in the society is a significant mark of esteem amongst others who appreciate wine.

Some wine societies structure their events as a full evening with a tutored tasting followed by a meal, and in that case the meal may be at least as important to members as the tasting; others operate as after-work groups for busy professionals who want the event to finish in time to get home or to make their own arrangements for eating. Some of the longest established societies bring together relatively affluent professionals in a similar field – for example, doctors, lawyers or academics. As an example, the Harrogate Medical Wine Society (based in Yorkshire, UK) has been operating for more than 20 years, and has its own website and an annual programme of events, but there are many societies that have been operating much longer.

Wine societies can have an enormous role in developing consumers' understanding of wine, and particularly their willingness to invest in serious and more expensive wines: Fattorini (1994) refers to the 'professional consumer' whose knowledge of wine has been developed in this way.

Some wine societies also operate as buying groups (allowing members to buy wines they have tasted through specially negotiated bulk prices with wine merchants) – indeed some so-called wine societies are simply tasting groups organised by particular suppliers, rather than organisations accountable to their members. However, one of the UK's largest wine merchants, The Wine Society (founded in 1874), is in fact a members' co-operative: it organises tastings and other events, but its main role is to supply wine to over 120,000 members for their personal consumption. Many wine societies are smaller local organisations, with a purely social and educational role, leaving members to purchase wines independently of the group.

Other educational wine events

Tutored wine tastings for interested consumers are not just the preserve of wine societies – they can also be offered as elements within other events, for example, as part of corporate hospitality events, or developing workplace teams in what is intended to be an enjoyable activity away from the office. Some professional wine educators specialise in offering events of this kind, often with some kind of competitive element such as 'guess the wine' with participants competing in teams. Consumers who have developed a serious interest in wine sometimes point to an occasion when they went to a wine tasting as part of another event as the spark which led to them wishing to learn more.

However, employers arranging wine-related events for staff in a particular organisation need to ensure the event does not lead to discrimination against the increasing numbers who do not consume wine for reasons of religion, health or personal choice (see Chapter 7 for more on these issues). Any kind of social event, whether in a work context or elsewhere, should always offer alternative drinks to non-drinkers or those on specific diets – this can include low-alcohol wines, non-alcoholic wines or specialist soft drinks. A voluntary wine society linked to a workplace, which staff can join or not as they wish, may be more appropriate than wine-focused events that all staff are expected to attend.

Trade tasting events

For those in the wine and hospitality trades, whether at trainee level or experienced professionals, participation in tasting events organised specifically for the trade can be an important part of their personal development. Attending one's first 'trade tasting' is a significant marker on the road to becoming a wine professional.

Most trade tasting events are organised by a generic body or public relations agency representing wines from a particular country or region, although major national retailers may also organise events in the hope of attracting press coverage for their wines. Leading wine merchants, especially those acting as importers, agents and distributors supplying trade customers, may also organise professional tastings.

Organisers of such events usually establish administrative barriers to ensure that participants are genuine professionals rather than interested amateurs. Invitations are normally sent in advance to suitably selected wine buyers and journalists, with a requirement for pre-registration, or at least some evidence of professional status if registration is accepted on the day. For the most prestigious trade tastings, invitations are strictly non-transferable, so that an invitation sent to a senior wine buyer cannot be transferred to a junior colleague.

A professional in the wine trade may attend tutored tastings from time to time in order to hear from an expert on a particular country or region, but most tasting events aimed at professional wine buyers involve many more wines than can be presented in a tutored tasting format. At a trade tasting the wines may be set out at tables around a room for participants to pour and taste at whatever speed they wish, known as a 'self-pour' tasting. In other cases, producers may be present at their respective tables to pour samples of their wines and to speak directly to participants about their methods of production. A printed tasting booklet is normally provided by the event organiser, which participants use to make their own notes.

It is not unusual for professionals to be attending trade tastings linked to a particular country or region, with perhaps 20 producers present, each with an average of six wines – so potentially 120 wines to consider (some events are much larger). Some attendees may only wish to taste wines from certain producers, or certain styles of wine, but for those wishing to taste the full range of wines on offer, a very rapid approach is needed: participants will take (or be poured) a sample of each wine, taste it, make a note, and move on to the next wine, perhaps tasting up to a hundred wines in an hour.

Sometimes wine consumers think it would be enjoyable to attend a trade tasting of this kind, and a few wine merchants set up smaller scale consumer events on these lines (with a charge to attend), or occasionally a trade tasting may be followed by a consumer event in the evening. But a full-scale trade tasting can be extremely demanding, and those new to the wine trade may need considerable guidance from a more experienced colleague or mentor to be able to apply themselves to such an event. Often the wines will be too young to drink for pleasure – they may be too tannic if red or too acidic if they are young whites – and the task is to consider how the wine will taste some months or years ahead once it is offered to consumers. It is possible to end up with a mouth feeling quite uncomfortable from all the tannins or acids.

For those building a career in the wine trade, large-scale trade tastings can be valuable learning experiences – especially in differentiating between the styles of different producers from the same region – but they can be challenging. The biggest challenge is not just to taste the wines, but to do so in a systematic way, evaluating both the nose and the palate of each wine, and making meaningful notes, which will be of use for buying decisions when one gets back to the office – or at least for deciding which producers warrant further discussions.

It is, of course, vital to use the spittoons effectively: in a large-scale tasting if one begins to swallow the wines it can be disastrous for concentration and even for health. For example, if a taster is evaluating 120 wines, even if he or she only takes a small 25ml sample of each (half the size typically served at a tutored tasting), that add ups to three litres (four bottles) of wine in all. Nevertheless, few people have the mouth control to spit every drop: the UK-based writer Jancis Robinson MW (1994) has estimated that around 10% ends up being swallowed no matter how effectively one spits – or one small glass for every 30 wines sampled. In this example that would mean around 300ml of wine is consumed (about four units of alcohol – see Chapter 7). So responsible professionals usually seek to avoid driving after major tastings, even if they are spitting all the samples.

At a busy trade tasting many spittoons will be placed in the room, but they can easily become congested with people, or they may become full if they are not emptied frequently. A taster holding a sample of wine in his or her mouth seeking access to a spittoon is, of course, unable to speak to say 'excuse me'. This creates a 'levelling effect' between those of different standings in the wine trade, with a new trainee perhaps elbowing a distinguished Master of Wine to get access to a spittoon!

Reading about wine

Of course, learning about wine is not always dependent on groups, classes and tastings: much can be learned from reading – although there is naturally a limit to how much can be learned solely from reading without tasting!

However, a wide range of newspapers and magazines have a wine column, often written by a journalist who has studied wine extensively and holds appropriate wine trade qualifications (see p. 187). Sometimes these are little more than recommendations for wines on sale through major retailers, but many wine columns provide a great deal of information on particular wine styles or wine-producing regions.

There are also many well-illustrated books about wine: some dealing with wines from the whole world, others focusing on particular regions. These are popular presents for wine lovers, and a huge amount can be learned from a book such as *The World Atlas of Wine* (Johnson and Robinson 2013) or *The Sotheby's Wine Encyclopedia* (Stevenson 2011).

Some consumers will also subscribe to in-depth wine magazines, for example, the UK-based *Decanter* magazine and the US-based *Wine Spectator* have both been successfully publishing for decades, though there are also many other titles available. In addition, those studying in the trade may have access to professional journals such as *Harpers Wine & Spirit* or *Drinks Business* or *Off-Licence News* (all UK-based but with international readership).

Beyond printed resources there is a vast range of internet resources devoted to wine, including some sites with reviews and tasting notes on a huge range of wines – as well as websites from specific producers or generic sites for particular wine regions. Some sites only provide information on a chargeable basis – one of the most famous sources is the website www.jancisrobinson.com from Jancis Robinson MW and a small network of writers working with her. Internationally, the tastings and ratings of the US writer Robert Parker have been hugely influential in determining wine prices and assisting those who only want to buy 'the best' wines: his magazine *The Wine Advocate* and the associated website www. erobertparker.com are seen as essential sources by many – see McCoy (2008) for an in-depth account of the work and influence of Parker.

Some commentators suggest that internet resources are now used more by wine connoisseurs than printed sources – indeed, an increasing number of wine bloggers are now extremely influential (Siddle 2014). However, whilst some wine bloggers are very good and knowledgeable, others have less experience, and it is not always obvious which are worth following.

Of course, only the most serious wine consumers will subscribe to wine journals or use internet sources regularly, but for those wishing to develop a serious knowledge of wine, the potential resources are immense.

Wine tourism

Whilst a consumer can learn a great deal about wines through widespread use of books and attending tastings, much more can be learned by visiting a wine region, especially as part of an organised group with detailed visits to wine producers.

To be taken round a vineyard by the owner, pointing out the lie of the land, the type of soil, and the methods of pruning and training the vines can be a very powerful learning experience. Then to visit the '*cave*' (to use the French term) or winery: to see how the grapes are crushed, the type of fermentation vats used, and the cellar where the wines are aged in barrel (if applicable) can be a quasi-religious experience. Especially for someone who has already developed a real interest in the wines of a region, a visit to the area may well been seen as an act of pilgrimage. To be invited into one of the top châteaux or estates may be akin to entering the 'holy of holies'.

Even without special visits, the mere fact of travelling around a wine region using a suitable map can add greatly to one's understanding simply by observing the steepness of the hills, the distances between villages, the sense of climate at whatever time one is visiting, the buildings and lifestyle. Time spent in a wine region can enable an individual to gain some real sense of the terroir, especially for those who spend time in the vineyards (see Chapter 5 on the role of wine tourism in the development of wine identity).

More broadly, wine tourism is extremely important economically to many countries (see Hall and Sharples 2002), and many wine-producing regions see the development of tourism linked to wine as a key to developing prosperity – both in making the wines better known, but also by supporting other local businesses such as hotels, restaurants, and transport providers.

Some people like to visit wine regions to buy wines 'from the cellar door' to take home. For a consumer to be able to serve a wine to his friends and say 'We visited this producer of this wine – it was just a small farmhouse down a tiny lane' gives a great sense of connection with the origin of the wine and a sense of its terroir while simultaneously increasing their reservoir of cultural capital. (Also, for those travelling from countries such as the UK or Scandinavia with high levels of duty compared to those in the wine-producing country, considerable savings can be made – but the risks of transporting wine long distances in a hot car must also be considered.)

However, simply visiting a region as a tourist, even if one calls on a few producers, may only give a limited understanding. Except for the largest producers with their own visitor centres, few winegrowers have the time to give in-depth tours to a visitor who may have only a casual interest. Moreover, many tourists lack the language skills to converse with wine producers in the local language. Those estates that specialise in receiving visitors often focus on certain parts of the process that they think will impress: almost every producer likes to show off their barrel cellar even if only a tiny fraction of their wines are oak aged.

There are some companies that specialise in providing in-depth wine tours with much more detailed explanations that can be very educational. But a short visit to a region does not teach you how to be a grower or a winemaker. Even those of us who write about wine professionally need to remember that it may take many years of living and working in a wine region to fully understand its terroir, how to get the best from the grapes in good years and bad years, and all the associated subtleties of winemaking practice. This doesn't mean that producers have to be old to produce good wine: most wine regions also have a new generation of young winemakers who are making great wine through having studied and gained experience for only a few years. But they will normally have worked a number of vintages on other estates or perhaps on their parents' properties, often with extensive work both in the vineyard and in the winery, before they seek to make wine on their own.

Wine examinations and qualifications

In almost any profession, fundamental markers of status are established through professional qualifications and access to membership of professional bodies. The wine trade is no different, although it was perhaps only from the late twentieth century that it became normal for those working in the wine field to hold professional qualifications. Until then many wine producers were trained by knowledge passed down from one generation to another and many wine merchants learned their trade as apprentices or through succeeding their parents in family-owned businesses.

However, somewhat unusually compared to many other professions, many of the qualifications associated with the wine trade are not restricted to those directly dealing in wine, and it is relatively common, for example, to find those with a keen amateur interest in wine studying for Wine & Spirit Education Trust (WSET) qualifications (see pp. 188–90) alongside those in the trade.

Historical bodies

Specific professional recognition in the wine field is certainly not new. Amongst wine producers, many wine-producing regions, especially in Europe, have ancient guilds or companies that had the power to set standards for the production and sale of wine and some of these continue to have important ceremonial or marketing roles even in the present day. In France such orders exist in almost every region or appellation, but the Jurade de St Émilion claims to be the oldest such order still in existence with a clearly documented history.

The Jurade was established in 1199 with extensive powers to govern the ancient town of St Émilion in the Bordeaux region (see pp. 68–9) and in particular the quality of its wines. It had the power to destroy barrels of wine that were deemed unworthy of that name (an early precursor of the modern system of controlled appellations: see Chapter 1). Although the Jurade declined in the Middle Ages it was revived in the twentieth century and leading châteaux-owners nowadays constitute most of the *jurats* (judges) who process through the streets of St Émilion in red robes on ceremonial occasions such as when the annual harvest is declared (the *ban de vendange*). Others can be admitted as honorary members in an elaborate ceremony (though the criteria are strict with each jurat only allowed to propose a maximum of three new members per year - unlike some wine guilds that will admit any tourist on payment of the relevant fee). The Jurade now has over 3,000 members throughout the world who act as ambassadors for the region – mainly people in senior roles in the wine and hospitality trade, but also a substantial number of individual wine connoisseurs (Wines of St Émilion 2015).

Many parts of the world where wine is bought and sold have long had systems of protection that determined who was allowed to sell wines. London, the traditional home of the international wine trade, has long had guilds whose members had special rights in undertaking a wide range of trades, and the Worshipful

Company of Vintners was granted a royal charter as early as 1364 – it stands only at 11th place in the list of 110 livery companies in the City of London. For many years, before the advent of professional qualifications in the wine trade, admission as a member of the Vinters' Company was the highest mark of status for a wine merchant in the UK. The Vinters' Company still provides extensive support to the wine trade, including maintaining Vintners' Hall – a major historic venue in London for wine trade events. Through its charitable arm, the Vintners' Foundation, it supports charities dealing with the social consequences of alcohol abuse (Vintners' Company 2015).

Modern wine qualifications

Nowadays young people looking to make a career in wine production are likely to study for a university degree in oenology, viticulture or similar sciences: most of the universities in the world's leading wine production regions offer a range of qualifications of this kind. Some of these universities are world leaders in oenological research. Very often the academic study will be enhanced by periods working with wineries well away from their home region in order to gain experience: it is not unusual nowadays to find a winemaker in Burgundy who has spent time in New Zealand, or a winemaker in Chile who grew up and studied in Bordeaux.

Those entering marketing or export roles linked to wine producers are more likely to study for degrees in business studies, languages (especially English) and communications, but will also find ways to gain in-depth understanding of the methods of wine production for the properties they represent.

Amongst those working in the wine distribution trade and wine retailing, new recruits are often selected for the combination of a passion for wine and willingness to work hard. Those in senior roles will normally be graduates but drawn from a wide range of disciplines. However, in terms of formal wine-related qualifications, those available from the WSET are seen as particularly relevant to people working with wines and spirits in many countries of the world. They are available at various levels ranging from the most junior to highly advanced (see p. 189) and are applicable both in wine retailing and to those dealing with wine in the hospitality industry. Many positions now require the appropriate level of WSET qualification – or recruits are taken on and sponsored to complete a WSET award. However, the ultimate professional qualification in the purchasing, selection and marketing of wine is the *Master of Wine* (MW) – awarded by the Institute of Masters of Wine (IMW).

The IMW was founded in 1953 as a result of an initiative by The Vinters' Company together with the Wine and Spirit Association (the UK-based trade umbrella body – later the Wine and Spirit Trade Association) to develop a modern high-level qualification for leading wine specialists. The Master of Wine examination was first held in 1953 and the Institute was launched two years later. However, the IMW and the Wine and Spirit Association subsequently identified a need for qualifications to cater for those at other levels in the wine trade and in 1969 the WSET (a registered charity with educational objects) was established to provide these. Although both WSET and IMW are UK-based organisations, their qualifications are highly sought throughout the world. WSET qualifications are offered through 'Approved Programme Providers' in 60 countries and the current list of Masters of Wine covers 24 countries (WSET 2015a; IMW 2015a).

There are also a number of other bodies offering professional qualifications in the wine field. The Court of Master Sommeliers (CMS) operates in a number of countries, offering qualifications specifically intended for those working as sommeliers in restaurants or working towards that status. The CMS, founded in 1969, offers four levels of qualification from an *Introductory Sommelier Certificate* involving three days of study, up to the *Master Sommelier Diploma* leading to the qualification 'MS' (CMS 2015). There are also some individual wine societies offering qualifications to members, notably the US-based French Wine Society which offers a qualification as a *French Wine Scholar* (designated 'FWS').

WSET and IMW qualifications

At the time of writing, the main wine-specific qualifications available from WSET and IMW can be summarised as follows. The levels in the WSET awards correspond to the levels in the 'Qualification and Curriculum Framework' set by the UK Government for vocational qualifications across numerous professions (WSET 2015b).

- The *WSET Level 1 Award in Wines* simply involves a one-day course on basic wine knowledge, assessed by a short multiple-choice test. It is intended for frontline staff who need confidence in the wines they deal with.
- The *WSET Level 2 Award in Wines and Spirits* covers the major grape varieties and where they are grown around the world and a systematic approach to tasting wine. No prior knowledge is required. Around 16 hours of class time is normally needed and similar time in personal study. Although most centres offering the award provide samples for students to taste this is not mandatory, so the qualification can be obtained even by those who do not wish to taste wines for reasons of health or religion, or those below the legal age to buy alcohol. Assessment is by a one-hour multiple-choice exam.
- The *WSET Level 3 Award in Wines and Spirits* is a more advanced programme designed, say WSET:

> To give a thorough understanding of the principal wines and spirits of the world and their commercial importance in the world's market. The qualification will assist those who are required to make professional evaluations of wines and spirits with regards to their quality and commercial value ... to advise management, and to answer customer queries authoritatively.

A typical study pattern would involve 12–15 weeks of two-hour classes, and a further 50–60 hours of personal study. Assessment is by a written examination of 1 hour 45 minutes involving both multiple-choice and essay questions, and a 30-minute practical examination involving the blind tasting of two wines.

- The *WSET Level 4 Diploma in Wines and Spirits* is the WSET's flagship qualification for those in demanding roles in the wine trade. The programme of study is normally taken over two years, with assessed coursework and around 11 hours of examinations, both theory and tasting. Candidates must pass six separate units in order to gain the Diploma. Holders of the Diploma are entitled to the professional qualification 'Dip WSET' after their names.

- The *Master of Wine* qualification – the 'MW' – is awarded by the IMW as a mark of outstanding 'theoretical knowledge and practical skills in the art, science and business of wine'. It is a highly exclusive qualification: at the time of writing there are only 322 MWs throughout the world. MWs are typically found as the top wine buyers in leading wine merchants or multiple retailers, though there are also many MWs working as consultants, journalists and educators. Candidates must already hold the WSET Level 4 Diploma or a similar level qualification such as a degree in oenology before they can enrol with the IMW. Study for the MW involves a minimum of three years. The examination process is extremely demanding where many enter but do not succeed: in total it involves 15 hours of theory examinations, seven hours of tasting papers (three separate blind tastings each involving 12 wines) and a research paper of up to 10,000 words. The costs of study – for the classes and for the world-wide travel and extensive wine samples – are also very substantial (IMW 2015b).

The significance of professional wine qualifications

For anyone who wishes to be recognised as a wine professional, the value of qualifications is self-evident. However, the difference between WSET Level 1 Certificate on the one hand (which might be taken by waiting staff in a modest restaurant or shop assistants in a local wine shop) and the Master of Wine on the other (which implies a career devoted to wine at the highest level) are so enormous that it seems misleading to describe them both as 'wine trade qualifications'.

However, none of the WSET qualifications require that candidates must be working in the wine trade. It is not unusual for committed members of wine societies to study for the WSET level 2 or level 3 awards, and a small number of committed wine connoisseurs have achieved the WSET Diploma purely for personal interest. Candidates for the MW must have 'at least three years professional work experience in the global wine industry' (IMW 2015b), but in a few cases those whose main career is not in wine have been accepted on the programme.

Nevertheless not everyone accepts the need for formal qualifications. There are many able people working in the wine trade who have gained extensive personal knowledge over time without sitting examinations leading to specific qualifications.

Wine educators

For anyone to learn about wine, except from existing published material, a teacher of some kind is needed. Of course, not all teaching is formal: many members of the wine trade provide informal guidance and mentoring to those entering the profession. Many consumers learn a great deal by means of conversations with experienced staff at their local wine shop, or simply by exchanging notes and experiences with other wine lovers.

But beyond these informal settings there is a need for wine educators – professionals whose role it is to present an understanding of viticulture, vinification and different styles of wines at an appropriate level. For example, the WSET generally requires that tutors at each level must hold the next higher qualification (WSET 2015c), and most employers seeking wine-related training for their staff would want assurance that the trainer is properly qualified. Even wine societies will place a premium on sessions presented by those with real knowledge and experience, able to convey their topic with clarity and authority: the ultimate is to get a speaker who is an MW, but a presenter holding the WSET Diploma would also be seen as a very significant speaker.

However, holding a wine-related qualification is not sufficient on its own to make an effective wine educator. A wide experience of visiting regions and wineries gives a speaker much more in-depth knowledge to draw on and usually makes for a more interesting presentation. Considerable skills are needed to share wine-related knowledge in an interesting way with a diverse audience. Moreover, most wine presentations also involve a tasting of some kind, and leading a tutored tasting where the aim is not just to comment on one's own perception of a wine but also to encourage participants to develop their own observations requires considerable skill. Wine educators also need experience in the practicalities of sourcing and presenting wines in a class session that may involve considerable logistical issues (transport of the wines, sourcing and washing of glasses, etc.) and issues of licensing law. They also need to maintain their own professional development – for example, through attending trade tastings, making periodical visits to major wine regions and reading appropriate journals to keep up to date with any changes and new developments.

As well as presenting formal classes and speaking to wine groups, some wine educators also offer more informal wine-related events – for example, corporate hospitality events or wine-related charity fundraising events. Some run their own 'wine schools' either for consumers or for trade participants. Wine educators are also regularly used on a freelance basis to undertake specialist presentations for trade bodies. Some wine educators are also active as wine writers.

To support and recognise wine educators working at the highest levels, an Association of Wine Educators (AWE) has existed in the UK since 1993 and now has a number of overseas members. Similar associations exist in several other countries, in particular, the Society of Wine Educators based in the USA.

Full members of AWE are required to hold at least the WSET Diploma or an equivalent qualification (and a number are MWs); they must have considerable experience in wine education, they must subscribe to a code of ethics, and they have to undergo a personal assessment by an experienced AWE member of a class they are leading to ensure they are capable of delivering interesting and engaging classes or tastings (AWE 2013).

Learning about wine: a summary

We have seen that people have a huge range of reasons for learning about wine, whether it is simply to enhance their personal enjoyment of wine, or to take on specific roles in the wine trade. However, an in-depth knowledge of wine marks a clear distinction between the casual wine drinker and the wine connoisseur: it can be a major marker of esteem.

For staff in wine shops or serving wines in the on-trade, there is a huge difference between those who simply know the bottles by their appearance, and those who can speak authoritatively to customers about the origins of a wine, how it was aged, how long it should be kept, and the most appropriate foods with which to drink it. For those at the highest levels of the wine trade, making major decisions about which wines to buy, and possibly even specifying to producers how wines are to be made or blended, in-depth knowledge underpinned by qualifications is normally essential.

Learning about wine can take place in a wide variety of settings from informal tasting groups and personal reading, to wine societies with their own rules and procedures, to classes in colleges, universities or specialist centres leading to formal qualifications. Experienced wine educators may play a significant role in any of these contexts.

We have noted that the various wine qualifications available can have a very powerful effect in signifying status in the community of those concerned about wine, both amateurs and professionals. The uniquely exclusive status of the MW is unusual compared to other professions, but the WSET Diploma and even the WSET Level 3 Award are qualifications that clearly label someone as a wine professional (or at least as a professionally qualified amateur).

For discussion

1. How important is it for (a) those working in wine retailing and (b) those working in the hospitality trade to hold formal wine qualifications?
2. Is education the main route to esteem in the wine world?
3. Why do people join wine societies?

4 If you have been to a wine society or wine class, did you make good use of the spittoons or did you end up drinking more alcohol than you intended? If the latter, what can be done to counter such risks?
5 What makes a good wine educator?
6 How does the MW survive as such an exclusive qualification?
7 Should students below the age where they can legally buy wine be allowed (or encouraged) to attend wine classes?
8 What are the benefits of trade tastings (a) for participants and (b) for the producers whose wines are offered? What can be learned if you have to taste over 100 wines in half a day?
9 What are the benefits of consumer tastings (a) for participants and (b) for the producers or wine regions represented in the wines tasted?
10 If you have no previous experience of wine tastings, try organising an informal wine group with some friends, where a number of people each bring a bottle to share. How much do you really learn about wine in this situation?

References

AWE (2013). *Association of Wine Educators – Application Process* [online] www.wineeducators.com/apply-for-membership/.
CMS (Court of Master Sommeliers) (2015). *Qualifications* [online] www.courtofmastersommeliers.org/qualifications/.
Donovan, J.E. and Molina, B.S.G. (2008). Children's introduction to alcohol use: Sips and tastes. *Alcoholism: Clinical and Experimental Research*, 32(1), 108–19.
Fattorini, J. (1994). Professional consumers: Themes in high street wine marketing. *International Journal of Wine Marketing*, 6(2), 5–13.
Hall, M. and Sharples, E. (eds) (2002). *Wine Tourism around the World* (London: Taylor & Francis).
IMW (Institute of Masters of Wine) (2015a). *History of the Institute* [online] www.mastersofwine.org/en/about/history-of-the-institute.cfm.
IMW (2015b). *The MW Examination* [online] www.mastersofwine.org/en/education/the-mw-examination/index.cfm.
Johnson, H and Robinson, J. (2013). *The World Atlas of Wine* (7th edn) (London: Mitchell Beazley).
McCoy, E. (2008). *The Emperor of Wine: The Remarkable Story of the Rise and Reign of Robert Parker* (revised edn) (London: Grub Street).
Robinson, J. (1994). Spitting. In: Robinson, J. (ed.), *The Oxford Companion to Wine* (Oxford: Oxford University Press).
Siddle, R. (2014). Wine bloggers risk becoming 'dinosaurs' unless they become more professional. *Harpers Wine & Spirit* [online] www.harpers.co.uk/news/wine-bloggers-risk-becoming-dinosaurs-unless-they-become-more-professional-hears-dwcc/373164. article.
Stevenson, T. (2011). *The Sotheby's Wine Encyclopedia* (New York: Dorling Kindersley).
Vintners' Company (2015). *The Worshipful Company of Vintners: Origins and Development* [online] www.vintnershall.co.uk/?page=origins_development.
Wines of St Émilion (2015). *The Jurade* [online] en.vins-saint-emilion.com/discover/jurade/creation/jurade-guardians-tradition

WSET (Wine & Spirit Education Trust) (2015a). *Welcome to the Wine & Spirit Education Trust* [online] www.wsetglobal.com/about_us/default.asp.
WSET (2015b). *Qualifications* [online] www.wsetglobal.com/qualifications/default.asp.
WSET (2015c). *WSET Approved Programme Providers* [online] www.wsetglobal.com/how_to_run_a_course/471.asp

10
THE SEMIOTICS OF WINE

In Chapter 8 we looked at the marketing of wine and we noted that the labels on wine bottles are extremely important in purchasing decisions. The information provided and the style of the label are important in both guiding our understanding of the wine and ultimately influencing purchasing decisions.

In many sectors of the wine trade, especially in the mass market, it is not possible to taste or smell the wine prior to purchase. So the consumer is guided by various influences such as the design of the wine label, the information and description of the vintage, and the various undertones describing both the taste and bouquet on the rear of bottle. This chapter explores how this information guides our behaviour, and also how as consumers we read labels and wine marketing.

The style of the label and the colour of the bottle directly informs how we read, understand and find meaning, as Barber, Almanza and Donovan (2006:118) state:

> The purchase of a bottle of wine is often challenging decision for most consumers. The marketing of a wine's package, which consists of several interrelated cues (bottle, shape, color, closure and label design), interfaces with the key factors of the consumer's experience, knowledge of wines, self-confidence and the occasion at hand to form buying decisions.

We read these clues and then, through a process of negotiation and interpretation, we find our individual meanings of what we think the wine will taste like and whether it will be appropriate for a situation or person or group of people. We can think of these interrelated cues as part of the semiotics of wine. Semiotics is very simply the study of signs and systems of representation through which meaning is generated and communicated, and it can be argued that every consumer product or sector of business or human interaction has its own language that is used by producers and are understood by us as consumers.

Celhay, Folcher and Cohen (2014:4) couch this in terms that wine labels contain a set of visual codes that mean something to the consumer. They go on to state 'The use of the word "code" implies that there is something to "decode". That is to say: a meaning or a significance that is contained within the sign.'

Wine is often devoid of packaging beyond the bottle itself, and the marketing of wine in magazines, on television and even in the form of in-store posters is usually limited to larger brands. The wine bottle, therefore, becomes the focus of interpretation and although the labels are relatively small they are rich in information and semiotic meaning. 'Signs are simply anything that stands for something (its object/referent), to somebody (interpreter), in some respect (its context, i.e. in an advert, label, package, servicescape or retail environment)' (Mick 1986:198). In the instance of wine, the object is the bottle, the referent element of the bottle is what it stands for, the interpreter is the consumer and the context is either in a servicescape (buying wine in a restaurant) or in a retail environment (such as a supermarket).

Living in the modern world we are surrounded by signs from the moment we awaken in the morning until we go to bed at night. Signs essentially make the world intelligible and meaningful to us; they tell us when we can cross the road, which door to use and whether we would like a wine, whether we want to be associated with it or whether it is suitable for the cuisine that is being served at dinner. In the main, we all understand the meaning of these sorts of signs. This is possible because we read, interpret and comprehend them. Comprehension is made possible from belonging to a shared cultural context and system of meaning that frames and directs our reading and understanding, which in literature is sometimes referred to as the code (e.g. Alexander 2000; McCracken and Roth 1989; Holt and Cameron 2010) or in other words, a cultural lens through which wine is contextualised and understood.

Within the wine sector there is a formalised language of appreciation, a language that unpacks and tells us what the wine will taste and smell like, its provenance and its significance. Essentially this language of wine is a code or template that provides an interpretive or organising framework through which signs located on the bottle and the bottle itself makes sense. For example, the front and rear labels of wine bottles utilise a set of codes, language and representations that tells the consumer how old it is, where it comes from, how strong it is, whether it is red or white, dry or sweet. Codes also allow us to read into the seller or producers communicative intentions even when drawing upon the most arbitrary of signs. For example, the use of an animal, a coat of arms or a bunch of grapes signifies something to the consumer, often symbolising luxury and heritage (see Boudreaux and Palmer 2007). According to Manning (2012:45–6):

> The statute of many a drink builds on the handicraft nature, i.e., the artisanal form of manufacturing the drink ... with a clearly visible label

materialising the brand, serves as both an index to the originality or naturalness of the drink, but also as a sign vehicle for something more profound in today's global market.

In a world that is dominated by the visual, pretty much anything and everything can be treated as a sign and can be seen to hold semiotic potency and value. In this way the information contained on the bottle can be treated as text or narrative and can be read and understood. For example, even the shape of a Champagne bottle means something – we recognise it for what it is as well as associating all of the experience and cultural significance that is associated with Champagne. The bottle itself carries symbolic significance even without exploring the label or the branding.

The products and activities that surround wine consumption themselves carry and communicate meaning. For example, according to Hope and Patoine (2009), the semiotic relation between the sommelier and the wine is subject to a significant multi-layered chain of meanings, compared to that of a novice drinker. In other words, the sommelier's wine-tasting experience has been enriched by previous sign-making that has been developed over a number of years, through interacting, studying and gaining experiential understanding, which has led to the sommelier developing a complex set of personal preferences, behaviours, habits and knowledge. This sign-making 'opens up' various neural networks, allowing access to a higher number of features of the object, all of which underpin the appreciation and study of wine. In this case over the years the sommelier has developed a nose and palate, knowledge of vintages, of terroir and the customer, etc., consequently making it more and more complex.

Throughout this book, specifically in Chapter 3 where we looked at the status of different wines and Chapter 9 on wine education, we have seen that wine consumers engage in different behaviours and practices that give them skills and knowledge to extract deeper and sensually heightened meanings from the wine product and is a clear strategy deployed by consumers in their efforts to extract value and meaning from using and interacting with them (Holt 1998). Interpersonal interactions that occur through engagement with a sommelier or membership of a wine society or wine education organisation, also have symbolic significance (Solomon 1983). People search for meaning and understanding, both through verbal and non-verbal forms of communication.

The service setting or 'servicescape', the rituals that surround the purchasing of wine and the language used on a wine menu, all contribute to the staging and contextualisation of wine within the restaurant setting. The meanings generated from this are also mediated and transferred from the service staff to the customer through their actions and interactions.

Semiotics and wine

Semiotics is simply the study of signs, understanding what they mean to the reader and what type of message is being sent. Signs can inform us, but critically signs can make us behave in certain ways. A good example of this is that we all stop (or should stop) at a red traffic light: it makes us behave in a particular way. Likewise, the words and images used in wine marketing or the information placed on a wine label will often direct the way in which we behave.

There a number of different semiotic approaches, traditions and schools of the thought. One of the first pioneers of semiotics was Ferdinand de Saussure (1857–1913) who identified that the relationship between signs consisted of two elements (or in his words dyadic), which consisted of the form of the sign (the signifier) and its meaning (the signified). The best way to conceptualise this is that the picture of flames or a fire is the signifier, but what it stands for is the signified; in the case of flame or fire it could stand for warmth, comfort or even danger (Saussure 1983). Generally this is guided by social rules or conventions, so in the case of wine studies, the images contained on a wine label are understood as they are culturally, historically and socially embedded. For example, the image of a château is the signifier: it may be no more than a modest French house, but within the semiotic language of wine it stands for (signifies), luxury, tradition and 'Frenchness'. This is an important development as the images and words used on a wine label mean more to the consumer than just words.

The second pioneer of semiotics is Charles Saunders Peirce (1839–1914) (pronounced *'purse'*). For Peirce (1934), signs can be organised or classified into three general categories: icons, indexes and symbols. Each of these can clearly be understood and applied within wine studies, and can be defined as follows:

- *Iconic signs*: This is the type of sign that imitates or has a resemblance or close correspondence to its object, for example, the image of a château or a bunch of grapes. They are integral to both the substantive and communicative staging of servicescapes of restaurants and especially in wine bars and retail environments where empty wooden wine cases, bunches of grapes, maps of French vineyards, false vines and used wine barrels are frequently used to commutatively stage spaces. 'Substantive staging' refers to the physical creation of contrived environments, that is, their material configuration, whereas 'communicative staging' includes the role performances of the wine waiter, sommelier or wine dealer and interactions that signpost and pattern consumer experiences in servicescape environments (Arnould, Price and Tierney 1998:90). Such icons are also important constitutive elements and component parts of advertisements, promotional materials, websites and, most significantly, on wine labels and other ancillary packaging.
- *Indexical signs*: This type of sign identifies the relationship between an object and an indexical sign, and is marked out by a causal relationship. For Echtner (1999), this is best explained in terms that a suntan is an indexical sign of sun exposure, or drunkenness is an index of excessive drinking. Within the context of wine studies there are a number of extremely famous wine producers throughout the world such as Château Lafite and the other first growths in Bordeaux, Château St Michelle in Canada, Keenan, L'Ecole No.

41 in the USA, Bindi or Giant Steps in Australia, A.R. Valdespino in Spain, as well as famous Champagne producers such as Krug or Louis Roederer, just to mention a few. Their names act as a sign that is indexical with quality and exclusivity. Also, in contemporary culture, other consumers may make an indexical link with a name such as Louis Roederer in relation to the ostentatious expression of wealth and power within 'Rap' culture (see Chapter 4). However, to understand the indexical link a consumer has to possess the requisite levels of knowledge to understand the cultural or oenological code that awards this particular indexical relationship between wine and its classification as possessing quality or alternatively not possessing quality.

- *Symbolic signs*: The idea of the symbolic sign is similar to Saussure's idea of the signified and signifier whereby a sign that sometimes possesses a random association to its object, a symbolic sign relates to its object in an entirely conventional manner and, as such, requires the participative presence of an interpreter to create the signifying connection. Thus, a point-of-purchase display for wine depicting a young couple lounging by a fireplace may represent 'the good life' or decadence, love or licentiousness, depending upon the codes of the interpreter's background (Mick 1986:199). In addition, symbolic signs are shaped and informed by a process of social and cultural convention, whereby meaning has been embedded in that society or culture (these do not need to be geographical, but can be societies of interest, for example, wine societies; it can also be argued that there is a recognisable oenological culture). For example, some New World wines will have an image of a kiwi or kangaroo on wine labels – these are symbolic signs that symbolically transfer information or meaning that they originate from either New Zealand or Australia. The symbolic meaning of this transfers from the wine bottle to the consumer, and will consist of a denotative element and a connotative element.

- *Denotative meanings*: Denotative meanings are concerned with what a sign symbolises. For example, if we continue with the kiwi or kangaroo examples, these symbolically represent country of origin and their categorisation as a New World wine, but its denotative meaning signifies various potential consumer experiences. For some this may mean a lack of formality, a wine that is realised from the seriousness and stuffiness of the Old World, or even just fun and sun, or the promise of a wine that is richer, with bolder fruit flavours and a more 'polished' taste than Old World wines. Alternatively, for others it may mean a wine that lacks the depth of taste and nose that can only be produced from a vineyard that possesses an ancient, authentic and historical terroir. It is important to recognise that although we may make the symbolic link between the kiwi and New Zealand, this will signify something different to each individual or consumer whether that is a positive or negative interpretation.

- *Connotative meanings*: The interpretation of wines is also informed by personal individualised connotative associations and significance. In other words, interpretation will be informed by whether a particular wine was used to celebrate a birthday, wedding or was drank during a particularly memorable or significant evening with friends or family. The connotative element is extremely important in forging people's relationship with wine. The writer Maggie Hoffman (2013) asked 25 sommeliers 'What was the greatest wine you have ever tried?' Only a small proportion of the sommeliers concentrated on the taste or nose of the wine; the majority described how it was linked to a particularly significant event or experience, or how it marked a transition in their lives (e.g. setting out on their own business). Others identified that they had tasted some of the greatest wines of all time, wines that they could never afford to personally buy but the most memorable glass of wine they had ever had was a *Vilmart 'Grand Cellier' NV*. 'It was what I drank on the night that I proposed to my wife'. What came through from this article is the significance of the context and connotative element within the interpretations. For one sommelier wine was 95% emotion for them, and for another the wine and the context are of equal importance.

These personal connotative meanings are dynamic and may change over time. For example, you may choose a particular wine for your wedding supper and this wine will be important to you for a number of years. However, if later you got divorced the connotations of the wine may change. The semiotics that surround wine not only inform our preferences or purchasing choices, but they can also inform how we interpret the wine in terms of taste.

The impact of signs on tasting

One of the major reasons professional wine tastings are often conducted blind is that the images and signs contained on a wine label, or even the shape and colour of the bottle, can impact upon the perception of the taster. Although it is easy to chart and explore people's connotative and denotative relationship and interpretation of wine and the semiotic language that surrounds it, it is much more difficult to chart the impact it has upon how people believe the wine tastes. For Spinelli (2012), it is a hidden aspect of signification.

A number of studies have identified that the information on the label directly influences people's perception of the quality and attributes of the wine. One of the most famous studies was undertaken by Frédéric Brochet (2001), who identified that when people are incorrectly told that the wine is expensive they virtually always report it as tasting better than the very same wine when they are told that it is inexpensive. In his study, Brochet decanted a mid-range Bordeaux into two different bottles, one labelled as a cheap table wine, the other bearing a 'grand cru classé' label. Tasters described the alleged grand cru classé wine as 'woody, complex, and round' and the alleged inexpensive wine as 'short, light, and faulty'. In a similar vein, Sester *et al.* (2013) examined a study in which the same wine was presented to a panel of regular wine drinkers who were either told that the wine had been given a positive rating (an expert score of 92 out of 100 points) or a negative rating (i.e. they were told it had only scored 72 out of 100 points). This information was provided prior to each tasting. The consequence was that the negative rating resulted in negative perceptions of the wine by the drinkers, while the wine that was positively rated resulted in positive assessments of the wine.

Signs can come in many forms and do not just have to be images or words – they can also include colours, style and even music. North (2012) explored the idea that the 'emotional connotations of music' acting as a symbol influenced people's perception of taste and other characteristics of a wine. Specifically, the research investigated whether the emotional connotations of pieces of music that were characterised as 'powerful and heavy', 'subtle and refined', 'zingy and refreshing', or 'mellow and soft' could have a corresponding effect on the perceived taste of a red wine and a white wine. It was found that the type of music played largely correlated to people's perception of the wine. It can also be argued that music influences emotion, and as identified earlier in this chapter, the taste and perception of wine is directly influenced by the emotions of the consumer and the relationship or connotations they have to a particular life experience, piece of music or type of wine.

As can be seen from this discussion, the information on the front and back labels of wine have a significant impact upon how the wine is perceived, evaluated and consumed, so the next section explores how wine labels are semiotically read and constructed.

The wine label

Although wine suppliers have considerable choice in the design of labels, wine law is very specific about what information must appear on labels (some of the basic requirements were explained in Chapter 1). Some information is mandatory and some discretionary, but even on back labels the rules about what is permitted are quite strict to prevent producers using terms that are not permitted – for example, under European Union (EU) law a varietal wine (a wine with no PDO or PGI) such as a 'Vin de France' cannot mention any geographical details other than the country of origin (and the producer's address in small print). However, in this chapter we are concerned with the semiotics of wine labels rather than the legal requirements.

According to De Luca and Penco (2006), the wine label fulfils the same role as packaging on other food goods. The description of the wine on the back label, the colour theme, the feel of the physical material used for the label and other factors creates a multi-sensory and bi-directional communication to the consumer, who consumes signs and symbols on the wine bottle in order to produce individual and social meaning.

De Luca and Penco state that information on a wine bottle engages the purchaser in at least five narrative programmes: individuation on display (or in other words making the initial choice of which wine to pick up); reading in hand (reading bottle prior to purchase); purchase (during the purchase process); consumption (when the purchaser takes the cork out, presents it and drinks it); and post-consumption (often revisiting the bottle to read the label again as part of the evaluation process). As such, the consumption of wine is as much a semiotic exercise as it is an oenological one.

According to Paradis (2013) the nominal and concrete meanings of wine are constructed and focused around either its constitution or function, defined as follows:

- *Constitution*: This involves the fixed or static aspects of a wine, for example, wine is an object, wine is a liquid, wine has colour, and so on. Therefore by defining through an expression such as 'red wine', the constitutional role is defined.
- *Function*: This involves more dynamic aspects related to the production, for example, how an entity such as wine was produced, the nature of the grape variety, the vineyard that produced it, etc., came into being or how wine is used, for example, with red meat or fish or cheese.

Research undertaken by Thomas and Pickering (2003) unpacked the significance of the contents of a wine label by breaking down its constituent parts into fourteen distinct areas. These were then ranked according to the importance and significance of each of the constituent parts (Table 10.1).

TABLE 10.1 Constituent parts of wine labels

Order of label importance	Significance
1 Wine company	Origin, recognition and trust
2 Wine brand name	Origin, recognition and trust
3 Expert opinion, awards, medals	Endorsement, recognition
4 Wine's attributes	Differentiates and status
5 History of winemaker	Origin, heritage, history reduces risk
6 How wine was made	Nature of wine
7 History of wine region	Origin
8 How wine should be used	Defining usage
9 Image, picture, logo	Attractiveness
10 Colours used on labels	Attractiveness
11 Alcohol level	Nature of wine
12 Unique, unrivalled wine	Status
13 Type of situation wine made for	Defining usage
14 Type of person wine would appeal to	Defining usage

Source: Adapted from Thomas and Pickering (2003)

In a more simplistic version Thomas (2000:61) identifies the information components that appear upon wine labels:

- *Attributes*: The features of benefits of the wine. This outlines the character of the wine and includes how it appears, smells or tastes.
- *Nonpareil*: A reflection of the quality of the wine. Nonpareil also identifies that the wine is unrivalled or unique.
- *Parentage*: This reflects the history of the wine, the terroir, history of the winemaker or region. Sub-categories of this include brand, company or person.
- *Manufacture*: This is how the wine was made and often includes sub-categories of process, ingredients and design.
- *Target (end user)*: This identifies who the product was made for in terms of a person type and the type of situations or end uses for which the product was made.
- *Endorsements*: This highlights expert opinions or the recognition of awards and medals.

All of these attributes form an important framework of knowledge that is contained on a single wine label. It is rich in data, codes and cultural significance, and as such, it is important that we understand what type of information is contained on the wine label and its semiotic significance for the consumer.

The meaning of each sign for the consumer is also directed and influenced by the use of a number of modes, including the style of writing, the font used, the layout and the colours on the label. Each of these plays a semiotic part in defining the semiotic significance of the wine: the writing tells us about the wine, the image shows us denotative and symbolic meanings, the colour frames highlight and intimate the quality and experience of the wine, while layout and lettering are used in part for reasons of compositional arrangement and in part for reasons of 'taste', which like colour, intimates quality and experience. Each mode is used in ways that draw on its potentials in the overall design of the messages. Moreover, to write what the images show on the wine label in narrative text would take up too much space and take too much time to read.

The front label

As can be seen from the research of Thomas and Pickering (2003) in Table 10.1, the name of the wine company (the producer or shipper) on the front label is the most significant piece of information on a bottle of wine. The front label is the first line of communication with the consumer and as such is particularly important in drawing the consumer to it (Barber, Almanza and Donovan 2006).

Additionally, the wine label contains a great deal of information and wine consumers prefer to read the label rather than ask for help (Olsen, Thompson and Clarke 2003). The level of knowledge held by consumers will impact upon their understanding and recognition of the significance of the information presented, but most importantly, the label tells consumers what is in the bottle. As such, consumers may interpret the same label in many various ways. For some it may just be helping them to identify the colour or the geographical derivation, for others it may be the ability to recognise the significance of the wine, etc. Thus it can be argued that the label holds various layers of information that can be accessed, but the level of access depends upon the knowledge of the consumer and the purpose of consumption.

The reading or interpreting of a wine label commences with a basic or cursory reading or, in De Luca and Penco's (2006) terms, assimilating the 'individuation on display'. In his research into the significance and effect of the 'country of origin' (coo) on the consumers' perception of a wine, Brijs (2006:122) explore this semiotic:

> Let us translate this case of 'semiosis' to a concrete, daily life example. Imagine a person looking for a good quality wine, entering a supermarket. He goes to the wine department and finds himself confronted with a large variety of wines. This particular supermarket doesn't offer the possibility for consumers to taste wine and, additionally, the person in question is not a wine specialist. So, what will he do to estimate the quality of the varieties offered? A first possibility might be to look for the price. The person in question might reason that expensive products are of a higher status and that, consequently, higher priced bottles will be of better quality. But what if, after a first selection based on price, there are still different options left? In such a case, one might turn to the wine's coo [as referred to on the label].

It can be argued that for some consumers the country of origin is the first factor in narrowing down the choice. For others it may be the wine brand or any of the other factors identified by Thomas and Pickering's (2003) themes listed in Table 10.1, or it could be something as simple as that the label is attractive.

Although different labels may contain the same levels of basic information, we often see this presented in different ways according to the country of production, or whether the wine is the product of the Old or New World. It is interesting to note here that the use of English and French has become the *lingua franca* of wine. Even if the wine comes from Chile, China or Japan, the labelling is dominated by the English and French language of wine. However, according to Robert (2014), English is the dominant language throughout the world and has been used extensively in the marketing of alcohol. For Robert, even the marketing of French products such as French AOC wines, Cognac and Champagne, the expression of their 'Frenchness' is still often articulated via the intermediary of English. The familiarity with the semiotic construction of European wine labels has led to French and English words, phrases and descriptions dominating the world of wine.

Sherry and Camargo (1987:177) categorise this process as the using of 'borrowed words'. These borrowed words are utilised within marketing and description of consumer goods in their packaging – these words transcend cultures and languages and are understood by consumers globally.

The major elements of information contained on the front label include the following.

Country of origin

At the initial stage of analysis the country of origin simply tells you where the wine has originated or, in other words, where it was made. As we noted in Chapter 1, under EU law, and in many other countries, a bottle of wine must show 'Product of X', giving the name of the country where it was produced (or, where necessary, a statement that it is a blend from several countries). In Brijs's (2006) analysis the country of origin information is charged with various meanings. He explores this by using the example of wines identified as French as a semiotic example, showing that this sign contains two elements: the appraisive signifying mode, and the designative signifying mode. He goes on to state:

> through its association with descriptive country features (like good weather), the Made-in-France label can be charged with affective tags (like feelings of joy, pleasure or optimism) because most people like (i.e., 'appraise') a warm and sunny climate. This way, the label comes to signify not only at the denotational but at the connotational level as well (Brijs's 2006:125).

However, this can also work at another more political level. For example, Beverland and Lindgreen (2002) explored the phenomenon whereby New Zealand consumers boycotted purchasing French goods, including wine. This boycotting was as a result of the French Government's decision to organise a nuclear test programme in the Pacific, and the attack on the Greenpeace ship, *Rainbow Warrior*, in Auckland, New Zealand. Thus the label of French origin now possessed negative connotations, so rather than the semiotic association being dominated by notions of sun and joy, it becomes replaced by connotations of violence, destruction and anger. Therefore the country of origin is informed by various conative factors that may be formed socially, but also individually.

Vintage

The vintage is the year the grapes were grown for a wine and is often important in defining the quality or taste according to the climatic conditions of that harvest, as we considered in Chapter 1. So even with the same wine produced by the same producer, the quality and taste of the wine will differ according to the vintage. Except for some entry-level wines, or with non-vintage blends at premium levels, the year of the vintage is normally shown prominently on the label. In some cases the date may be on the neck of the bottle or on the rear label. For the wine collector or aficionado the vintage is particularly significant (see Chapter 3 for more on vintage in relation to the status of wines).

Specific geographical indication

Identification of the region with a country is important as it allows the consumer to identify the characteristics of place. Under EU wine law, geographical names must be recognised as PDOs or PGIs to appear on wine labels (see Chapter 1). Sometimes the geographical indication may simply refer to an entire region such as *Bourgogne* (Burgundy in English); in other cases it may be as small as a single grand cru vineyard (see pp. 70–5 for discussion of the appellations and classification in Burgundy). As we saw in Chapter 5 when considering the importance of terroir, the regional identity may be extremely important as a recognisable brand.

However, the statement of region upon the wine label can sometimes be confusing to less experienced consumers. On many New World wines the region is clearly marked and is clearly separate from the name of the wine. However, often the reading of Old World wines requires a level of understanding and knowledge of wine regions and sub-regions, as many European wines are named from the region or village they come from, as explained in Chapters 1 and 3. Where, as with most wines, a PDO or PGI designation is given it will always be a geographical name, but, as we noted in Chapter 1, different local terms are permitted in each country so French wine will typically show *Appellation d'Origine Contrôlée* (AOC) below the geographical name of the PDO or Italian wines will have *Denominazione di Origine Controllata* (DOC). This information is designed to enable consumers to identify the region definitively.

Producer (domain, château, etc.)

The name of the wine producer can be presented in a number of ways and can be as simple as the personal name of the owner, a domain, a château or even a supermarket brand. The producer is usually easy to recognise. As can be seen from Table 10.1, for many consumers the name of the producer or brand is the most important piece of information on the front label and is the primary means of initial choice.

For New World wines, the name of the producer is usually very prominent on the label: examples of this include Echo Falls, Hardys and Kumala in Australia; Helan Mountain, Silver Heights and Grace Vineyard in China; or brands such as E & J Gallo and The Prisoner Wine Company in America. In Europe, this can be more confusing as the name of the producer is often small if it is not a prestigious château, with most significance being placed on the region as indicated by the PDO. With wines from co-operatives and large bulk wine producers, the name and address of the producer may only be in very small print, and is sometimes only given by means of codes that have to be checked on a database of producers.

Vineyard

A small number of wines in addition to the name of the producers, region and the vintage, will also identify the particular vineyard where the grapes have been produced. As we saw in Chapter 3, this is particularly important in regions such as Burgundy where great importance is placed on the distinctions between vineyards or 'climats' with the best climats designated premiers crus or grands crus. If the vineyard has been identified this means that all the grapes used to produce the wine were grown in a single vineyard, rather than blended from several sources.

Wine name – brand

There is an increasing trend to apply branding principles to wine and for producers to attach a proprietary name to the wine that is not related either to the producer or the vineyard it came from, but is rather part of a branding or marketing strategy. Often these names derive from local cultural attributes, the personality of the grower or of even the wine. Sometimes brands are simply used to distinguish different cuvées from the same producer in the same year.

In a recent article Silver (2013) explored the use of unusual wine names, the purpose of which is to attract the consumer attention in a crowded market place. Some of the American wine names he identified included, Three Blind Moose, Middle Sister, Marilyn Merlot, Little Black Dress and Dracula's Blood. This trend is not merely restricted to the New World wines, but can also be witnessed in Europe, particularly from countries such as Hungary where the geographical names do not have the same distinction as the regional names of France and Italy.

Yet the strategy of breaking with the visual and semiotic codes of using traditionally formulated names is not without risk. Adopting an unusual or provocative wine or brand can be rejected by consumers if the product is not perceived as belonging to the product category or a category they wish to be associated with, and is thus not considered for purchase. A good example of this is provided by Celhay and Trinquecoste (2014), who identified that when brands attempted to break with the traditional semiotic French wine codes, using brand names like e-motif, Chamarré, and Rock'n Rhône, these daring attempts to differentiate their products through the label graphics were summarily rejected by consumers.

Grape variety

As consumers develop their wine knowledge and understand the type of grape they like, the grape variety often becomes the first element of information they seek on the wine label. When learning how to read wine labels, beyond the issues shown in Table 10.1, the grape variety used in the wine is often the first thing people look for. The type of grape or combination of grape varietal is usually very clearly listed on New World wines, as well as countries such as China, Germany, Alsace and Chile. As such, people say that they like Zinfandel (Primitivo), Cabernet Sauvignon or Merlot. Often the grape variety is given equal significance of prominence on the label so that choice is made simpler for the consumer.

In other regions the grape variety may not be mentioned at all on the label (or perhaps only on the rear label). This is because in major regions such as Bordeaux, Burgundy and Champagne identified by PDOs, it is usually the case that only specific grapes are allowed by law to be used in wines of that PDO. So the wines are named by the vineyard or village where the grapes were grown, rather than identifying the variety of grapes. For example, all red wine producers in Burgundy have to use 100% Pinot Noir grapes if they wish to market their wine as *AOC Bourgogne* (although a lesser appellation, *Bourgogne Passe-Toute-Grains* allows a blend of Pinot Noire and Gamay). Therefore, in the case of a top Burgundy such as Chambertin Grand Cru, to put both 'Chambertin' and 'Pinot Noir' on the label would be redundant. Also, for these wines most aficionados agree that it is the place where the grapes are grown that is most important to the quality and characteristics of the wine.

The rear label

Although consumers may undertake a small amount of research before purchasing wine, the primary means of gathering information are in store, and the rear wine label has a major role in this (Chaney 2000). Although the rear label carries the most information in terms of the characteristics of the wine, the front label is still the primary stimulus in encouraging purchase (Thomas 2000; Boudreaux and Palmer 2007).

Tasting notes

The most detailed and dense information is left for the description of the wine on the rear label, and often contains descriptions of the wine that are characterised by the synaesthesia of the wine including smell, taste and visual qualities. For example, olfactory perceptions are described in terms of things and events that we perceive through our eyes.

Many of the descriptors semiotically denote everyday flavours and aromas that most consumers can relate to, such as various fruits (blackberries, apple, lemon), herbs and spices (vanilla, nutmeg), flowers and plants (violet, cedar), sweets (chocolate, jam), beverages (coffee, tea) and minerals (chalk, earth), and descriptors that relate to human beings (body, backbone, nose). The descriptors may also seek to explain the wine in relation to people's personalities and behaviour, such as masculine, shy, intellectual and voluptuous (Paradis 2013).

TABLE 10.2 Examples of the semiotic language of wine

Development	Youthful – grape aromas – aged bouquet (tired – oxidised)
Acidity	Flabby – low – balanced – sharp
Character	Sexy – naughty – opulent – muscular – voluptuous – soothing, aggressive – smooth – an old friend

Wine education bodies such as the Wine & Spirit Education Trust (WSET) (see Chapter 9) produce guides to wine tasting, including suggested terminology that can help to explain the style of a wine on the nose or palate. Using the work by Paradis and others, it is possible to develop the normal tasting language into a broader semiotic language of wine – see Table 10.2 for some examples (the last line of the table illustrates more creative language that is sometimes used on rear labels).

Stylistic qualities of labels

Images

The images that are utilised on labels have the strongest impact upon consumers. Boudreaux and Palmer (2007) reported that symbolic images of grapes and châteaux have the greatest appeal, whereas coats of arms are markers of upper class and high values. In their research traditional label layouts were found to have an advantage over the modern ones in terms of consumer preference and purchase intent. In their study of Bordeaux grands crus classés labels, Celhay, Folcher and Cohen (2014) identified that there were two different aspects to the images found on wine bottles:

- *The illustration visual*: For example, an image of castle, a vineyard, a coat of arms, an animal or a leaf, etc. They found that 55% of the labels contained a castle and 27% contained a coat of arms, monogram or crown. Such images produce a sentiment of nobility and social distinction, at the same time signifying tradition and history. These sentiments are also supported by the font choice and colour (see p. 210).
- *The illustration display format*: For example, an etching, a photograph or a painting. In their study 70% of wine producers chose to represent their illustration through an etching. According to Cavassilas (2007), the choice of etchings amongst other styles of illustration signifies a tradition of detail and craft-work, compared to modern printing techniques and photographs.

For Celhay, Folcher and Cohen (2014), the Bordeaux grands crus classés labels, through their illustrations, convey nobility and social distinction, tradition and history, and craft-work.

Colours

High-quality deep, rich colours signify quality, whereas bright colours represent fun and frivolity. In their analysis of 117 Bordeaux grands crus classés labels, Celhay, Folcher and Cohen (2014) found that wine labels that utilised burgundy, navy and neutral palettes generated the highest scores for intent to purchase by consumers, and they represented traditional values and success. Bright colours such as red-orange and wasabi green also received high scores in terms of intent to purchase, and wines using these colours were perceived as exciting, daring, spirited, imaginative and modern. In fact all warm pallets such as burgundy, red-orange and neutrals signified success, desirability and expense. They found that wine colours in the pink palette received the lowest intention to purchase scores.

From this study, Celhay, Folcher and Cohen (2014) found that it was possible to identify two distinct forms of labels in their sample. They found that 52% of the labels use a pristine white background, then black, bordeaux/red, grey and gold for the text, the illustrations and the frames. According to Blanchard (1980) the whiteness of the label denotes the quality of the wine: the whiter the white the higher the quality. Another 44% of the labels used a yellowing white as a background colour then black, Bordeaux red, grey and gold for the text, the illustrations and the frames. In this case, the yellowing white denotes heritage and tradition (Cavassilas 2007). It appears that most of the labels use the same range of colours: white, pale yellow, ochre, bordeaux/red, black, grey and gold. The use of red or bordeaux is related to the nature of the wine, whereas the usage of white, black and grey produce signify classicism and elegance (Ares *et al.* 2011; Cavassilas 2007). Celhay, Folcher and Cohen (2014) finally identify that the gold colour used by 73% of the labels signified luxury and social distinction (Lawes 2002).

Font

Further in Celhay, Folcher and Cohen's (2014:8) analysis of Bordeaux grands crus classés labels they observed that 68% of the labels use capital serif letters, 15% formal scripts letters, 5% capital non-serif letters and only 3% gothic letters. Also, the wine brand element used a thin font in 82% of the cases, typefaces with stroke modulations in 94% of the cases and that it appears in italic only in 18% of the cases. In conclusion they identify three main lessons to be learnt:

1 *Capital letters are preferred over lowercase letters.* Ares *et al.* (2011) observe that the use of capital letters is a way to give more importance to the word that is capitalised. For example, a 'grand vin de Bordeaux' (a term that has no legal meaning) would seem more 'GRAND' if it appears in capital letters. Therefore, the use of capital letters for the brand and the region is a way to signify the greatness, the prestige and the importance of the wine and its region of origin.

2   *Serif letters are preferred over sans serif fonts.* The use of serif letters, because of their similarity to antique Roman letters, signifies both classicism and tradition comparing to non-serif typefaces that signify something more modern (Pohlen 2011). It is interesting to note that the use of serif lettering on new wine brands can add heritage and credibility to its brand value.
3   *Thin letters with stroke modulations are preferred over bold regulars ones.* This form of typeface imitates handwriting, thus it creates a sentiment of a hand-made or artisan product rather than a wine that has been produced using modern techniques. Additionally, Cavassilas (2007) suggests that typefaces known for their fineness could signify a subtle and delicate taste with a long finish in contrast to the bold and large fonts that are more likely to signify a strong and powerful taste. Thus, 'the Bordeaux Grands Crus labels, signifies greatness, prestige, classicism, tradition, and seriousness' (Celhay, Folcher and Cohen's 2014:8).

Wine semiotics: a summary

It can be argued that there is a semiotic language of wine that is constructed through a set of signs and images that not only tell us the significance and nature of wine, but can also impact upon our senses and thus impact upon how we taste the wine. There are a number of signs that construct the semiotic language of wine. These do not always need to be seen on a wine bottle, advertisement or website, but are used as a semiotic staging, as a background to both the purchasing and consumption of the wine.

Therefore the sommelier's uniform or their *tastevin* is part of this staging, as are the empty wine cases or wine barrels at a wine merchants or wine bar. Thus, within wine studies it is as important to understand the semiotics of wine as it is the wine itself, because the semiotics socially and culturally contextualise the wine and give it external meaning.

However, it can be argued that the most important lesson to be learnt from this chapter is that the way we enjoy wine, find meaning within it or even taste it are subject to our own personal view, emotions and memories, and that these can personally elevate a poor wine to the level of a grand cru. Someone once said that there is no bad wine only bad company!

For discussion

1   Define your most important wine experience. To what extent was this influenced by the social situation the experience took place in?
2   What do you think the purpose of the semiotic language of wine plays within wine appreciation?
3   What props would you use to semiotically stage a wine event?
4   What are the key messages for consumers in interpreting wine labels?
5   In marketing how important is the country of origin compared to the brand?

References

Ares, G., Piqueras-Fiszman, B., Varela, P., Morant, M.R., Martín López, A. and Fiszman S. (2011). Food labels: Do consumers perceive what semiotics want to convey? *Food Quality and Preference*, 22, 689–98.

Alexander, A. (2000). Codes and contexts: Practical semiotics for the qualitative researcher. Proceedings of the Market Research Society Annual Conference, London: MRS, pp. 139–46.

Arnould, E., Price, L. and Tierney, P. (1998). Communicative staging of the wilderness servicescape. *Service Industries Journal*, 18(3), 90.

Barber, N., Almanza, B. A. and Donovan, J. R. (2006). Motivational factors of gender, income and age on selecting a bottle of wine. *International Journal of Wine Marketing*, 18(3), 218–32.

Beverland, M. and Lindgreen, A. (2002). Using country of origin in strategy: The importance of context and strategic action. *Brand Management*, 10(2), 147–67.

Blanchard, G (1980). *Pour une Sémiologie de la Typographie*, Thèse de doctorat, Université deParis la Sorbonne

Boudreaux, C. A. and Palmer, S. E. (2007). A charming little Cabernet: Effects of wine label design on purchase intent and brand personality. *International Journal of Wine Business Research*, 19(3), 170–86.

Brochet, F. (2001). Chemical object representation in the field of consciousness: Application presented for the grand prix of the Académie Amorim following work carried out towards a doctorate from the Faculty of Oenology, General Oenology Laboratory, Talence Cedex, [online], available from: http://web.archive.org/web/20070928231853/http://www.academie-amorim.com/us/laureat_2001/brochet.pdf.

Brijs, K. (2006). Unravelling country-of-origin: Semiotics as a theoretical basis for a meaning-centred approach towards country-of-origin effects. PhD thesis, Radboud Universiteit Nijmegen, [online], available from: http://hdl.handle.net/1942/1819.

Cavassilas, M. (2007). *Clés et Codes du Packaging – Sémiotique Appliquée* (Paris: Hermès Sciences – Lavoisier).

Celhay, F., Folcher, P. and Cohen, J. (2014). Decoding wine label design: A study of the visual codes of Bordeaux Grand Crus.; Academy of Wine Business.com [online], available from http://academyofwinebusiness.com/wp-content/uploads/2013/04/Celhay-Folcher-Cohen.pdf

Celhay, F. and Trinquecoste, J.F. (2014). Package graphic design: Investigating the variables that moderate consumer response to atypical designs. *Journal of Product Innovation Management*. doi: 10.1111/jpim.12212.

Chaney, I. (2000). External search effort for wine. *International Journal of Wine Marketing*, 12(2), 5–21.

De Luca, P. and Penco, P. (2006). The role of packaging in marketing communication: An explorative study of the Italian wine business. In: *Proceedings of 3rd International Wine Business Research Conference*, Montpellier, France, 6–8 July.

Echtner, C.M. (1999). The semiotic paradigm: Implications for tourism research. *Tourism Management*, 20(1), 47–57.

Hoffman, M. (2013). Ask a sommelier: What's the greatest wine you've ever tried? *Serious Eats* [online], available from http://drinks.seriouseats.com/2013/07/ask-a-sommelier-the-greatest-wine-in-the-world.html.

Holt, D. (1998). Does cultural capital structure American consumption? *The Journal of Consumer Research*, 25(1), 1–25.

Holt, D.B. and Cameron, D. (2010). *Cultural Strategy: Using Innovative Ideologies To Build Breakthrough Brands* (Oxford: Oxford University Press).

Hope, J. and Patoine, P.L. (2009). Does a glass of white wine taste like a glass of Domain Sigalas Santorini Asirtiko 2005? A biosemiotic approach to wine tasting. *Biosemiotics*, 2, 65–76.

Lawes, R. (2002). Demystifying semiotics: Some key questions answered. *International Journal of Market Research*, 44(3), 251–64.

Manning, P. (2012). *The Semiotics of Drink and Drinking* (London and New York: Continuum).

McCracken, G.D. and Roth, V.J. (1989). Does clothing have a code? Empirical findings and theoretical implications in the study of clothing as a means of communication. *International Journal of Research in Marketing*, 6(1), 13–33.

Mick, D.G. (1986). Consumer research and semiotics: Exploring the morphology of signs, symbols, and significance. *Journal of Consumer Research*, 13(2), 196–213.

North, A.C. (2012). The effect of background music on the taste of wine. *British Journal of Psychology*, 103, 293–301.

Olsen, J., Thompson, K. and Clarke, T. (2003). Consumer self-confidence in wine purchases. *International Journal of Wine Marketing*, 15(3), 40–51.

Paradis, C. (2013). Touchdowns in winespeak: Ontologies and construals in use and meaning-making. In: Goded, M. and Luelmo, A. (eds), *Proceedings for the 1st Congress on Linguistic Approaches to Food and Wine Descriptions*, pp. 57–72 (Madrid: UNED University Press).

Peirce, C.S. (1934) *Collected Papers of Charles Sanders Peirce*, vols. 1–6, Charles Hartshorne and Paul Weiss (eds), vols. 7–8, Arthur W. Burks (ed.)(Boston: Harvard University Press).

Pohlen, J. (2011). *Letter Fountain, the Anatomy of Type* (Cologne: Taschen).

Robert, J. (2014). Oppositional symbolic values of language display, or the case of 'English' drinking in France. *Social Semiotics*, 24(2), 209–24.

Saussure. F. (1983 [1915]) *Course in General Linguistics* (Baskin, W., transl.) (London: Duckworth).

Sester, C., Dacremont, C., Deroy, O. and Valentin, D. (2013). Investigating consumers' representations of beers through a free association task: A comparison between packaging and blind conditions. *Food Quality and Preference*, 28(2), 475–83.

Sherry Jr, J.F. and Camargo E.G.C. (1987). May your life be marvellous: English language labelling and the semiotics of Japanese promotion. *Journal of Consumer Research*, 14(2) 174–88.

Silver, C. (2013). Wine names are getting wackier and wackier. And at no extra price! *Forbes Magazine*, 16 August, [online] available from: http://www.forbes.com/sites/craigsilver/2013/08/16/wine-names-are-getting-wackier-and-wackier-and-at-no-extra-price/

Solomon, M.R. (1983). The role of products as social stimuli: A symbolic interactionism perspective. *Journal of Consumer Research*, 10(3), 319–29.

Spinelli, S. (2012). The hidden aspects of signification. Semiotics of practices and sensory science. In: *Proceedings of the 10th World Congress of the International Association for Semiotic Studies (IASS/AIS)*, pp. 313–20 (A Coruña, Spain: Universidade da Coruña); available from: http://ruc.udc.es/bitstream/2183/13323/1/CC-130_art_30.pdf.

Thomas, A. (2000). Elements influencing wine purchasing: A New Zealand view. *International Journal of Wine Marketing*, 12(2), 47–62.

Thomas, A. and Pickering, G. (2003). The importance of wine label information. *International Journal of Wine Marketing*, 15(2), 58–74.

11
THE IMPORTANCE OF WINE IN CONTEMPORARY SOCIETY

This book has attempted to bring together a number of theoretical and practical aspects of the role of wine in contemporary society. It has sought to combine various forms of knowledge and subject areas into one accessible source to reflect the idea of what critical wines studies is or should be.

We refer to the field of 'critical wine studies' as an approach that can see both the positive and negative aspects of wine in society, and which challenges some of the assumptions of the wine trade and wine marketeers. However, this critical stance comes from an approach that recognises the enormous significance of wine as a cultural symbol, and which takes account of the enormous care exercised by individuals across the globe in the fields of viticulture and vinification. We have seen that through their labours, often with a huge respect for the terroir in which they are working, and increasingly with concern for the environmental impact of their work, it is possible to produce a product that, at the least, can greatly enhance a wide range of social occasions and in some cases can bring extraordinary levels of sensual enjoyment by those who consume it.

The complexity of wine in terms of its production, consumption, social and cultural significance and its administration warrants a multidisciplinary approach. This book presents three fundamental recurrent themes that are woven throughout, interlinking chapters to create a logical progression of ideas and concepts. These three themes are very simply:

- the definition of wine and what it means to different people;
- how consumers understand and use wine as part of their everyday life or lifestyles; and finally
- how wine is sold and regulated.

It is to these themes that we now turn.

What is wine and where does it come from?

One of the major recurring themes within this book has been the exploration of the elements that constitute a definition of wine. The complexity of social, cultural and symbolic significance and meaning that surrounds wine in contemporary society is reflected in the fact that there are four chapters dedicated, or partially dedicated, to defining wine. Chapter 1 asked the question 'What is wine?', providing a practical technical definition of wine that includes its legal definitions, regulations as to what constitutes 'a wine', the introduction to grape varieties and the component elements such as acids, tannins and polyphenols that give wine its character. This chapter also explored the legal definitions of wine in terms of factors such as the maximum and minimum alcohol and how wine regions define and protect their wines.

These themes are further developed in Chapter 3, 'Fine wine or plonk?', which attempted to identify the various factors that define the quality of wine and its status as an anthropological object, considering factors such as the price of wine, its scarcity and the formal classifications used in major wine regions. These characteristics allow for a wine to be classified as either 'plonk', a commercial wine, a mid-range wine, a wine for drinking on special occasions, a highly exclusive wine or a trophy wine. We considered how the status and providence of many of these wines are protected by law. These two chapters provide a very practical definition of what wine is and an assessment of its significance to purchasers.

However, in order to provide a definitive understanding of 'what is wine', it has to be contextualised in the debates that see wine elevated from a simple beverage to a drink that is revered, collected and sometimes even coveted. Both Chapter 2, 'Understanding the significance of wine' and Chapter 5, 'Terroir' identify the various social and cultural factors that have helped provide wine with its contemporary context. Chapter 2 explores how the historical significance of wine has provided the foundations for the embedding of wine as a special, celebratory and even mythical cultural product. This celebratory and mythical element is not a new one, rather these themes emerge out of ancient Rome and Greece, where wine even had specific gods (Bacchus and Dionysus).

We examined how wine was celebrated and cherished and used widely in religious rituals, which subsequently became absorbed into the Judeo-Christian tradition. In particular, we considered the significance of wine in the Christian Eucharist, which led to the huge focus on wine growing by abbeys and monasteries throughout Europe and even in some parts of the New World, notably Chile. Over the centuries, this led to huge improvements in standards of wine production and the differentiation of one vineyard from another.

This idea of sacredness has also transferred into the secular realm, whereby wine is used to commemorate special occasions and is central to any celebration in alcohol drinking cultures. Wine is also used as a marker of identity and status for individual consumers, regions and even countries.

These practical and cultural factors merge and are utilised within the contemporary appreciation of wine as the product of a particular location, as expressed in the philosophy of *terroir*. Chapter 5 explored the conception of terroir. Although it is a French term, it has become adopted by many other countries when attempting to explain the geographical, historical and cultural attributes of a wine. It is argued that the terroir of the vineyard provides wine with its particular characteristics. However, as such, the term means much more the just the territory from which a wine originates – it encompasses a huge range of factors, many of which have deep anthropological significance.

In short, terroir represents the geographic, topographic and climatic condition that a wine has been subject to, and also the characteristics of the soil and the minerals contained in the earth. For some, terroir also includes the history and culture of the region, so that when we taste wine, we taste both human and environmental factors. In essence, the notion of terroir brings together both the practical elements that constitute a wine and the social and cultural context of the wine and the region's history: it is as much a philosophical concept as much as it is a practical one.

Wine, knowledge and identity

It is clear that wine forms an important role in contemporary society. Apart from generating many jobs and supporting many regional and national economies, wine is also used to reinforce individual and regional identities. Consequently, there is a body of knowledge surrounding wine that is accumulated, generated and utilised by the wine industry and marketeers to target individuals or groups with various goods and services.

Chapter 4, 'Wine consumers' explored first how individuals are categorised and identified as potential consumers according to the consumer resources they possess. From this it is possible to ascertain and develop an understanding of the consumption patterns of various types of consumers. This approach provides the wine industry and marketeers with the ability to assign characteristics to different groups of consumers and, as such, to define and categorise them into identifiable market segments. Second, Chapter 4 explored the idea of consumption and identity – that is, the principle that individual consumers have the ability to define their own identity, for example, through the consumption and appreciation of wine.

Wine has become a lifestyle marker that enables people to express their cultural knowledge and identity. This is important as people come together into consumption groups or tribes that they choose to join rather than having group membership imposed upon them. In short, wine becomes a means for individuals to express their own identity and status, through the generation and exchange of knowledge. The result of this is that people search for wine experiences that will add to their reservoir of cultural capital or so they can exchange it with other culturally motivated consumers.

This search for knowledge is supported by the wine industry in many forms. Chapter 9, 'Wine societies and wine education', examines how consumers learn about wine – sometimes purely for reasons of personal interest but with support in various forms by the wine industry. Consumers and professionals who need to learn about wine have the ability to gain various levels of knowledge in the form of informal tasting events, wine societies and tutored tastings, wine tourism, wine books and magazines or through the formal qualifications and educational systems of bodies such as Wine & Spirit Education Trust or the Institute of Masters of Wine.

The desire by consumers to understand wine, its characteristics and nuisances, and to have the ability to talk knowledgeably about it has enormous significance in understanding the place of wine in society.

The home remains one of the most important places in which to express the consumer's knowledge, cultural capital and wine-related material resources. The ability to produce the correct glasses, decanter or to show someone a wine collection or wine cellar is a clear expression of the individual's cultural capital and wine knowledge that has been gathered from engaging with the various knowledge sources in the field of wine. The home also offers a space in which cultural capital can be freely exchanged with friends, guests or members of one's habitus or consumption tribe, thus demonstrating both one's lifestyle and identity.

Marketing, ethics and control

The information within the first two themes of the book provided a platform for Chapter 7 'Licensing law, duty and the ethics of alcohol' as well as Chapter 8 'Marketing of the wine experience' and Chapter 10 'The semiotics of wine'.

These issues are underpinned by the cultural and social significance of wine, in conjunction with the resources, knowledge and needs that consumers possess. Chapter 8 provided an overview of the function of the marketeer: fundamentally this involves the creation of the marketing offer (how the wine is to be defined and what messages will be used to express the characteristics of the wine to the consumer), creating awareness of the product and then the process of removing barriers to the purchase of wine. However, one of the other major roles of the marketeer is to create addition value for the consumer. Within the context of Chapter 8, marketeers are not just marketing executives based in offices separated by distance from the product, but also includes wine merchants, shop assistants, waiters, sommeliers, etc. who directly add value to the marketing process by becoming part of the servicescape. They co-create value with the customer through the exchange of wine knowledge and performance of the roles and rituals that surround the consumption and appreciation of wine. However, the marketing of wine is a particularly complex area of activity, as wine is sold through many different channels, including on-premise, retail sites, through the internet, etc. All of these provide a different context to the wine, creating different understandings and expectations by the consumer. This complexity is further compounded by the nature and various motivations wine consumers possess, thus there is no one right or correct method with which to sell and market wine, although there are important ethical issues as considered below. One of the key requirements for effective marketing is to ensure that the right messages are communicated to the right consumers: if this does not take place then the marketing process falls down.

Chapter 10 explored the semiotics of wine. Semiotics is not just the study of signs and images but it understands the varying factors that both add value to the product and signpost experience. It can be argued that there is a specific language of wine, and that consumers understand this language (although this may be at different levels). This language underpins wine marketing, the wine label and packaging and the servicescape in which wine is bought and sold. There is a complex use of images, the sommelier's uniform, the staging of experiences in shops and restaurants, the words chosen to describe the wine, the colours used on the label and even the shape of bottles all help to communicate what type of wine experience we will have.

The information on the label or labels of a wine bottle directly inform how the consumer interprets the taste of wine. Semiotics can change perceptions, and as such the semiotics of wine plays a significant role in contemporary marketing and wine studies. However, one of the dominant discourses that underpin the semiotics of wine is a hedonistic one.

As seen in Chapter 2, wine has always been associated with hedonistic practices, celebrations, luxury and often overindulgence. The characters of Bacchus and Dionysus are still used to represent many of these meanings associated with wine. Consumers are programmed to be pleasure seekers and will always engage in the things they find most pleasurable. For many (but by no means all) the consumption of wine is a particularly pleasurable thing, but there are significant risks when consumption is excessive or when it impairs judgement in crucial activities such as driving. Because of these risks, throughout history there have been many attempts at rationing wine (and alcohol more generally), so as to discourage over-consumption and to mediate hedonistic urges.

Chapter 7, 'Licensing law, duty and the ethics of alcohol', explored many of the methods that have been employed to regulate wine production and consumption. This need to recognise the implications of the over-consumption of wine is not only recognised by governments, but it has also been adopted by many other organisations including the wine industry itself as through an increased awareness of its ethical duty to society. The ethical production and consumption of wine is becoming an ever more significant factor in a world where the cost of healthcare is becoming increasingly expensive and where alcohol is contributing to the pressure placed on the healthcare system. So the ethical questions surrounding wine are become ever more pertinent. In addition to this, as we saw in Chapter 8, there has been a growth in the 'ethical' or 'green' wine consumer, where customers are actively searching for ethical, sustainable or organic wine options.

Society's dance with wine: a summary

As can be seen from above, wine is a complex product that has major social, cultural, religious and regional significance. There is little doubt that wine holds an important place in contemporary society.

Although it may be merely a drink made from fermented grapes, every wine has a different characteristic. Often wine reminds us of experiences, people and celebration – it is part of all our lives. As we noted at the start of this book, this exploration of how people's lives and patterns of behaviour engage with a product such as wine can be seen in anthropological terms as a dance.

The way in which society 'dances with wine' can take many forms. When we take a sip of wine we can enjoy it on many levels. Each of us finds our own pleasure and significance whether we are a connoisseur drinking a trophy wine or a beverage drinker sipping on a glass of house white. The consumption and appreciation of wine can be seen as one of life's small pleasures and its elevation to the level of the extraordinary is fully justifiable.

INDEX

Note: References to specific châteaux or domains are listed under the individual name, rather than under "c" or "d".

abstinence 137, 144, 151, 182, 189
acidity 6–8, 12, 19, 24, 27, 107, 175, 184, 209, 215; by grape variety 15; effect of ageing 78, 126; for sparkling wine 14; volatile 56
alcohol 2, 36, 76; duty 52; in fortified wines 13
alcohol by volume 31, 178
alcohol consumption patterns and risks 132, 135, 137–52, 158, 188, 218
alcohol drinking culture 33, 215
alcoholic strength 3–6
alcohol units *see* units of alcohol
Alsace 58, 208; Crémant 14; grand cru 75
Amarone della Valpolicella 2
Angélus, Château 69
anthocyanins 8
AOC *see* PDO
AOP *see* PDO
aspirational drinkers 89–90, 95, 170
Asti 5, 14
Ausone, Château 69
authenticity 40–3, 109
AWE (Association of Wine Educators) 192

Bacchus xvii–xviii, 36, 38–9, 46, 215, 218
Barolo 27, 30, 58
Biblical references to wine 38
blood of Christ *see* Eucharist

Bordeaux 27, 51, 122, 179, 200; ageing 23, 78, 126–7; AOP 56; appellations 66; barrel 23; classed growths 61, 67–8, 198, 210; classification of châteaux 65–70; cru bourgeois 24, 30, 57, 67–8; decanting 129; en primeur 59–60; grape varieties 17–18; labels 209–10; map 66; pricing 57–62; second wines 54; storage 122; vintages 77, 126–7
Bordeaux blend 17, 22
Bourdieu, Pierre 40, 45, 97, 99, 159
Bourgogne Passe-Toute-Grains 208
Bourgogne PDO 25, 206; *see also* Burgundy
branding 207
brandy 13
Brettanomyces 127
Brix scale 4
Broadbent, Michael 19, 126
Burgundy 9, 31, 54, 65; appellations 27–8; aromas 127; classification 70–3; climats 207; en primeur 59; geology 107; grand cru 25–6, 42, 51, 62, 65, 72–3, 75; grape varieties 16–17, 208; large formats 125; maps 26, 71, 74; PDOs 27–8; premier cru 28, 61, 72; pricing 27, 57–62; yields 20

Catholic Church 37
Cava 14, 57

Champagne 9, 14, 27, 41, 57, 59, 77, 94, 134, 204; bottle shape 197; distribution 163; échelle des crus 75; ethical scores 162; grand cru 75; labels 208; large format bottles 125; non-vintage 78; opening 129; premier cru 75; producers 162, 199; vintage and special cuvées 61
Champagne method *see* traditional method
chaptalisation 2, 5, 7
charities in field of wine 144, 152, 188, 189
charity fundraising tastings 177, 191; licensing of 147
Cheval Blanc, Château 69
Chianti 27, 57, 76
children and wine 132–4, 142, 146–8, 176
Christianity and wine *see* Eucharist
classed growth châteaux *see* Bordeaux: classed growths
Clos de Vougeot 25–6, 73
CO_2 (carbon dioxide) 3; in sparkling wines 5, 13, 132
communicative staging 93
communitas 43
communities 111
connoisseurs 56–64, 73, 74–5, 77, 88–9, 95, 99, 119, 121, 125–7, 133–4, 153, 168, 175, 180–1, 192, 219
consumer classification 99
consumer resources 81
consumers as resources 94
consumption tribes 90, 99–101, 165
Côte de Beaune *see* Burgundy
Côte de Nuits 73; *see also* Burgundy
Côte d'Or *see* Burgundy
country of origin 205
Crémants 14
crime 142, 146, 149
cru (definition) 65; *see also* grand cru; premier cru
cru bourgeois see Bordeaux: cru bourgeois
cru classé châteaux see Bordeaux: classed growths
cultural capital 96–9, 112
cultural embedding 41
cultural expression 111
cultural intermediaries 196

dance and wine xvii, 1, 146, 219; *see also* Bacchus
decanting 129–30
definition of wine 2
demand manipulation 55

Dionysus *see* Bacchus
DO *see* PDO
DOC *see* PDO
DOCa *see* PDO
DOCG *see* PDO
DOP *see* PDO
Douglas, Mary 132–3
DRC *see* Romanée Conti
Drinkaware 144
driving 139–40, 149, 184, 218
Durkheim, Émile 40
duties on wine 52

English language 204
English sparkling wine 14, 59
English wine 3, 29, 150
en primeur 59–61, 122, 125, 127, 157
ethics 161
Eucharist 36–8, 139, 215
European Communities Act 1972 2
EU (European Union) wine law 2–3, 6–9, 13, 20, 26–7, 58, 64, 106, 138–9, 140, 201, 205–6; comparison with New World 76; derogations 3; protected geographical names 24–9, 108; wine imports 119; wine zones 3; VAT 52, 150–1
events 111
exchange principle 165

Fairtrade 163–4
farmyard nose 127
festivals 111
fine wine 55
flabby wines 107
fortified wines 6, 13

geographical identity 110
geology *see* terroir
goods dominant logic 165
grand cru 65; *see also* Alsace: grand cru; Burgundy: grand cru; Champagne: grand cru; St Émilion: grand cru
grape varieties 9, 12, 15–18, 30, 215; blending 22; for specific PDOs 27; terroir 107
green marketing 163
greenwashing 164–5
gustemology 113

habitus 97
Haut-Brion, Château 68
Haut-Médoc 55, 65

health and wine 35, 132, 134, 138, 141–5, 151, 153, 182, 184, 218
history of wine 33, 109
Hunter Valley 17

iconic signs 198
imperiale 126
IMW *see* masters of wine
indexical signs 198

J-curve 144–5
jeroboam 125
Judaism 38
Jurade de St Émilion 68, 187

knowledge 85, 96

labels 30–1, 160
Lafite-Rothschild, Château 68, 198
large format bottles 125
Latour, Château 68
law 138, 157, 215; classifications 63–76; duties 122, 150–1; education 191; labelling 30–1; licensing 146–9, 201, 205–6; personal imports 119; protected designations 25–9, 54–5, 108; wine definition 2–13
licensing the sale of wine 146–9
lifestyle 85, 99, 158
liqueur wines *see* fortified wines
low-alcohol wines 4, 145, 182
luxury 196

Margaux 26, 27, 58, 65, 75; grape varieties 30
Margaux, Château 68, 74
marketing offer 166
masters of wine 180–1, 188–92
material resources 84
Médoc classification of châteaux 65–8
minerals 9–10
minimum pricing 152
Mouton-Rothschild, Château 68
myths 41

Oechsle scale 4, 76
online purchasing 157
on-premises purchasing 158
operand resources 82
operant resources 82
organic wine 162
organoleptic assessment 28

packaging 160
Passover 38, 139

Pauillac 65, 67
Pavie, Château 69
PDO 5, 20, 25–8, 30, 58, 65–73, 75, 108, 206
Peirce, Charles Saunders 198
personal identity 44–6, 95, 101
Pétrus, Château 51, 55
PGI 5, 28–9, 206, 208
polyphenols 8–9
Pomerol 51, 70
Portman Group 144
post-modernism 111
Prädikatswein 28
premier cru *see* Burgundy: premier cru; Champagne: premier cru
price 25, 82–3
Prosecco 14, 39, 57
protected designations *see* PDO; PGI

racking 22
religion 35; *see also* Biblical references to wine; Eucharist; Passover
retail purchasing 157
Rioja 27, 57, 76
risk 86–9
risk reduction 88
ritual 62
Robinson, Jancis 25, 78, 126, 184, 185
Romanée Conti, Domaine de la 51, 73

saccharomyces cerevisiae 10
sacred 36
St Émilion 27, 68–9; classification of châteaux 68–9; grand cru 58, 65; *see also* Jurade de St Émilion
St Estèphe 65
St Julien 65
Saussure, F. 198
Sauternes 13, 59
secular 39
segmentation 82, 89, 100, 158
semiotics 165
senses 43–4, 112
sensescapes 112
service delivery 92
service dominant logic 166
service personnel 92
servicescapes 43, 93, 197
SO_2 (sulphur dioxide) 10, 22
social media 158
social resources 85
soils *see* terroir
sommelier 93, 158, 196–7
sparkling wine 5, 13–14, 15, 18, 56, 57, 90, 119, 120, 134, 135, 143, 163; duty

on 151; in Buck's fizz 134; opening 129; storage 132; *see also* Asti; Cava; Champagne; Crémants; English Sparkling Wine; Prosecco
spitting 84, 178–9, 184
status 101
storage 84
sugars in wine 4, 6
sustainability 160
sweet wines *see* sugars in wine
symbolic signs 199
symbolic value 165
synaesthesia 112–13

tannins 8–9, 12, 19, 126, 175, 178, 184, 215; by grape variety 17; effect of ageing 24, 77–8; effect of decanting 129–30
tartaric acid 7
tartrate crystals 10, 129
tasting 18, 28, 53, 83, 84, 88, 127, 128, 157, 168, 169, 175, 200, 217; blind 84, 200; charity 147, 177, 191; en primeur 59–60; examinations 190; food-matching 176–7; glasses 84, 103n1; horizontal 62; informal 175–6; self-pour 183; techniques 19; terminology 43; trade 183–4; tutored 177–9, 181; vertical 62, 78; wine merchants 189; wine society 177–82; WSET techniques 189–90, 209
tasting notes 59, 102, 126, 158, 179, 208; internet 185
tasting research 78, 201
tasting rooms 54
teachers of wine *see* wine educators
terroir 9, 16, 20–1, 25, 42–3, 46, 65, 70, 93–4, 106–14, 163, 167, 199; identity 46; in wine tourism 186; labelling 203, 206, 214, 216

toasts 134
tourism 112–14, 186
traditional method: for sparkling wine 14, 59
tutored tastings 177–9, 183, 191, 217
type fonts 210–11

under-age sales 148
units of alcohol 138, 141, 178

value creation 92, 165
values 159, 161
varietal wines 29
VAT 52–3, 122; en primeur sales 60; EU country variations 150–1; minimum pricing 152
vintage 205
Vitis vinifera 15, 34

wine cellar: home 23, 120–2, 125, 127, 133, 217; restaurant 167
wine connoisseurs *see* connoisseurs
wine definition 2
wine educators 177, 179–80, 182, 191–2
Wine in Moderation 145
wine labels 201–17
wine marketing 156
wine societies 177–82
wine studies field 1, 89, 96–7, 102, 108, 158–9, 160–1, 169, 198, 211, 214–18
wine tasting *see* tasting
wine tourism *see* tourism
WSET (Wine & Spirit Education Trust) 187–91

yeast 3, 5–6, 10–11, 141; in sparkling wine-making 13–14